Library of Medieval Women

Goscelin of St Bertin
*The Book of Encouragement
and Consolation
[Liber Confortatorius]*
The Letter of Goscelin to the Recluse Eva

Library of Medieval Women   ISSN 1369–9652

Series Editor: Jane Chance

The Library of Medieval Women aims to make available, in an English translation, significant works by, for, and about medieval women, from the age of the Church Fathers to the fifteenth century. The series encompasses many forms of writing, from poetry, visions, biography and autobiography, and letters, to sermons, treatises and encyclopedias; the subject matter is equally diverse: theology and mysticism, classical mythology, medicine and science, history, hagiography, and instructions for anchoresses. Each text is presented with an introduction setting the material in context, a guide to further reading, and an interpretive essay.

We welcome suggestions for future titles in the series. Proposals or queries may be sent directly to the editor or publisher at the addresses given below; all submissions will receive prompt and informed consideration.

Professor Jane Chance, Department of English, MS 30, Rice University, PO Box 1892, Houston, TX 77251–1892, USA. E-mail: jchance@rice.edu

Boydell & Brewer Limited, PO Box 9, Woodbridge, Suffolk, IP12 3DF, UK. E-mail: editorial@boydell.co.uk. Website: www.boydellandbrewer.com

Previously published titles in this series are listed at the back of this book

Goscelin of St Bertin
The Book of Encouragement and Consolation [Liber Confortatorius]
The Letter of Goscelin to the Recluse Eva

**Translated from the Latin
with Introduction, Notes,
and Interpretive Essay**

Monika Otter
Dartmouth College

D.S. BREWER

BX
4210
.G61713
2004

First published 2004
D. S. Brewer, Cambridge

ISBN 1 84384 015 4

D. S. Brewer is an imprint of Boydell & Brewer Ltd
PO Box 9, Woodbridge, Suffolk IP12 3DF, UK
and of Boydell & Brewer Inc.
PO Box 41026, Rochester, NY 41026–4126, USA
website: www.boydellandbrewer.com

A catalogue record for this book is available
from the British Library

Library of Congress Cataloging-in-Publication Data
Goscelin, of Saint-Bertin, ca. 1035–ca. 1107.
 [Liber confortatorius. English]
 Goscelin of St. Bertin : The book of encouragement and consolation / translated
 from the Latin with introduction, notes, and interpretive essay [by] Monika Otter.
    p. cm. – (Library of medieval women, ISSN 1369–9652)
 Includes bibliographical references and index.
 ISBN 1–84384–015–4 (hardcover : alk. paper)
  1. Monastic and religious life of women – Early works to 1800.   2. Spiritual
 life – Early works to 1800.   3. Hermits – Early works to 1800.   I. Otter, Monika.
 II. Title.   III. Series.
  BX4210.G61713 2004
  248.8'943–dc22   2003027384

This publication is printed on acid-free paper

Printed in Great Britain by
Antony Rowe Ltd, Chippenham, Wiltshire

Contents

Acknowledgements

I would like to thank the colleagues at the International Medieval Congress at Kalamazoo, and at the Medieval Club of New York who listened to my several exploratory papers on Goscelin and made valuable suggestions, particularly Georges Whalen, Tom Head, David Townsend, and Rebecca Hayward; the wonderful undergraduate research assistants who contributed their linguistic skills, ingenuity and enthusiasm: Curtis Dozier, Lilly Wollman, Davida Wegner, Tara Thompson, Kristina Mendicino, and Jeff Beardsley; Jane Chance, the editor of this series, Caroline Palmer at Boydell and Brewer, and the anonymous reader for the press; Dartmouth College, for providing an environment conducive to writing and research, and especially the library; and my friends and colleagues at Dartmouth, especially Peter Travis and Manuele Gragnolati, who read drafts of this project and provided much appreciated comments and encouragement.

Abbreviations

AASS	Acta Sanctorum
CCSL	Corpus Christianorum Series Latina
CSEL	Corpus Scriptorum Ecclesiasticorum Latinorum
EETS	Early English Text Society
KJV	King James Version of the Bible
MGH	Monumenta Germaniae Historica
PG	Patrologiae Cursus Completus, Series Graeca
PL	Patrologiae Cursus Completus, Series Latina

Introduction

The *Liber Confortatorius* [the Book of Encouragement and Consolation] is an idiosyncratic and extraordinarily rich document from the late eleventh century. A letter of guidance to a female recluse by her male spiritual adviser, a guide to meditation and prayer, and an anthology of spiritual and meditative texts, it is also a personal letter and an account of a deep, desperate, only half sublimated love between a man and a woman in religious orders. Taking up the tradition of St. Jerome's letters of spiritual guidance to holy women, it anticipates better-known medieval advice literature for anchoresses, especially Aelred's *De Institutione Inclusarum* and the *Ancrene Wisse*.[1] Many of Goscelin's concerns and rhetorical strategies will sound familiar to readers of these later works. But the *Liber Confortatorius* is sui generis, criss-crossing and deconstructing all the dividing lines that are so important to the *Ancrene Wisse* and similar texts: inside-outside, teacher-pupil, male-female, parent-child.

Anchorites, Anchoritic Literature, and the *Liber Confortatorius*

The late eleventh and twelfth centuries were a time of religious experimentation, a time when many people attempted to fashion new and often independent ways to act out their personal religiosity, the right "rule" to live by.[2] The great monastic movements of the previous centuries had concentrated on reforming coenobitic (communal) monasticism, to return it to stricter observance and to its pristine, austere origins. These efforts continued, and generated new movements and new religious orders. At the same time, many people were attracted to eremitic lifestyles, inspired in part by the immensely popular literature of the early Christian "Desert Fathers" of the Near East. Even

---

[1] Aelred of Rievaulx, "A Rule of Life for a Recluse," trans. Mary Paul Macpherson, in *Aelred: Treatises and the Pastoral Prayer*. Cistercian Fathers Series 2 (Kalamazoo: Cistercian Publications, 1971); Anne Savage and Nicholas Watson, eds., *Anchoritic Spirituality:* Ancrene Wisse *and Associated Works* (New York: Paulist Press, 1991).

[2] See Caroline Bynum, "Did the Twelfth Century Discover the Individual?" in *Jesus as Mother: Studies in the Spirituality of the High Middle Ages* (Berkeley: University of California Press, 1982), 82–109.

those who remained in communal life or were very much involved in active politics and administration often drew heavily on the rhetoric and imagery of "the desert," of seclusion and asceticism.[3] Some put these ideals into practice. They might withdraw to a "desert" or wilderness in imitation of the early Christian desert fathers, or they might live as anchorites or anchoresses in cells attached to churches or monasteries, often in the middle of town yet solitary and unseen.[4] The latter form in particular attracted many women, indeed more women than men. Some anchorites and hermits were true solitaries, others had companions or servants, or (like Eva, the addressee of the *Liber Confortatorius*) lived in small colonies of recluses who might share some devotions or practical arrangements and offer each other some rudimentary support.[5] Regardless of individual arrangements, the recluse's practice included voluntary imprisonment, self-imposed restrictions, and minimal human contact in order to find God.

The most widely read and most thoroughly studied anchoritic texts are Aelred of Rievaulx's letter to his sister, a recluse (c. 1160); and, partly based on Aelred, the thirteenth-century Middle English *Ancrene Wisse* ("Guide for Anchoresses"). In both texts, a male cleric dispenses advice to female recluses, ranging from the very practical (what to wear, how to organize one's day, how to support oneself, how to avoid distractions) to the theoretical and philosophical. Both texts are born of personal intimacy, affection, and respect;

---

[3]   See John of Fécamp's "Lamentation," in *Un maître de la vie spirituelle au XIe siècle: Jean de Fécamp*, eds. Jean Leclercq and Jean-Paul Bonnes (Paris: Vrin, 1946), 183–97, and the introduction, pp. 19–29; Giles Constable, "Eremitical Forms of Monastic Life," in *Istituzioni monastiche e istituzioni canonicali in occidente (1123–1215)* (Milano: Vita e pensiero, 1980), 239–64; L. Raison and R. Niderst, "Le mouvement érémitique dans l'ouest de la France à la fin du XIe et au début du XIIe siècle," *Annales de Bretagne* 55 (1948): 1–46. On the anchoritic community at St. Laurent, Angers, see Therese Latzke, "Robert von Arbrissel, Ermengard und Eva," *Mittellateinisches Jahrbuch* 19 (1984): 139–40.

[4]   The terms "anchoritic" and "eremitic" are essentially synonymous, denoting a religious discipline practiced by individuals in isolation. But in medieval usage, "anchorite" and "anchoress" came to mean the solitary who lived in a cell attached to a religious house (an "anchorhold"), as opposed to the "hermit" who lived in a remote wilderness.

[5]   For an introduction to high medieval anchoritism, see Giles Constable, "Eremitical Forms of Monastic Life," *Istituzioni monastiche e istituzioni canonicali in occidente (1123–1215)* (Milano: Vita e pensiero, 1980), 239–64; Ann K. Warren, *Anchorites and Their Patrons in Medieval England* (Berkeley: University of California Press, 1985); Roberta Gilchrist, *Gender and Material Culture: The Archaeology of Religious Women* (London: Routledge, 1994), 177–81.

nonetheless, the male advisor unmistakably speaks from a position of priestly authority, often adopting a fatherly tone. Both Aelred and the anonymous *Ancrene Wisse* author stress the recluses' commitment to a life of virginity; indeed they see their choice of living enclosed in a cell as a natural extension and a perfect metaphorical embodiment of that commitment.[6]

The *Liber Confortatorius* is interesting, among other things, as an early anchoritic text anticipating these better-known twelfth- and thirteenth-century successors.[7] It has many themes, images, and rhetorical features in common with them but is also significantly different. For instance, unlike his successors, Goscelin is only marginally interested in the anchoress's virginity, her untouched and unseen body.[8] But the *Liber Confortatorius* is also itself heir to a rich tradition of meditative and advisory spiritual literature. Augustine's meditations are a palpable presence in the work. Augustine bequeathed to his medieval students a personal, prayerful approach to theological and philosophical thought. His meditations proceed at a leisurely, reflective pace, like a dialogue the writer is having with himself or, more accurately, with God. Questions are posed, and solutions emerge slowly, incrementally, associatively. The meditations are very much written "in the first person." The voice of the thinker is always present; his doubts, his fumblings, his anguish, his search for an intellectual and spiritual path are as much part of the work as the outcome of that search. This style of thought perfectly suited medieval monastic thinkers, for whom reading, meditation, and prayer form one indissoluble spiritual practice.[9] The eleventh century saw a re-flowering of this Augustinian style. Anselm, roughly contemporary with Goscelin, was long held to be the initiator of this revival but is, as is being recognized these days, really an early high point, drawing in particular on the work of John of Fécamp.[10]

---

6   Another engaging and highly illuminating twelfth-century text on anchoritism is C. H. Talbot, *The Life of Christina of Markyate*, Oxford Medieval Texts (Oxford: Clarendon, 1959) – not an advice book but a biography of a recluse.

7   Even though they do share many themes and concerns, there is no evidence that the *Liber Confortatorius* directly influenced either Aelred of Rievaulx or the author of the *Ancrene Wisse* – or indeed that it circulated much at all.

8   For a further discussion, see the interpretive essay at the end of this book.

9   The classic description of monastic thought, study, and spirituality is Jean Leclercq, *The Love of Learning and the Desire for God* (New York: Fordham University Press, 1961).

10   Jean Leclercq and Jean-Paul Bonnes, eds., *Un maître de la vie spirituelle au XIe siècle: Jean de Fécamp* (Paris: Vrin, 1946), esp. the "Confessio Theologica."

Another important model for Goscelin are Ambrose's and especially Jerome's letters of advice to women, a natural choice for a male cleric finding himself in the position of advising religious women. (Abelard, being asked by Heloise to advise her and her nuns, also invokes St. Jerome.) Perhaps the most famous of the advice letters, Jerome's letter to Eustochium (letter 22) is a major source of the *Liber Confortatorius*.[11] These letters, too, had found imitators in Carolingian and more recent times (for instance, John of Fécamp writing to Empress Agnes). But most of these medieval examples are short letters, highly formalized and rhetorical; none approaches the *Liber Confortatorius* in length, ambition, and intimacy.[12]

Finally, the *Liber Confortatorius* finds much inspiration in the *Vitae Patrum* ("Lives of the Fathers") tradition, a body of literature pertaining to the fourth-century monks of the Egyptian desert which includes collections of edifying anecdotes, collections of sayings ("Verba Seniorum") and longer biographies of major figures.[13] The Desert Fathers' (and Mothers') extreme asceticism, their miracles and spectacular encounters with demons, and their sparse, gnomic wisdom have thrilled readers from the fourth century until our times. To anchorites and ascetic monks, the Desert Fathers were an unreachable but fascinating ideal as well as a literary model for their own self-definition: no one could seriously hope to duplicate the Fathers' ascetic feats, but they were an inexhaustible source of narrative patterns and images.

(It seems likely to me that Goscelin also knew John of Fecamp's work.) For other examples of eleventh-century devotional writing, see André Wilmart, ed., *Auteurs spirituels et textes dévots du moyen âge* (Paris: 1932); Thomas Bestul, "St. Anselm, the Monastic Community at Canterbury, and Devotional Writing in Late Anglo-Saxon England," *Anselm-Studies* 1 (1983): 185–97.

[11] Joan M. Petersen, trans., *Handmaids of the Lord: Contemporary Descriptions of Feminine Asceticism in the First Six Christian Centuries* (Kalamazoo: Cistercian Publications, 1996), 169–217.

[12] E.g., John of Fécamp's letters to Empress Agnes and to an unnamed nun, in *Un maître de la vie spirituelle*, 205–17; a little bit later than Goscelin, Robert of Arbrissel's letter to Ermengarde, and Marbod of Rennes' and Hildebert of Lavardin's quite extensive correspondence with women.

[13] For an overview of this literature and its eleventh-century reception, see Peter Jackson, "The *Vitas Patrum* in Eleventh-Century Worcester," in *England in the Eleventh Century: Proceedings of the 1990 Harlaxton Symposium*, ed. Carola Hicks (Stamford: Watkins, 1990), 119–34. A convenient translation of some of the major texts is Helen Waddell, *The Desert Fathers*, Vintage Spiritual Classics (New York: Random House, 1998; rpt. from London: Constable, 1936).

Goscelin and Eva

Goscelin, the author of the *Liber Confortatorius*, was a Fleming from the important abbey of St. Bertin. He had come to England in 1058 (or soon thereafter) together with the Lotharingian Herman, who had been appointed bishop of Ramsbury. Goscelin was to spend the rest of his fairly long life in England, at first as part of the bishop's "familia" (household, entourage, staff). His activities during that time appear to have included a stint as chaplain at the prestigious royal nunnery of Wilton. Herman's death in 1078 deprived him of protection and patronage, so that Goscelin's career became uncertain and unstable. He moved around the country, spending time at various monasteries (with varying degrees of certainty, scholars have identified Winchester, Peterborough, Barking Abbey, Ely, and Ramsey) before settling at St. Augustine's in Canterbury. During this time, Goscelin undertook most of his considerable hagiographic work. The decades after the Norman Conquest were a period of upheaval, transition, and reorganization for many religious houses, and many saw a need for updating their records, including the materials pertaining to their most important saints: scattered materials were collected, oral traditions were put into writing, old *vitae* ("lives," or biographies) were rewritten in a form more pleasing to modern tastes. Goscelin was entrusted with this work by several of the religious houses where he stayed. Among other major efforts, he composed a series of *vitae* and other hagiographic materials on the early abbesses of Barking Abbey; a *vita* and collection of miracles of St. Yvo at Ramsey; a major body of hagiographic and liturgical works concerning the founding fathers and early abbots of St. Augustine; a series of works on St. Mildrith; and, closest in time and subject to our text, a *vita* of St. Edith of Wilton, a work of some literary ambition that combines prose and verse. His work brought him fame as one of the foremost hagiographers and church musicians in his adopted country.[14]

Eva, the addressee of the *Liber Confortatorius*, had entered Goscelin's life relatively early in his English career. Born c. 1058, at the time he first arrived and therefore perhaps twenty or twenty-five

---

14 For discussions of Goscelin's life and works, see Antonia Gransden, *Historical Writing in England, c. 550 to c. 1307* (Ithaca: Cornell University Press, 1974), 64–65, 107–11; Frank Barlow, ed., *The Life of King Edward Who Rests at Westminster*, 2nd ed (Oxford: Clarendon, 1992), 133–49; C. H. Talbot, "The *Liber Confortatorius* of Goscelin of Saint Bertin," *Studia Anselmiana* 37; *Analecta Monastica*, 3rd ser. (1955): 5–22; André Wilmart, "Eve et Goscelin," *Révue Bénédictine* 46 (1934): 414–38 and 50 (1938): 42–83; esp. II.42–51.

years younger than him, she became his friend and protégé. As a little girl she entered the convent of Wilton, where Goscelin, in his capacity as chaplain, became her tutor and mentor.[15] He saw her take her vows there while still quite young. His emotional attachment to her is unmistakable. He insists that this attachment was mutual, but in the absence of any word from her we cannot be sure. In about 1079 or 1080, after the death of bishop Herman had sent Goscelin on his wanderings through ecclesiastical England, Eva abruptly left Wilton. Without consulting Goscelin or anyone else, she went to France to become a recluse at the church of St. Laurent at Angers, where there was a small community of anchoresses. Devastated by her decision and hurt by her secrecy, Goscelin wrote the *Liber Confortatorius* a few years later, perhaps 1082 or 83.[16] We do have considerable information about Eva's later life, most importantly a letter by Abbot Geoffrey of Vendôme and a commemorative biographical poem by Hilary of Orléans, written shortly after her death.[17] Thus we know that after about twenty years at Angers, she moved to an even more secluded life near Vendôme, sharing a cell with a monk-hermit named Hervé. Medieval and modern commentators alike are quick to assure us that there was nothing disreputable about the arrangement, and indeed, she must have been a highly respected religious figure for Abbot Geoffrey to address a letter jointly to her and Hervé.[18] But all this was long after the *Liber Confortatorius*.

Another Abelard and Heloise?

High medieval spirituality accommodated and encouraged passionate spiritual friendships, between friends of the same sex as well as

[15] On Wilton and Goscelin, see Georges Whalen, "Patronage Engendered: How Goscelin Allayed the Concerns of Nuns' Discriminatory Publics," in *Women, the Book and the Godly*, eds. Lesley Smith and Jane H. M. Taylor (Cambridge: D. S. Brewer, 1995), 124–27.

[16] This may or may not mean that he had not known of her departure until then; he may simply have taken some time to conceive, plan, and execute the work. The work gives the impression of great spontaneity (albeit in a stylized, rhetorical form); but, as with any work of art, it is risky to infer biographical details from literary form. The dating depends on one of Goscelin's references to contemporary events: the marriage of the Flemish princess Adela to the Danish king Knut IV in 1081 or 82 (Wilmart, "Eve et Goscelin (II)," 62 n. 1).

[17] *Hilarii versus et ludi*, ed. John Bernard Fuller (New York: Holt, 1929), 97–100. Therese Latzke also edits and discusses the poem in her article "Robert von Arbrissel, Ermengard und Eva," *Mittellateinisches Jahrbuch* 19 (1984): 148–54.

[18] Wilmart, "Eve et Goscelin, I," 418–19. On Eva's career, see Wilmart; Therese Latzke, "Robert von Arbrissel, Ermengard und Eva," *Mittellateinisches*

between men and women, in language that to our ears often sounds erotically charged.[19] But even allowing for differences of perception, most readers will feel that Goscelin's love for Eva goes beyond such spiritual soulmateship; indeed Goscelin himself seems quite worried about having gone too far.[20] While the *Liber Confortatorius* is not exactly a love story, Goscelin's passionate love and desire for Eva and his pain at losing her make for an absorbing subplot. Readers may well be reminded of Abelard and Heloise, perhaps the most famous pair of clerical lovers in the Middle Ages. A comparison is indeed instructive, as long as one remains conscious of the considerable differences. The two books together would make a splendid unit in a course on love and gender in the Middle Ages, or medieval spiritual literature or intellectual culture. Both involve a teacher-student pair, an intellectual cleric and a convent-trained, well-born young woman of exceptional intelligence, very much his junior. In both cases the love relationship takes its origin precisely in the erotics of teaching; and this pedagogical setting, together with the age difference, brings about an imbalance of power that (to us at least) is somewhat uncomfortable. Both affairs are known to us only through correspondence after the lovers' separation, filtered through the pain of loss.[21] After the separation, both men take on the role of spiritual adviser in the mold of St. Jerome's letters to women – Goscelin to console himself, Abelard, one feels, to distance himself. (Heloise says as much.) The two couples belong to roughly the same geographical and cultural area (Northern France, Flanders, and post-Conquest England) and they are close in time: Eva and Abelard must have been roughly contemporaries, with Goscelin about a generation older and Heloise a generation younger.

Jahrbuch 19 (1984): 136–47; Sharon Elkins, *Holy Women of Twelfth Century England* (Chapel Hill: University of North Carolina Press, 1988), 21–27.

[19] Aelred of Rievaulx wrote a dialogue on this subject (*Spiritual Friendship*, trans. Mary Eugenia Laker [Kalamazoo: Cistercian Publications, 1974]). See Brian Patrick McGuire, *Friendship and Community: The Monastic Experience 350–1250* (Kalamazoo: Cistercian Publications, 1988). McGuire stresses, though, that the boundaries between spiritual friendship, eroticism, and sexuality were fluid, and that this fluidity was frequently felt to be problematic. Aelred is his chief example.

[20] For further discussion, see the interpretive essay at the end of the book.

[21] Unless, that is, Constant Mews is correct in attributing the Troyes Ms. 1452 correspondence to Abelard and Heloise at an earlier stage of their relationship. (*The Lost Love Letters of Heloise and Abelard: Perceptions of Dialogue in Twelfth-Century France* [New York: St. Martin's Press, 1999].)

Yet, even though they are only about a generation apart, the two couples could not be more different in their spirituality, their intellectual style, their *mentalité*. Abelard and his pupil Heloise not only belong to but embody the nascent culture of the universities and early scholasticism. They certainly are as conversant with the Bible as Eva and Goscelin are, and as likely to resort to its language and imagery. But they are far removed from the world of monastic reading and meditation. They are debaters, logicians, dialecticians, rhetoricians. They are urban and urbane, with a pronounced taste for the secular intellectual culture of their time. They relish controversy and can be aggressive in their writing and reasoning.[22] Monasticism is simply not their milieu. Heloise had been educated at the convent of Argenteuil (perhaps not unlike Wilton in its social and educational aspirations), but as a secular boarder, not a nun. Abelard was in lower orders, as he had to be to study and teach in the schools, but he was not a priest and certainly not a monk. Both entered monasteries only after their debacle, quite reluctantly, and both remained at odds with monastic culture.

Goscelin and Eva, by contrast, are steeped in monastic culture. Eva had been brought to Wilton as a little girl, a child "oblate," with the express intention that she should become a nun. She seems to have made her formal vows at a very young age (see p. 23, n. 9). Goscelin had been a monk all his life; we do not know at what age he entered the monastery, but his training and self-understanding are thoroughly monastic, even if he did spend a lot of his career in what might be called public life as part of the entourage and staff of Bishop Herman. Eva's and Goscelin's intellectual style is of the cloister, not the schools. It involves slow, ruminative reading, meditation, a lot of memorization; the aim was to make the text one's own, incorporate it fully into one's mental furnishings. Like Abelard and Heloise, Goscelin and Eva are well read in the Latin classics as well as the Bible and the Church Fathers, but their main point of reference is the liturgy, and particularly the Psalms, which are the core of the monastic offices, the prayer services performed at set times throughout the day and night. Through this steady, prayerful routine, they not only memorized the liturgy and the Psalms, but appropriated and inhabited them. Their thinking and writing is meditative,

---

[22] Andrew Taylor, "A Second Ajax: Peter Abelard and the Violence of Dialectic," in *The Tongue of the Fathers*, eds. David Townsend and Andrew Taylor (Philadelphia: University of Pennsylvania Press, 1998), 14–34.

prayerful, associative, colorful, and image-rich.[23] It is closely linked to their reading: quotations come to mind as readily as the next word in a sentence. They do have a vivid interest in the intellectual debates of their time (such as the question of why God became man, which shortly afterwards led to Anselm's celebrated treatise, "Cur Deus Homo"); but they treat them in the style of an Augustinian meditation or theological reflection, not as a scholastic debate. These differences in intellectual style are not just accidental or personal; they are a sign of the times. Between them, Goscelin and Eva and Abelard and Heloise bracket a major shift in Western religious and intellectual history, from monasticism to scholasticism, from cloister to university.[24]

Another major difference between the couples – which renders direct comparison difficult, if not problematic – is that we do not know very much of Goscelin's and Eva's history together. Abelard provides us with a detailed, if one-sided and tendentious, account of their affair in the *Historia Calamitatum*; both his letters and Heloise's offer corrections and additions to this account. There are, moreover, independent witnesses to their story.[25] Of Goscelin and Eva, we know only what Goscelin tells us. We are quite well informed about each of their lives individually. Goscelin, apart from what he himself tells us in his other works, is mentioned by contemporary writers.[26] Even Eva's life, as we have seen, is relatively well documented.[27] None of these sources, however, seem to be aware of any connection between Eva and Goscelin, or if they are they do not say so. It is particularly striking that Hilary, who is undertaking to tell Eva's entire life and is sufficiently well informed to know her parents' names and national origins, does not even mention Goscelin.

---

[23] A fascinating account of the intellectual tradition of monastic meditation is Mary Carruthers, *The Craft of Thought: Meditation, Rhetoric, and the Making of Images, 400–1200* (Cambridge: Cambridge University Press, 1998).

[24] Jean Leclercq, *The Love of Learning and the Desire for God* (New York: Fordham University Press, 1961), 72–75; Ivan Ilich, *In the Vineyard of the Text* (Chicago: University of Chicago Press, 1993), ch. 3; Andrew Taylor, "A Second Ajax" (see n. 22 above).

[25] See Peter Dronke, *Abelard and Heloise in Medieval Testimonies*, W. P. Ker Memorial Lecture, No. 26 (Glasgow: University of Glasgow Press, 1976).

[26] Notably William of Malmesbury, *Gesta Regum Anglorum: The History of the English Kings*, ed. and trans. R. A. B. Mynors, R. M. Thomson and M. Winterbottom (Oxford: Clarendon, 1998), 590–93.

[27] See above, at nn. 17 and 18.

Most importantly, we have only one side of the correspondence. If Eva ever replied to Goscelin's long missive, her response has not survived; we do not even know if she ever received it.[28] One of the chief interests of the Heloise and Abelard correspondence is the give-and-take between two extraordinarily intelligent and passionate people, the struggle between two very different perspectives on the same sequence of events, and the painful difficulty of getting the conversation started. Here, we have only Goscelin's pain, Goscelin's thoughts, Goscelin's desire. We can infer some idea of Eva from the picture he paints of her and for her, but we must frequently read between the lines and always remember that much of the emerging picture may be his projection. Silence, one-sidedness, and difficult, indirect access are of course what we are accustomed to in our study of medieval women; Heloise is the immensely attractive exception. As readers and historians, we must proceed with tact and caution, succumbing neither to the fatalism or smugness of earlier generations who simply declared that there was nothing to know about medieval women, nor to the temptation of reading more into the text than it is able to yield.

It may be tempting to form theories about what "really happened" between Goscelin and Eva. But it is important to remember that such reconstructions are pure speculation, and dangerously open to modern projections. Most readers will at times be uncomfortable with the vehemence of Goscelin's eroticism, especially when he looks back and recalls his feelings for a very young Eva. One can see controlling and even threatening elements in Goscelin's emotional relationship with Eva (and these are discussed more fully in the essay at the end of this book). But it seems important to avoid seeing it through the lens and describing it in the language of our modern conceptions of coercive love and sexual abuse, which in their present articulation are quite specific to our time. I prefer to follow Goscelin's own imagery, emotions, and judgments, and let the medieval text speak to us, rather than superimpose our own conceptual grids on what may be a quite different emotional landscape. In her valuable article on male advisors of religious women, Therese Latzke reacts strongly to Goscelin's overheated language, and possibly over-reacts. She imagines Eva fleeing Wilton *because* of Goscelin's fervid, even abusive love, and all but constructs a gothic novel out of the *Liber Confortatorius*'s scanty data. But there is no evidence to support this

---

[28]   Wilmart, "Eve et Goscelin II," p. 55, and Therese Latzke (p. 143) surmise she did.

reconstruction.[29] For every passage that seems to hint at a guilty sexual relationship, there are others that speak against it, and all of Goscelin's penitential comments, both on his behalf and on hers, make equally good sense if they refer to guilty desires rather than a love affair. And in the absence of any word from Eva, we have no indication one way or the other how Eva felt about Goscelin.

How to Read the *Liber Confortatorius*
Goscelin and Eva were both raised in a tradition of slow, meditative, reiterative reading that aimed at committing the text to memory, savoring each word and phrase and pausing for imaginative association and emotional elaboration. Modern readers need to be patient and re-learn these techniques (at least up to a point), but will be richly rewarded if they do. To find a way into this not instantly accessible book, it helps to understand what kind of book it is. It is a consolation and a self-consolation; it is an Augustinian meditation, or series of meditations. One might almost think of it as a textbook of meditation, modeling associative, imaginative thought for the reader. It is also a textbook of psalmody. Goscelin not only quotes and annotates numerous psalm texts, but he reflects extensively on what it means to be reciting the Psalter (pp. 99–100). The recitation of the Psalms, as we have seen, was the defining religious practice of monks and nuns, the "opus dei," the work of God, par excellence. Goscelin is assuming that Eva, like many anchoresses, will retain this practice ("reweaving the Psalter," as he calls it at one point). Since they had recited the Psalter constantly all their lives (and very likely had been taught to read by memorizing it), both Goscelin and Eva knew it inside out. This explains Goscelin's liberal quotation from the psalms, freely weaving in and out of the Biblical text. It was a shared storehouse of images, a shared language, so much part of both Goscelin's and Eva's mental fabric that it would be more accurate to say that they did not so much quote the psalms as they thought with them. Moreover, meditation and psalmody are seen as an antidote to depression ("taedia," "acedia"), one of the chief "demons" that plagued the solitary from the Desert Fathers onwards and which, as the Desert Fathers insisted, is best overcome by keeping busy, with one's hands or with one's mind. In that sense, the *Liber Confortatorius* is also a textbook of asceticism, even though it lacks

---

[29] Besides, Goscelin seems to imply that he had not seen Eva for years when she decided to move to Angers and become an anchoress.

the practical, rule-like advice of Aelred, the *Ancrene Wisse*, or Abelard's letter on nuns.

The book has to fulfill so many functions because anchoresses (and indeed most medieval readers outside of the major monastic centers) had to make do with few reading materials. At the same time, the book's compendium-like quality also makes it very personal: it is a "desert island" anthology of shared favorites. (As a modern analogy, one might think of the sampler tapes or CDs teenagers make for each other of their favorite music.) There is a kind of anchoritic sparseness about such a compilation, but at the same time it claims and invokes fullness: you must make do with just this *libellus*; it is all you have, but also all you need.[30] This creates a kind of intellectual intimacy between compiler and reader. The sampler is a token and a practical necessity, but also a synecdoche for the friendship and all its shared interests. It is in some way an authoritative and even slightly controlling gesture: the compiler claims to know exactly what the addressee needs, to be able to make knowing and sufficient selections on her behalf. But it is also a participatory gesture and a soul-baring one: the compiler reveals what most matters to him and offers to share these personal choices, not with the world in general but with the addressee alone. The compactness of the compilation implies that it is only a small selection of the intellectual treasures the two of them share; the addressee is invited to supply the rest, re-constitute the totality of their shared mental world and of their friendship.

For all these reasons – the tradition of "ruminative," "mulling" monastic reading; the tradition of associative, imaginative meditation; the special language of monastic worship, and the special language shared by these two friends – we must read as they did, slowly and imaginatively. There are, to our mind, long and dry stretches in the *Liber Confortatorius*. Even Goscelin is aware of his prolixity, and he explains it very poignantly: writing the book is his last real connection with Eva, and when he is done it will be all over; he does not *want* to stop writing.

If we read patiently and imaginatively, we enter a world that in some ways is instantly accessible on a very human level. We can recognize Goscelin's love and sense of abandonment, his longing for affection; we recognize, perhaps better than he could, his

---

[30] Not literally so: Goscelin does assume that Eva will have other books at her disposal, and in fact outlines a rather ambitious reading program for her in Book III.

half-acknowledged sexual desire. With a little imagination and empathy, we can learn to respond to the beauty of the Psalms or the Song of Songs, the joy of knowing them so intimately, of ranging freely over them and recombining them in new and unexpected ways; we can share the wonder of the images, the little stories and vignettes that arise at times – the story of the Danish murderer who escapes from the courtroom; the down-to-earth description of how one can revive a spent vine and make it bear fruit again; the strangely erotic meditation on the Angel Gabriel's annunciation to the Virgin; the story of Perpetua and Felicitas and other bracing tales of the early Church.

In other respects we are entering a radically strange world. In fact, it was quite strange, and deliberately so, even to Goscelin's and Eva's contemporaries. Those who sought out the "desert" wanted – as Goscelin frequently states – to leave the world behind as completely as possible, and they reveled in their estrangement. They seem to have felt the need to find image after image of what they had become: a pelican in the desert and a night-raven on the house; a prisoner; a champion fighter against demons; a mariner on a vast sea in a tiny skiff; Mary of Egypt, alone, naked and unsheltered, her skin withered and blackened by the desert sun – images that suggest confinement and seclusion as well as exposedness and vulnerability. Augustine had stressed the idea of spiritual exile: we are never truly at home in our lives until we return to God. Anchorites wanted to literalize the metaphor of exile, not only to think it but to live it.

Often when we begin to think we recognize a somewhat familiar image or idea, we are brought up short by a recognition of startling otherness. For instance, we may be tempted to read in the sometimes sharp inside-outside, soul-body dichotomy an asceticism we ourselves might be comfortable with. Most of us can understand that one might choose to forego material and even physical comfort in exchange for psychological or spiritual well-being. Many of us in our modern consumer society fantasize – as even Goscelin does at times – about simplicity, about trading material things for inner peace and inner fulfillment. Yet we need to remember that to anchorites, psychological wholeness and personal fulfillment is not the goal. Medieval ascetics will put their psychological well-being on the line just as readily as their material comfort. Fighting depression ("acedia," "taedia," "tristia") is one of the chief activities of the Desert Fathers and the medieval anchorites; but in the first place they actively invite these conditions, put themselves in harm's way, in order to test themselves and emerge victorious.

Likewise, when Goscelin retells the anecdote from the *Vitae Patrum* about "seeing oneself" in a calm water surface, he is not talking about a modern self-discovery, a modern "finding oneself," in its largely narcissistic meaning. Indeed, he is not talking about a modern self at all, a core personality that is uniquely, valuably, and in a certain sense self-sufficiently "us." The discovery, as Goscelin immediately goes on to say, is of one's own insufficiency, even (if left to oneself) one's worthlessness. Self-recognition is an occasion for humility and penitence, and the fulfillment sought lies entirely outside oneself, in God.

Despite this self-abnegation, ancient and medieval anchoritism is nevertheless expressive, performative, poetic.[31] When ancient monks or nuns went "into the desert," they acted out a spiritual metaphor: that of exile, of being utterly alone with their God, in an arid, thirsty environment of physical, emotional, sensory, and even spiritual deprivation.[32] When anchoresses or anchorites had themselves walled up in a small cell, they acted out a spiritual metaphor: that of being enclosed, within the world but not of it; of being untouched and untouchable, unseen and invisible. In later anchoritic literature for women – not yet so much in Goscelin – the anchoress is also acting out her own virginity, her physical and sexual untouchedness: the cell becomes a metonymy for her body, surrounding, defending, and imprisoning her body as her body does her soul.[33] In all these instances, although the precise emphases may vary, the ascetics do not only sacrifice material comfort, they do not only deprive themselves, but they also create something: they actively stage and enact their way of being in the world.

---

[31] Margaret Hostetler, "Designing Religious Women: Privacy and Exposure in the *Life of Christina of Markyate* and *Ancrene Wisse*," *Mediaevalia* 22 (1999): 206–207.

[32] Unlike their medieval successors, the Desert Fathers did not cultivate a colorful, image-rich inner life; they shunned too much thought, too much imagining, as they did anything visual or material. Their wisdom is sparse and aphoristic, not homiletic and associative like the *Liber Confortatorius*.

[33] Elizabeth Robertson, "The Rule of the Body: The Feminine Spirituality of the *Ancrene Wisse*," in *Seeking the Woman in Late Medieval and Renaissance Writings: Essays in Feminist Contextual Criticism*, eds. Sheila Fisher and Janet E. Halley (Knoxville: University of Tennessee Press, 1989), 109–34; Jocelyn G. Price, " 'Inner' and 'Outer': Conceptualizing the Body in the *Ancrene Wisse* and Aelred's *De Institutione Inclusarum*," in *Medieval English Religious and Ethical Literature*, eds. Gregory Kratzmann and James Simpson (Cambridge: D. S. Brewer, 1986), 192–208.

These lived metaphors are the poetic nucleus of anchoritic literature, and one of its enduring attractions. Goscelin and Eva were
fascinated by the Lives of the Desert Fathers, and despite or because
of their strangeness these Lives still speak to us today. (They are cor-
dially recommended as a background and counterpoint to this book.[34])
The anchoritic works of the high Middle Ages, and Goscelin's book
in particular, may have much to puzzle, alienate or even repel
modern readers: but they will also be unexpectedly compelling
and accessible to anyone willing to read imaginatively and listen
patiently.

Some Notes on the Text and the Translation

The *Liber Confortatorius* survives in a single manuscript, BL Ms.
Sloane 3103, apparently a mid-twelfth century copy. The only edition to date, the basis of this translation, is C. H. Talbot's 1955 print-
ing, which is not widely available.[35] Goscelin's Latin is artful and
complex to the point of being convoluted. It follows a stylistic ideal
that was already somewhat old-fashioned in his own time.
Nonetheless – in this book more than in Goscelin's other works – his
convoluted style has a poetic force and appropriateness all its own.
After some acclimation, it is not necessarily difficult to read (though
quite difficult to render into good English), and one begins to savor
its pleasures. In translating, I have cautiously smoothed the syntax
and broken up endless sentences, to produce legible English; but I
have tried not to obliterate Goscelin's characteristic periods and
cadences, and I have aimed for a tone that preserves both the artful-
ness and the fervent intimacy of the original.

Goscelin, for reasons already explained, liberally quotes the Bible,
especially the Psalms; he excerpts long passages from Patristic literature, sometimes acknowledged and sometimes not; to a much lesser
extent, he quotes the more commonly read Classical authors.
Especially with Biblical material, he effortlessly moves in and out of
quotations, paraphrasing, condensing, inserting explanations. It would

---

[34] See n. 13 above.

[35] C. H. Talbot, "The *Liber Confortatorius* of Goscelin of Saint Bertin," *Analecta
Monastica*, 3rd ser. 37 (1955): 2–117. A much-needed new edition is, I hear,
being prepared. I have not systematically collated or corrected Talbot's edition,
though I have checked some of the more puzzling readings against the manuscript (in microfilm). In the few instances where my reading differs from Talbot
(and the even fewer instances where I have taken it upon myself to emend the
text), I have so indicated in the notes.

be excessive to try to identify every quotation, echo, and reminiscence; I have reported those identified by Talbot, and added a few more, but I have not aimed for completeness. It is equally pointless to attempt to distinguish precisely between verbatim and free quotations. (Talbot, who attempts to use italics for "real" quotations as opposed to paraphrases or verbal echoes, quickly becomes embroiled in inconsistencies.) I have kept quotation marks to a minimum (like most medieval manuscripts, Sloane 3103 has no punctuation corresponding to our quotation marks), using them only where Goscelin explicitly introduces a sentence as a quotation. For Biblical quotations, I have followed – but not slavishly – the wording of the Douai version, an English translation of the Latin Vulgate (since that is the text Goscelin uses) in preference to the King James Version [KJV]. I have also based all references on the Douai version. Users of the KJV or more modern translations based on it should keep in mind that slight discrepancies are possible; that the Vulgate and Douai versions include some Biblical books omitted by KJV as apocryphal (e.g., Wisdom, Ecclesiasticus); that the Vulgate text counts as 1-4 Kings what appears as 1-2 Samuel and 1-2 Kings in KJV. The biggest discrepancies will be found in the Book of Psalms, where there are two different underlying original texts. KJV follows the "Hebrew" text; Goscelin, as is usual for his time and place, uses the "Gallican Psalter," based on the Septuagint, an early Greek translation of the Hebrew Scriptures. The two versions count the psalms slightly differently. Thus, for most of the Psalter, except at the very beginning and end, the Vulgate count will be off by one with respect to KJV; i.e., looking for a reference to Ps. 22:1, try Ps. 23:1 in KJV. Wording of individual verses may differ slightly, and occasionally considerably.

The Book of Encouragement and Consolation

Prologue

The first volume speaks of complaint and comfort.
The second confronts our lusts and prevails in the battles.
The third book inflames desires and conquers dejection.
The fourth, in humility, heads for the stars in a chariot.

The excluded to the enclosed; the solitary in the world to the solitary from the world; one who is known to Christ and to Love, writing to his only soul.

The Eva of whom I speak is Christ's darling,[1] left alone in the house for God's sake; she is become the night raven in the house.[2] Far from her homeland she seeks her true home. Or, rather, she has escaped from the turbulence of the world to the peace of God; escaping from mortal sufferings, she is seeking the eternal joy, which is God. May he receive her who received Mary Magdalene, who in the inexhaustible bosom of his kindness gathers and embraces every soul that comes to him. May he receive his darling and stranger; for the Lord has heard the poor, and has not disdained the prisoners.[3] If by any chance this pilgrim letter, entrusted to uncertain winds but commended to God, should stray into alien hands, I pray that it may be returned to her for whom alone it is manifestly intended, lest someone appropriate what is not meant for him. This secret between two people is sealed with Christ as mediator, offering in sacrifice nothing but virginal simplicity and pure love. Far be from this pure encounter the whisperer of scandal, the lecherous eye, the pointing finger, the spewer of hot air and the dirty snickerer. The story is long, the words are awkward and feeble; he who does not like it should not

---

[1] The Latin *pupilla* allows for a similar double meaning as English *pupil*: "ward, protégée, student, disciple" – surely the primary meaning here – and "apple of the eye."

[2] Ps. 101:8. (References to the Book of Psalms are according to the Vulgate/Douai version; the corresponding citation in the King James Version would be 102:8, and the text may vary considerably, as it does in this instance. See Introduction, p. 16.)

[3] Ps. 68:34.

read it, and should leave alone what was not written for him. But whatever happens, I would rather be ridiculed by the raised eyebrows of strangers than not do justice to love. Since this exhortatory letter is growing beyond moderate length, let it be divided into four segments, like way stations where it may pause on its journey and catch its breath.

HERE ENDS THE PROLOGUE.

Here Begins *The Book of Encouragement and Consolation* by the Monk Goscelin, Sent from England to Eva, Enclosed in Christ's Name at St. Laurent in Angers

O my soul, dearer to me than the light, your Goscelin is with you, in the inseparable presence of the soul. He is with you, undivided, in his better part, that part with which he was allowed to love you, that part which cannot be hindered by any physical distance. He salutes you in Christ with an everlasting greeting. See, his hand has touched us, with its all-discerning and all-disposing wisdom; and separating us for a time taught us higher purposes, namely that we may pant for that homeland and hurry to be reunited in that place where we cannot ever be separated again in all eternity. The farther he has separated us in body, the more inseparably he will refashion as a single soul what used to be one soul in two people. In the same way, long ago, the fountain of love himself sorely wounded the love of his disciples through his bodily absence; but he made their love flare up all the more splendidly in spiritual charity. Therefore, since your soulmate cannot and does not deserve to visit you in the flesh, he now seeks you out with anxious letters and long laments. God's provident mercy has afforded us that consolation, that, though distant in space, we can be present to each other in faith and in writing. And these torments of separation, which I deserved through my crimes – a letter shuttling back and forth can reconnect us and keep us warm.[1] Also, the tenacious page will speak more edifyingly than the fluid tongue. You have relinquished me and banished me from your sight, but your love will be able to see me in your reading and to take in my voice and my sighing words, using your eyes for ears. Therefore do not think me cut off from you. Whenever, thinking of me in Christ, you will deign to look at these my letters, you will believe me with you at Wilton, before our holy Lady Edith, sitting chastely by your side, speaking with you, admonishing you, consoling

---

[1]   The theme of the traveling letter that can make up for the lover's absence echoes Ovid's letters from exile, especially *Tristia* 1.1. The Latin sentence is awkward and not altogether logically constructed. I have kept the logical break in my translation.

you, and with the languishing desire of a wounded love infusing your breast with Christ.

But see, as I was writing this, my sorrow swelled up and could not be repressed.[2] My hand and my pen dropped; a moaning and sobbing overcame me. I rushed before the altar of your St. Lawrence, as I was sitting in his remote chapel.[3] In a flood of tears, I called out again and again, as if buffeted and beaten by the Lord: Lord have mercy, Lord have mercy. I snatched up a psalm, "Miserere mei Deus," and intoned it amidst sobs: "a contrite and humble heart"; and again from another psalm these verses that seek you out: "I am made like unto a pelican in the desert," and "The Lord looked down from Heaven onto the Earth, to hear the groans of them that are in fetters."[4] With loud wails I forced out, "Holy Mary, come to the aid of the miserable and help the dejected."[5] Now, as I take up again my interrupted speech – interrupted by sorrow – please do not disdain to receive my devotion. If you are moved by any feelings of affection, accept this consolation as if I were present.

Now let me, for our mutual refreshment and for our everlasting remembrance, rehearse the story of our affection and confirm our unending love. This is more a book than a letter, but do not let that deter you; no matter how long it is, it cannot contain my great desires. And unless I am mistaken, insatiable fervor and anxious love will make the longest discourses seem short to you as well. Hear me, speaking to you, as it were, from the sickbed of my sorrow.

---

[2] The following passage, describing Goscelin's emotional collapse while writing, is confusing in its tense system, though probably with good artistic reason: he is thinking both of a breakdown that is occurring simultaneously – or almost – with his writing, and of his recurrent tearful prayers over the previous days, weeks, or months. Synchronizing the recitation of the psalms with one's emotional life or daily routine is a recurrent theme in the book. The quotations here are from the five penitential psalms, which monks and nuns would recite every morning before matins. Linda Olson points out that the passage as a whole echoes the conversion scene in Augustine's *Confessions*. ("Did Medieval English Women Read Augustine's *Confessiones*? Constructing Feminine Interiority and Literacy in the Eleventh and Twelfth Centuries," in *Learning and Literacy in Medieval England and Abroad*, ed. Sarah Rees Jones [Turnhout: Brépols, 2003], 76.)

[3] I.e., Goscelin visits a chapel and altar dedicated to St. Lawrence in the church where he is currently staying (presumably Peterborough, see Book II at n. 10), in order to feel connected to Eva at the church of St. Laurent in Angers.

[4] Ps. 50:1, 50:19, 101:7, 101:20–21.

[5] "Sancta Maria, succurre miseris": the opening line of a Latin hymn to the Virgin Mary.

The Birth of Affection

You remember, my sweetest soul, how I first vexed you when you were a child, quite certain I could easily correct such a pious soul.[6] It is as with the bees: they prefer to make honey from bitter juices. I won you over with talk; you won me over with favors and gifts. You gave me books I very much wanted; you spoke affectionately of my Saint Bertin; you hastened to do all the offices of charity. Yet so far my love for you was only external, and bearable; it was a love in the good hope of Christ. But when you walked up to the Lord's wedding,[7] with trepidation, the penultimate of fourteen virgins, with glittering candles like the stars and constellations above; when, before a large crowd waiting in solemn silence, you put on the sacred vestment, it was as if from the fiery throne of God sitting above his cherubim, I was struck to the quick with this wondrously beautiful epithalamium: "I am given in marriage to him whom the angels serve, and he has wedded me with his ring."[8] I was touched by the heavenly dew and wept in tearful fervor. And as I continued to witness your silence, your careful continence, your singing of the psalms and the praises of your teacher, my desire was inflamed even more. I arranged for you to be present at the upcoming dedication of the church, since I wanted you to benefit from such a great sacrament.[9] Do continue to practice diligently what I then, as if giving birth,

---

6 Goscelin is thinking back to the time when he was chaplain at the nunnery of Wilton and tutored Eva as a little girl; she entered the convent of Wilton as a child "oblate" and was educated there. Apparently their relationship got off to a rocky start.

7 I.e., as she was making her profession, her formal vows as a nun (but see n. 9 below).

8 Antiphon of the Vespers office on the feast of St. Agnes, a virgin saint.

9 It is hard to say whether Goscelin is here thinking of Eva's oblation (i.e., the dedication of a young child to the monastic life by his or her parents), or Eva's profession (her formal vows as a nun). The church of Wilton was rebuilt by Queen Edith, wife of Edward the Confessor (who herself had been educated at Wilton), and was dedicated on October 3, 1065. If Wilmart's conjecture about Eva's birth date is correct, she would have been about seven years old. The ritual described here clearly recalls a profession, not an "oblation" (the dedication of a young child to monastic life), and seven seems extremely young for a profession; the age usually recommended for girls was twelve or older. But regulations were erratic, and apparently honored mostly in the breach, especially with child oblates, whose legal status as monks or nuns was murky. Since they had made no vows themselves, but their parents had acted on their behalf in dedicating them to the religious life, there was considerable controversy at various times over whether oblation was binding on the child; whether it superseded profession or whether it had to be reaffirmed by formal vows as the oblate neared

instilled in your ear: "Weep before the Lord." That is, you should ask of God only one thing: that you may desire Christ alone in wounded love, and that you may with full concentration of your heart and with all your soul wish for him alone as your dowry. "Thus," I said, "my dearest soul, thus you should implore your Lord with the privilege of eternal love: 'Give yourself to me.' That is the locus of your only prayer. You entered here alone to receive him alone. Shout, wail, knock, so that the door may be opened to you. Struggle with the Lord as long as you have life; push violently to enter the kingdom of heaven. If the Lord himself offers himself to you in charity, be sure to spare no effort on your part." Then, when our bishop processed in with the smoking censer, chanting, "Let my prayer be directed as incense in your sight,"[10] what was it that I then instilled into your heart? "This," I said, "is the model of how you must enter before the Lord: not with a cold sense, not with an empty breast, but set ablaze by burning love, scented with the burnt spices of virtue. In heaven, the angel who carries the golden thurible is given many pieces of incense: the uncounted wishes and sighs of all pious minds, carried

adulthood; whether at that time the oblate had a genuine option of leaving the monastery, and if not, whether these vows were anything more than a pro forma ceremony. Partly for these reasons, the practice of oblation was discouraged and finally abandoned from about the twelfth century onwards. See Mayke de Jong, *In Samuel's Image: Child Oblation in the Early Medieval West* (Leiden: Brill, 1996), esp. 176–91; Giles Constable, "The Ceremonies and Symbolism of Entering Religious Life and Taking the Monastic Habit, from the Fourth to the Twelfth Century," in *Segni e riti nella chiesa altomedioevale occidentale* (Spoleto: Centro italiano di studi sull'alto medioevo, 1987), 771–34. It is therefore not inconceivable that the nuns of Wilton had their oblates profess at a very young age, or even made oblation and profession coincide. It is also possible that Eva was a few years older than scholars have surmised; or that Goscelin misremembers the sequence of events; or that he fictionalizes them to suit his poetic purposes (cf. his account of the oblation-cum-profession of the two-year-old St. Edith, with a sweetly sentimental "epithalamium": A. Wilmart, ed., "La légende de Ste Édith en prose et vers par le moine Goscelin," *Analecta Bollandiana* 56 [1938]: 43–47). Needless to say, one would also like to think that Goscelin did not have such strongly erotic feelings for a seven-year-old. The liturgy for the dedication of churches, like that for the profession of nuns and the feasts of virgin saints, makes use of the nuptial metaphors of the Song of Songs and Ps. 44: the church, or the virgin, is seen allegorically as "the bride of Christ." See my "Closed Doors: An Epithalamium for Queen Edith, Widow and Virgin," in *Constructions of Widowhood and Virginity in the Middle Ages*, eds. Angela J. Weisl and Cindy Carlson (New York: St. Martin's Press, 1999), 70–76, and the references provided there.

[10] Ps. 130:2.

before God by the angelic hand like scented smoke, heated by the burning and boiling of tears." And when, through the generosity of your father, you and your mother attended the banquet,[11] I passed you a platter of fish and enjoined upon you the mortification of the flesh with these words: "Piscis assus, Christus passus."[12] And then we went to the solemnities of another church dedication.[13] Again, I was granted the favor of taking you along, like the three-year-old Mary:[14] not purpled, not jeweled, not gilded, standing out from the crowd of girls not by the beauty of your face. But I attended only to you, in that beauty which the King of Chastity desired, black in clothing like the daughter of Zion but beautiful in faith.[15]

Then the festive assembly dispersed. But the arrowheads imbedded earlier still stuck; wounded with love, my insides continued to smart. My parchments and tablets frequently brought Christ to you; and chaste letters from you were not slow in coming. I frequently visited to talk to you, pushed by both my own and your loving impatience. Your own heart, full of the Lord's arrows, knows full well what I suffered, with sighs, disappointments, feverish anticipation, empty days and nights, with the inaccessible love of my most desired soul, when I sometimes came running for the holy conversation that could save me, but left frustrated. In our mutual conversations, you, although most eloquent, silently drank in the pious admonishments. Whatever I counseled, I found accepted, not in your replies but in your deeds. Do you remember when you told me your dream, in

---

[11] This could refer either to Eva's biological parents – who, as well-respected, wealthy lay people, might well have been present at a major solemnity with royal involvement – or to Bishop Herman and the abbess of Wilton, who are referred to as Eva's father and mother a little later on.

[12] Literally, "the fish is roasted, Christ has suffered." Apparently a mnemonic jingle used to teach children the connection between Christ's passion and Lenten or Friday fasting (when meat is forbidden and only fish is allowed).

[13] The dedication of the new Westminster abbey church, built by King Edward I ("the Confessor") and dedicated 28 Dec. 1065. Goscelin describes this occasion in the dedication of his Life of St. Edith. (It was during this celebration that the king took ill, dying a few days later and thus setting the stage for the Norman Conquest.)

[14] "Triduana Maria": literally, "three-day" (not "three-year") Mary; but the reference is presumably to the story in the apocryphal Infancy Gospel of James, which has the Virgin Mary being dedicated to the temple in Jerusalem as a small child (and the precise age is an issue in the narrative). See Edgar Hennele, *New Testament Apocrypha*, ed. Wilhelm Schneemelcher, trans. P. McL. Wilson (Philadelphia: Westminster Press, 1963), 1:380.

[15] Ps. 44:12.

which I was feeding you with snow-white bread, and as you ate you
found golden morsels in your mouth, which you collected in your
lap? See, that is the bread of life and the word of God that is more to
be desired than gold. From that gold fashion yourself a necklace, and
like Mary, keep all the Lord's words and ponder them in your heart.[16]
Whenever our Bishop greeted you with an embrace and these words:
"Eva, Mother of all the living," I, alluding to the name, responded,
"No, the other Eva was the mother of the living; this one will be the
daughter of the living."[17] By God's grace, your ways, your places,
your pursuits smelled sweet to me like nectar and balsam. It would
take too long to retell everything; your memory is strong enough and
will not be weakened by living in a faraway land. After the death of
our father, I was much consoled by talking with you about our common bereavement, until that king arose who knew not Joseph; and
your devoted friend was forced to wander the land for a long time,
forced out by the envy of vipers and the cruelty of a stepfather.[18]

A Model of Affection

Therefore I need to change my tune; for even though reason
approves of your virtue, love, the nurturer of all virtues, is injured.
The mother soul who gave birth to you with heaving womb, who
shunned her desired homeland for your sake as if it were an exile,
and loved her exile as a homeland,[19] who did so much and bore so
much in the hope of our mutual presence, now complains that you
have left her behind, in a cruel and insulting manner of which she

---

[16] Luke 2:19.
[17] Gen. 3:20. Goscelin's reply is apparently intended as a learned joke, but I confess I do not understand it.
[18] Exodus 1:8. The "father" is Bishop Herman, who had brought Goscelin over to
England in his entourage, and had sponsored his ecclesiastical career. His suc-
cessor, Osmund, apparently thought less highly of Goscelin, and Goscelin found
himself without a permanent appointment and little prospect for career advance-
ment for several years.
[19] Goscelin ("the mother soul") was from Flanders but spent most of his life as an
expatriate in England, Eva's native land. Note that Goscelin, here and throughout, describes himself predominantly in female terms and female images,
taking advantage of the grammatical gender of "anima," soul. For such gender-
crossing imagery in medieval devotional language, see Caroline Walker
Bynum, *Jesus as Mother: Studies in the Spirituality of the High Middle Ages*
(Berkeley: University of California Press, 1982) and Pamela Sheingorn, "The
Maternal Behavior of God: Divine Father as Fantasy Husband," in *Medieval
Mothering*, eds. John Carmi Parsons and Bonnie Wheeler (New York: Garland,
1996), 77–99.

thought your love quite incapable. While she was being held as a captive of the Lord, when she anxiously hurried to visit you with a gift that was particularly desirable to you, you had gone away forever. Did I say "gone away"? It would be more accurate to say that you kept your counsels hidden from your only soul as if from an enemy; you hit her hard with your hasty and unforeseen flight when she was least prepared for such great pain; you never considered that unforeseen blows are deadlier than expected ones, or what remedy your only soul would have for her wound. If God is love, it would seem holier to approach him with respect for love than in contempt of love. For he who follows the entire law but offends in only one thing, namely love – you know the rest.[20] Therefore I consider you to have sinned against charity. Your only soul does commend the courage of your new vows, but she deplores the cruelty of your silence. Instead of her daughter, you are become her parricide. Neither St. Martin nor St. Benedict nor many others who caused wounded love have allowed themselves to be stolen from their loved ones in this way or allowed them to be quashed by unforeseen pain. Instead, they were careful to give advance warning of their departure or death in order to forearm their loved ones in patience; for they knew their departure would leave them reeling. Nor did the wellspring of all love leave his charges behind like this. He told them on the one hand to let the dead bury the dead;[21] on the other hand he set an example by providing for those who had been touched by the breath of his spirit. For he knew that they, inebriated with the nectar of his sweetness and pierced with the sword of his love, would be shipwrecked by the pain of losing him. Therefore he had taken care, far in advance and many times over, to predict to them what was to come, so that they might be better armed with the shield of foreknowledge. For even as he was about to return to the Father, since he loved his own until the infinite end, since he was left in the world for the time of his mortality, he piously participated in the last supper, the new covenant of his body and blood, the eternal memory of his passion; in the eternal bond of love, he exhorted them to remain in him as he would give himself to them; he eased the fears of his foundering friends with a very long and most loving speech; he revived the buried ones with the hope of his speedy resurrection, as in the psalm: "Because of the misery of the needy and the groans of

[20] 1 Cor. 13:1–3.
[21] Mt 8:22.

the poor, I shall rise up now, says the Lord." "The time has come," he said, "for me to return to him who sent me, and therefore sadness is filling your hearts; but do not be sad, and let not your ears be disturbed." And, raising his eyes towards his heaven, as one who was returning from where he had descended, he carefully commended to God the Father those whom he was about to leave behind in the body. "Holy Father," he said, "keep them in your name whom you have given me, so that they may be one as we are one." And in order that we, his other and latest members, might partake of the same grace, he added, "not for them only do I pray, but also for all those who through their word shall believe in me. You are in me, and I am in you; may they also be one in us. Father, I will that they shall be where I am, that the love with which you have loved me shall be in them, and I shall be in them."[22]

Next to the cross stood that singular mother, regarding him with tearful gaze as he was transfixed with the sins of the world – him to whom alone she alone, peerless virgin, had given birth, the immaculate to the holy, the one to the one, the unique to the unique. Her eyes, like the springs of Esebon, poured forth a stream from the holiest of founts.[23] Her heart was pierced by the sword, her whole being was transfixed with the sufferings of her divine son, and her soul called out with the voices of the prophets: "My spirit is fearful within me, my heart is broken within me, and all my bones tremble. My eyes were dimmed by tears, for he who comforted me is far from me. All you who pass by the roads of this world, see if there is a sorrow like to my sorrow."[24] For nobody had ever borne such sorrow; never had so great a woman seen so great a man die. Jesus, in his mercy, took pity on the weeping woman and would have caught her as she fainted; but he remained, with both palms nailed to the cross, thus preserving the marks of his wounds to be kissed in his resurrection, for he did not want to void our redemption by descending. And even though Gabriel, well known to her, and all the angelic hosts were watching over her as their sovereign lady and the mother of their Lord, he nonetheless commended his mother to his favorite disciple, most special to him because of his virginity, as to another son. But her soul refused to be consoled. Although she loved the

---

[22] Ps. 11:6; John 16:6, 14:27, 17:11, 20–24. The whole passage is an extended paraphrase of one of the prefaces to the Consecration at mass.

[23] Song of Songs 7:4.

[24] Ps. 142:4; Jer. 23:9; Lamentations 2:11, 1:12.

virginal surrogate of her son, she desired only him, the unique exemplar of virginity. Note, by the way, how pious and holy it is that in our churches three virgins are seen converging at the cross, or a triple virginity: the Lord, his mother, and his disciple; or, if you want, the bridegroom and bride with the bridegroom's friend. Note how the Savior, who himself is the virgin's virginity, is placed in the middle, embracing with each arm a virgin of each sex. But when you hear "three," do not think of him as one of the three, but rather a third in addition to the two, lest you equate the Lord of Majesty in the middle with the two on the sides; that is the mistake Peter made as he suggested three huts, forgetting to exempt the Lord from the servants.[25] Shall I further recall how the Lord after his resurrection showed himself by many proofs for forty days to those who missed him,[26] offered himself to be seen and touched, ate and drank with them, made everything known to them as his friends, promised his holy spirit, and finally took himself up into heaven before a long line of spectators, blessing them and leaving behind the gifts of his grace and his peace? But by relating this great grace I would be exceeding my present purpose.

Therefore, my sweetest, even though this most sublime example of our Lord hardly fits the indignity of a humble servant, he has nonetheless deigned to offer himself as an exemplar to be followed; and from this you can see what you owed your mother in charity. There is a letter from the saintly women Paula and Eustochium to Saint Marcella (which does, though, recall the style of St. Jerome, their friend), beginning, "Charity knows no bounds, and impatience knows no measure and cannot sustain longing."[27] Who could express in words how shattered she was when she first heard the news of your departure? But she held herself together by some more palatable food, namely the hope that you might return, if God took pity on her. Meanwhile she fluctuated between hope and fear.

For at one time David fasted for his dying son, to ask that God might give him back in some way, yet feasted when the son had died, in order to temper his fatherly grief to God's will. For as a prophet, God's close friend, he knew God's heart intimately; he knew that what the good Lord did could not be bad for him, even though according to the sentence of the apostle he was guilty of

---

[25] Mt. 17:1–9.
[26] Acts 1:3.
[27] Jerome, Epist. 46.1.1–2 (CSEL 54, p. 392).

lese-majeste, for those who defile the flesh, blaspheme the Majesty.[28] What faith, presumptuous out of sheer piety! He even dared to pray for him whom he had conceived through adultery and murder, whom he had delivered up to a divine death sentence in punishment for a crime. Yet soon he received a distinguished reward for that same adulterous union, namely Solomon, not only an heir to the kingdom but himself an unequaled king of wisdom. Nor did he even lose that son who was punished, since God took him up into his eternal rest.[29]

But I, she said, like a broken reed cannot rise to the height of such an exemplar.[30] I am not sufficiently consoled by Abraham's grief over Isaac, nor Jacob's over Joseph, nor by Job, even more blessed after his loss in riches and in children, nor Tobias with Sara, nor a thousand other messengers of God's mercies. You have left behind much lamentation for the mother of Wilton, for your sisters, for your parents, and for all of us. But you, pious soul, rejoice always in God your savior. Give no room to sadness. You have gone to the fountain of joy, and you may exclaim with the faith of David: "But I have hoped in the Lord. I shall be glad and rejoice in your mercy. For you have regarded my lowliness; you have saved my soul from its distress; you have not enclosed me in the hands of my enemies; you have set my feet in a spacious place."[31] He has set you in a spacious place, for he has saved you from the afflictions of worldly desires and from those who descend to the lake; he has begun to close hell for you and open heaven for you, that you may enter the narrow path with a spacious heart and walk in the way of the Lord's commands. Walk in the way of his spacious commandments, spread out in the love of God and of your neighbor. Those are more straitened who are enveloped by the world, who are buried in the tumult of this mortal life. Their very freedom to sin has steeped them in luxury, their servitude to sin has enslaved them to Styx the tyrant,[32] and their bondage to lust has hurled them into the mouth of hell. You, however, do well to cling to your God. Put your trust in the Lord, and in the darkness wait for the sound of his trumpets; as the sun's face loses its color, wait for the iniquity of the world and the flesh to pass. And I, you may say, "shall be glad in the Lord and I shall rejoice in

---

[28] Jude 1:8.

[29] 2 Kings [KJV: 2 Sam] 12:16–24.

[30] Is. 42:3. "She said": i.e., Eva's "mother in charity," above (and see pp. 163–64).

[31] Ps. 30:7–9.

[32] Styx is, of course, a river rather than a ruler of the underworld. Either Goscelin has his mythology mixed up, or he is speaking metaphorically.

the Lord my Jesus."[33] The Lord God is my strength, and he will make my feet like the feet of the stag to run in the ways of his commandments, until he, the conqueror, will lead me unto the summits of the mountains, to the psalms and cymbals of Mary, singing the triumphs of Christ.[34]

The Fruit of Prayer

And warm me with your prayers, for I deplore not your salvation but only my desolation.[35] Indeed, I beg you, my lady, if you have ever loved my insignificance, offer up my mourning along with your tears to the goodness of the Most High, for whom alone you have gone into enclosure. Present my wretched soul to our most merciful savior himself. And as you give it to the Lord, ask that it be given back to you forever because of your special love; thus, for the worldly wounds that I suffer through your absence, may I possess eternal joys with you. Is there a brighter light in the constellations of the church than St. Paul? But it was the prayer of St. Stephen, the protomartyr, that turned a persecutor into the greatest of apostles.[36] The redeemer of the world himself not only prayed for forgiveness for his killers, but even gave them the kingdom of heaven, and shed his blood for the benefit of the very people who shed it. Can we not then with great confidence pray to God for those who love us, if he gave such inestimable goods to those who killed him? The great Augustine, creator of a thousand volumes, testifies in his Confessions that he was gifted with his mother's tears.[37] The holy lover wept for her heretic son and pleaded with a host of holy men to whom she could gain access. One of them once said to her, "It cannot be that the son of these tears should be lost." O blessed tears, which gave birth to such a triumph for the mother and such a great light for the church! O divine gifts, greater than any wishes and prayers we could use to ask for them! Not only did he emerge from the heresy, which was all his mother's fervent prayers asked for; but he also escaped from the

---

[33] Habac. 3:18.

[34] Ps. 42:2, 17:34, 118:32, Habac. 3:19; Exod. 15:20–21.

[35] The Latin uses first person plural here ("warm *us* with your prayers"); as frequently in this part of the book, it is hard to decide whether to translate "I" or "we." On the one hand, Latin freely uses plural "we" for singular "I," and the next sentence is clearly singular. On the other hand, Goscelin has been talking about the grief of the whole community, and indeed has been hiding behind that grief, as it were.

[36] Acts 6–8.

[37] Augustine, *Confessions*, 3.12.21.

Charybdis of lust and all the temptations of the world, and he shone forth as a great light among all people. That we might learn to persevere in our waiting and receive his long-awaited mercy the more abundantly, the Lord came after a ten-year delay and touched Augustine's heart. Converted, Augustine dissolved into tears; like a leper purified by the divine touch, like the paralyzed man who took up his bed and walked, he rose up, all cured, to the voice of the Lord. Thus, in an instant, dirt turned to gold, and soiled wool to scarlet cloth,[38] twice tinted with the precious dew of the Holy Spirit – that is, he was inebriated by the love of God and the love of his neighbor.

Let these and countless other proofs of God's gifts of love inflame you. Arm yourself with invincible faith, and stand ready to ask for all you want from the best and most generous giver of all. Approach him with faith, I tell you; your faith will become more confident as you will see yourself more and more amply indulged in your most long-held, most cherished wishes. For this fountain of goodness is truly inexhaustible: it allows itself to be tapped with prayers and will give amply, only to encourage more confident prayers for even greater gifts. It loves to be asked without pause, for it is prepared to give indefatigably. Ask, it says, and you shall receive.[39] What an untiring fulfiller of wishes! What has he not given to those who repent! By what merit? Simply the asking. For what returns? Our presumption. Therefore, my dearest, remember Goscelin, once your very own, to the clemency of that great father. It is true that I, who am nobody, do not deserve your prayers; but they will be the more meritorious for being offered on behalf of someone undeserving. The mother, as I said, offered up her son to God; may the daughter offer up her father with the same piety. Ask only this with your loving tears, that the Redeemer's goodness may make me his, that he may convert me to himself with all my heart, that he may give me a heart and a place to serve him in peace.

I cannot tell you how often I have sighed for a little refuge similar to yours (though one that would have a door for solemn exits, that I may not lack a larger temple)[40] where I might escape the crowds that tear at my heart; where I might pray, read a little, write a little, compose a little; where I might have my own little table, so that

---

[38]   This is an echo of Is. 1:18, though the image is inverted.

[39]   John 16:24.

[40]   He presumably imagines a cell like hers, attached to a church; but, being a priest, he would need access to the altar in the church in order to say mass.

I could impose a law on my stomach and on this pasture feast on books rather than food; where I might revive the dying, tiny spark of my little intellect, so that, unable to be fruitful in good deeds, I might yet be just a little bit fruitful by writing in the house of the Lord.

But the Lord has rejected me and destroyed me, and my days are vanished like smoke. He has made my soul to waste away like a spider's web, and cut short my years like a spider's thread. I wish I could point to my successes and say, "he who has made my foot fleet like the stag's," "with the pen of a scrivener that writes swiftly."[41] I have become more sluggish than a snail. Yet my Lord is a God who does not need what good I have to offer; he can take pity on me for no reason, and heal me for nothing. It is not up to him that wishes, nor to him that runs, but to God who shows mercy.[42] So please, my dearest, take action. Make God come between me and you, and have him take to us his bosom since, for the time being, he has separated us in the body. He has said, "Wherever two or three are assembled in my name, I will be in their midst. And if two of you shall consent on earth concerning anything whatsoever they shall ask, it shall be done for them by my father."[43] For the Lord, one in being with the Father, also wants us to be one in him. We, the lowliest members of his body, have been so dignified in his body that we must presume on this great goodness; we must ask that through the same mediator who made us both, we may be permitted to become one in perpetual love. Take action, I beg you, that I may one day rejoice to have found you again as my intercessor, just as I now mourn to have lost you, my life's joy; that, God willing, joy may bloom forth from our sorrows. May my daughter become my patroness, of whose prerogatives I am as unworthy as I am unlike her in holiness of life.

In that faith, that hope, that charity, and in that affection you have for me, commend me, readmit me, receive me after the quarrel caused by your going away. Look at me as I sit with you; listen to me as I talk to you. Indeed, as the bride of charity says, "set in order love within me"[44]: love, which is burning to say all, does not know how to keep order, does not know any measure or bounds. This is what the blessed Paula says, too, in that letter which I mentioned earlier.[45]

---

41 Ps. 88:39, 101:4, 38:12, 17:34, 44:2.
42 Romans 9:16.
43 Mt. 18:19–20.
44 Song of Songs 2:4.
45 Jerome, Epist. 46.1 (CSEL 54, p. 329–30).

Therefore, presuming on your indulgence, I let my speech flow forth uncensored. For love acts not so much from moderation as from willfulness; it does not speak measuredly so much as affectively; it does not think to set forth something good so much as it thinks to set forth a lot, everything if it can. Yet how can I console you in your loneliness with my exhortations, when I am more in need of consolation myself, or am even inconsolable? How can I, who am down, raise up the upright one? How can I, the sick one, help the healthy one, I, the troubled one, assist the secure one? But I have the building materials of comfort in you, which I do not find in myself. You are safely in the harbor, I founder. You sit at home, I am shipwrecked. You have built your nest in a rock, I slide about in the sand. You can already exult and sing: "From the ends of the earth I have cried to you my Lord; you have exalted me upon a rock. You have conducted me, for you have been my hope, a tower of strength against the face of my enemies. In your tabernacle I shall dwell forever; I shall be protected in the covert of your wings; for you, my God, have heard my prayer; you have given me an inheritance, that I may fear your name." So, as I languish, you call out to him: "God, may your mercy console me." And when he consoles you, say joyfully to him, "According to the multitude of sorrows in my heart, your comforts have gladdened my soul."[46] Food came from the eater, and sweetness from the strong one, says Samson's riddle.[47] So why could not joy break forth from sadness and the sun from the fog?

Let us Rise Up in Everlasting Glory
Rejoice greatly, o daughter of Zion; rejoice and be glad, for the Lord is your savior and the crown of your gladness, and the garment of your everlasting joy. He shall rend your sackcloth and surround you with joy, that your glorification may sing unto him and your earlier sorrows may no longer sting you; for the old has passed away. He will shower joy and exultation upon you. He will call out to you from the heights of his mercy: "Fear not, Daughter Zion, for I am with you."[48] I am your strength, your firmament, your refuge, your protector and the horn of your salvation; I am he who will take you up. I will not desert you nor abandon you who trust in me. And Zion said, "The Lord has forsaken me, and the Lord has forgotten me!" How many times have we said this in the poverty of our spirit! But

---

[46] Ps. 60:3–6, 118:76, 93:19.
[47] Judges 14:14.
[48] Is. 43:5.

what is God's answer? "Can a woman forget her child, and not take pity on the son of her womb? And if she should forget, yet will I not forget you."[49] I have left you behind only for a short time, but I will take pity on you forever. As a mother consoles her child, thus shall I console you, and you shall see and your heart shall rejoice. Eternal joy shall be on your head; you will reap joy and gladness; and sorrow and sighs shall flee, and God will wipe away all your tears and heal all your wounds. Rise up, then, Jerusalem, rise up and stand on the heights, and see the gladness that comes to you from your God.[50] Rise up from your earthly desires, from the bed of your sorrow, from the sleep of your torpor, from the languor of desolation. Rise up, stirred up by heavenly desires, inflamed by eternal love; kick away the world and stand on high, that you may sigh for the higher things, on the rock which Christ has exalted and established in holy Zion (which means "lookout mountain"), whence you will see the unthinkable joys of the world to come. Stand there firmly and expectantly, and see with the elevation of faith, with the far-reaching patience of hope, the encompassing breadth of charity; see the joy that will come to you from your God, when he shall come with his right hand full of gifts. You shall say to him, now in hope and then in fact: "Your countenance will fill me with joy, at your right hand are delights even to the end, for the needy shall not always be forgotten; the patience of the poor shall not perish forever."[51] Let this be your antidote and consolation: in the light of the glory to come you can not only dismiss all sorrows and pains, all the damages of death, but you may rejoice in them, embrace them in the expectation of the rewards of the crown and eternal prize.

Thus, consoling and exhorting, I desire you, my sweetest, to arm yourself to virtue – I, who myself am unarmed and empty of all virtue. I am like the noncombatant trumpeter, who, even though he cannot fight, nonetheless can give much to the fighters. He stirs up the strong ones, and strengthens them with the glory of victory, "never surpassed at rousing fighting men/with brazen trumpet, setting Mars afire."[52]

These arms and this fortitude to which you are called have nothing to do with sex or age or physical strength, but rather with greatness of mind, constancy, and an invincible spirit ready to overcome

---

[49] Is. 49:14–15.
[50] Is. 63:16, 51:10; Apoc. 21:4; Is. 30:26, 60:1.
[51] Ps. 15:11, 9:19.
[52] Virgil, *The Aeneid*, trans. Robert Fitzgerald (New York: Vintage, 1990) 6.165.

anything. I confess that my good will is weak and my diligence is soft. But nonetheless I have always wished, and I have given birth to you and loved you for this, that you may pass into Christ's womb,[53] and become totally Christ's sacrificial lamb. I wanted this to happen elsewhere than it is happening now and in a different way; I wanted you to live a holy life and become a useful vessel in the house of the Lord, a coenobitic pigeon, not a solitary mourning dove; or if that was what you preferred, a mourning dove in your own country.[54] Why would I have preferred that? That we may suffer less desolation, with you near. But the Lord has founded the earth in wisdom, and has stabilized the heavens in prudence, and through his dispensation the day will last, and he has done all that he wished, and he has done every thing well. And in the end, though I am reluctant to admit it, I see your refuge is so conducive to your well-being, that I believe it was prepared for you by God's goodness. Thus, I am forced to plant you and have you take root in the sorrows of my abandonment – even though, if it could happen with God's will, I would prefer to pull you out.

The Salvation of Holy Pilgrims

Hear, then, the voice of the Lord: "Listen, my daughter, and see, and incline your ear, and forget your people and your father's house," etc.[55] With Abraham, you have left the country of your kinship in order to arrive in the land which the Lord your God will give you, a land flowing with milk and honey, so that you may see the goodness of the Lord in the land of the living and that you may please God in the country of the living. You have arrived at the door of the paradise of true desire; be persistent and knock with tireless importunity, until the Lord comes and you can enter; and do not let the desires you have left behind lure you back. For it often happens to sick souls

---

[53] "Ut in Christi transieres uiscera." *Viscera* means literally, "bowels" or "entrails" (where the Vulgate uses it metaphorically, Douai usually translates "all that is in me") but is often used to mean "womb." It is true that translating this as "Christ's womb" tips the balance too far towards the image of a female Christ, which is only faintly suggested here; but to go for the more neutral "Christ's body" would lose the strong connotation of womb, motherhood, and (reverse) birth. The rather odd image is of Goscelin the "mother soul" giving up her child not so much to a father as to yet another male mother.

[54] I.e., he would have liked her to be part of a community of nuns ("coenobitic") rather than a hermit; or if she had to be a hermit, he would have preferred for her to stay in England.

[55] Ps. 44:1.

after their escape that those same bleak and bitter circumstances now appear much sweeter, and run through their minds clothed in deceptive splendor. With a pang you remember your homeland, flowing with milk; your family, flowing with honey; your loving relatives, your close friends, and sweet, bantering letters; your mother's devotion, your teacher's solicitude, your sisters' intimacy, the manifold beauties of the world and the manifold loveliness of things. You have laid all this aside for a brief time so that you may receive in eternity; that you may receive your true mother, your true sister, your true kinfolk, and your true friends inseparably in your true homeland. She loses nothing who gives up what she has for her savior's sake. Whatever has perished for Christ has not truly perished but has gained a thousandfold. It is a grain that has fallen for God: it goes to heaven and there will bear hundredfold fruit. Many saints found themselves transplanted into foreign lands by divine dispensation. Is this surprising? "While we are in the body," said the Apostle, "we are wandering far from the Lord." And, "We have here no permanent abode, but we seek the one that is to come."[56] And that clearest window of writers, Augustine, said, "Whoever belongs to the city on high is a pilgrim in this world."[57] Cain was the type of the worldly people: he founded a city for the teeming multitudes, thousands of humans. Abel, the type of those who await the reign of God, was a nomad.[58] To the earthly people, it is said: "Dust thou art and to dust shalt thou return." To those who prize heaven, "Blessed are the poor in spirit, for theirs is the kingdom of heaven." The former accumulate riches on earth, the latter in heaven. "Our conversation," they say, "is in heaven"; and also, "Your kingdom come."[59] Abraham, Isaac, Jacob, Joseph, Moses, the sons of Israel, and also Jeremy, Ezekiel, Daniel, and the other prophets; and also the apostles and the larger multitudes of apostolic teachers: they all went on pilgrimage or into captivity, such as Dionysius from Athens to Gaul[60]; Martin, the gem of confessors, from Pannonia to your region[61]; Augustine

---

[56] 2 Cor. 5:6; Heb. 13:14.
[57] Augustine, "In Evangelium Joannis," 28.9.
[58] Gen. 4:3, 4:17.
[59] Gen. 3:19; Mt. 5:3; Phil. 3:20; Mt. 6:10.
[60] St. Dionysius or Denis, the patron saint of France venerated in Paris (died c. 215), was frequently identified with the Dionysius "Areopagita" who appears in Acts 17:34.
[61] Angers is not too far from Tours, where Martin was venerated. Goscelin is clearly selecting his examples for their proximity to Eva's own history. For St. Martin, venerated at Tours, see the famous *Life* by Sulpicius Severus (trans.

from Rome to your own Britain.[62] But God never abandons those who seek him. Abraham became a great nation as numerous as the stars in the sky; in him all nations are blessed, for Christ was born from Abraham's seed. Rebecca, as a type of the church, followed her husband far from her kinship; and having been sterile before, with a single birth gave rise to two nations.[63] Jacob crossed the Jordan a poor man, with nothing but his shepherd's staff; and he returned very rich, with two divisions of men. With seventy souls he entered Egypt and returned with six hundred thousand grandsons, not counting children and women.[64] Joseph rose from servitude to the king's governor ruling the entire realm of Egypt, to which he had been a slave.[65] Ruth, a foreigner, leaving behind the gods of her native land to follow the God of Israel, not only joined the Israelites but also became the mother of kings from David onwards, and even merited a place in the kinship and genealogy of our savior.[66] From time immemorial, God's gifts have been as innumerable as his works.

You, too, have gone from your homeland with all these poor wanderers in the Lord, not only in the spirit of poverty and rejection of worldly lust, but also in geographical distance, so that you can commend yourself to God's care the more closely for being so far exiled. "Be not silent, for I am a stranger with you and sojourner. Suffer me to recover strength in your house. O Lord my God, to you have I fled; teach me to do your will, for you are my God. Be unto me a God, a protector, and a house of refuge. Make me whole, because you are my strength and my refuge, and for your name's sake you will lead me and nourish me. Lo, I have gone far off flying away, and I abode in the wilderness. I shall await him who will make me whole from smallness of spirit and from the storm. Friend and neighbor

Bernard Peebles, Fathers of the Church vol. 7 [New York: Fathers of the Church, 1949]).

[62] Augustine, the missionary bishop sent by Gregory the Great to convert Britain. See Bede's *Ecclesiastical History of the English People*, ed. and trans. Bertram Colgrave and R. A. B. Mynors (Oxford: Clarendon, 1969), 68–116. Goscelin wrote a Life of St. Augustine based on Bede, and an account of a translation of his relics (PL 155: 13–46); see also Richard Sharpe, "Goscelin's St. Augustine and St. Mildreth: Hagiography and Liturgy in Context," *Journal of Theological Studies* n.s., 41 (1990): 502–16 and David Townsend, "Omissions, Emissions, Missionaries, and Master Signifiers in Norman Canterbury," *Exemplaria* 7 (1995): 291–315.

[63] Gen. 25:21–23.

[64] Gen. 32:10, 46:27.

[65] Gen. 45:8.

[66] Book of Ruth; Mt. 1:5.

you have removed from me, and you have put far away my acquaintance. I am at the mercy of my enemies, and I shall not come forth. Protect me under the shadow of your wings, from the face of the wicked who have afflicted me," from the face of the African sun that makes souls swarthy, from the fire that burns forests among the people, and from the flame that burns the summits that stand out in the saintly virtues.[67] "Tear me from the hands of my enemies, from the slings of the demonic hunters, from the mouth of the lion that roars that it may strike its prey, from the dragon that lies in wait to devour the souls that have rebelled against you and fled."

From Vanity to Truth

What could you desire, my soul, in this world that is so contemptible that you have shunned it? All things in this world, said the Apostle, are vain. And "vanity of vanities," said Ecclesiastes, "all is vanity."[68] "Ecclesia" means "assembly"; "Ecclesiastes" means "he who calls to assembly." As you know, he is Solomon the wise man himself. He wrote three books: Proverbs, Ecclesiastes, and the Song of Songs.[69] The first sets down the discipline of fearing God and the rule for right living; the second preaches that all things are subject to the vanity of our various desires, in order to ravish us to the third stage: the eternal Song of Songs, where, freed from the servitude to vanity, the contemplative mind may rush towards the peace of its maker.[70] All the happiness and magnificence the world has to offer was found in Solomon's reign and contributed to his glory. He did everything, tried everything, experienced everything, tasted the delights of all things; he penetrated all worldly ideas and errors and saw through all stupidity; and in all the world he found nothing except vanity. Who can call to mind the powers, riches, delights of Solomon, the kings and kingdoms, the tributes and payments, the immeasurable gold, the silver so abundant that it was worth no more than rocks, the infinite treasures, the cities, mansions, palaces, the excellence of his rule, the magnificent temple, encased in gold inside and outside and made with workmanship that surpasses all human ingenuity, so splendid that no tongue can tell it and no eye exhaust it? From the farthest end of the earth came the Queen of Saba (standing for the Church), incited by the rumors of so

---

[67] Ps. 38:13–14, 142:9–10, 30:3–4, 54:8–9, 87:19, 87:9, 16:8–9.
[68] 1 John 2:16; Eccl. 1:2.
[69] Solomon was traditionally held to be the author of all three books.
[70] Origen, *Prologus in Cantica Canticorum*, PG, 13:74 a.

many wonders. Treasure this story in your memory; for the Book of Kings tells it not for the sake of royal ambitions, but for the wonderful, sacred love of Christ and the Church, as indeed every page of Holy Scripture is sanctified for us. The Queen saw the ivory roofs, the golden beds, the chambers of the three hundred queens (who signify the virginal souls wedded to the True Bridegroom), the golden tables, gilded meals, the crowd of noblemen who waited on the king, the masses of servants, the processions of purpled dignitaries, the army of counts. She listened to him as he proposed thousands of parables and gave the solutions to them, as he argued from cedar to hyssop, elucidating everything, transcending all human understanding and all human knowledge. She had come believing herself unsurpassed in riches and in knowledge, to test or perhaps to challenge the king with riddles; now she blushed as she recognized how small and provincial, how ignorant she was. She had not even regained her senses; still in a stupor, she said with blessings and greatest admiration, "how much greater is your glory than the fame which I heard in my land."[71]

In the same way the church, and every blessed soul, when she is admitted to the feast of Christ, the True Solomon, will be awestruck, stupefied, ravished by this inseparable light and joy. All those magnificent descriptions of his inestimable glory; all that we humans can now say of your splendors, o eternal city of Jerusalem; everything the world now proclaims about the bliss of heaven, and everything we are told by book after book – she will see, and marvel. Ravished beyond herself by such endless clarity and joy, she will count all earthly descriptions of it but an insignificant rumor she heard back in the world. King Solomon, that greatest flower and ornament, well versed in worldly glory and earthly lust, is our witness, together with the world-renouncing apostles, that all transient things are vain and will evaporate between the hands of their possessors, and that everything that is done on earth, except for the love of Christ and the Kingdom of God, is nothing but vanity and affliction of spirit. For the world, too, will pass, and all its concupiscence.[72]

Any friendship of the flesh and of the world, therefore, is as unstable as it is vain. Either – if it is present – it will grow tedious to the saturated heart; or, if absent, it will fall into oblivion. Out of sight, out of mind – and the nearer the dearer. An enemy murders a husband, and so "merits" to be married to the widow. The murdered man is dead and buried, trampled underfoot; the killer is loved more and

---

[71]   3 Kings [KJV: 1 Kings] 10:7.
[72]   1 John 2:17.

more, and accepted into the widow's embraces. The innocent victim is slandered as a villain; the villainous victor is cherished as an upright man. Affluence, no matter how criminal, is without guilt; poverty, no matter how innocent, is without pardon. A young, happy, handsome, charming man is loved – as long as no younger, happier, more handsome, more charming man comes along. When the next more powerful man comes along, the less powerful one is ousted; and, for suffering such violence, he is judged worthy not only of disgrace but even hatred. What he used to cherish is but a tale; what he loved above all else is but a dream. Only one thing will stay with him: the thing that (unless he die and be lost) he will never be asked to give back. Arrogant happiness is cherished; affectionate love is disdained. Adolescence supplants manhood; the latter is more venerable, yet the former is more cherished. But in the end, adolescence as well as manhood and all the favors of this world, as Ecclesiastes testifies, have been found vain. Only that love which is in Christ is true. That love does not change with place, time, person, sex, age, or beauty; nor is it diminished by plenty or want. It is true that love knows no envy, but neither will it let anyone come between the two friends except if he or she is pleasing to both. Therefore our wise caller to assembly, having declared so many different desires of so many different things to fall under the sin of vanity, then draws us towards the joy of eternal life by adding, "What has a man more of all his labor that he take under the sun, except to go thither where there is life?"[73] And finally he concludes all his proverbs with one key to salvation: "Let us all hear together the conclusion of my speech: Fear God and keep his commandments. This is the whole duty of man."[74]

Therefore, my soul, what further business could you have with the snares of the world you left behind?

From Transience to Stability[75]

If you are bound for the brightness of your eternal homeland, why would you worry about the land of your birth – or rather, the land of your death? The daughters of kings and princes, raised from infancy in all delights, knowing nothing beyond the splendors and the happiness of their homeland, marry into foreign nations and far-away kingdoms. They are destined to learn barbarous customs and strange

---

[73] Eccl. 1:3, 6:8.
[74] Eccl. 12:13.
[75] The manuscript (and Talbot) has "a fluxis manenti." On the analogy of the previous chapter title, "a vanis vera," I have assumed that it should be "a fluxis manentia."

languages, and to serve fierce lords and repugnant laws that go against nature, as for instance recently the daughter of the Margrave of Flanders married King Knut of Denmark.[76] These girls, having once said good-bye to their parents and their land, cannot or do not want to see their homelands ever again, for married love supersedes all else. Surely the soul that has followed Christ with all her heart should in perpetual love forget her land and the house of her father, that the king may greatly desire her beauty; and she will put on wisdom, the mother of fair love, that is, the beauty of the love of Christ.[77] How many have transferred their kinship and their birthright to faraway places for the sake of earthly gains, from Gaul to Galicia and Spain, from England to Apulia and Greece, setting their hearts on transitory things – and should we be shy about migrating to eternal bliss? Even entire peoples and kingdoms migrate, such as Israel to Egypt, from Egypt to Canaan, from Canaan to Assyria and Babylon; or the Cuthites to Samaria, the Trojans to Italy and Rome,[78] or nowadays the Normans to England or Britain, where the entire English people were once newcomers – including yourself who, the well-born daughter of a Danish father and a Lotharingian mother, turned out English. And not just humans, but even lands and seas change: where once there were signs of flourishing peoples and cities, vast and deep waters now reign, proclaiming everything to be as fluid and brittle as it is unstable and mutable. Thus all things are governed and ordained by the Lord's eternal counsel and wisdom, who rules pagans and Christians, unbelievers and faithful with his just scale, and simultaneously teaches by the mutation of things that we have no permanent city here but must seek the one that is to come.[79] One sun shines on all, one heaven is open to all, one earth warms us all in her bosom. The same stars shine on Anjou and England; rivers, fields, and groves and all the delights of things flourish there as well as here. If anything should be missing, then the things your land lacks will be made up for by other things. Hence, Prosper says, "I do not fear exile, for one world is home to us all." Everywhere is good and bad mixed together; everywhere are thorns and brambles, and everywhere Christ's roses.

[76] Talbot identifies her as Adela, daughter of Count Robert of Flanders (1071–93), who married Knut IV (1080–86).

[77] Ps. 44:11–12.

[78] Cuthites: see 4 Kings [KJV: 2 Kings] 17:24,30. Trojans: Rome, according to the Aeneid, was founded by refugees from Troy.

[79] Heb. 13:14.

Only heaven and hell know their places; only they completely split the patrimony. May the Redeemer and Judge of the world take us up into his own.

Hope for the Bereaved

But, knowing your heart, the cradle of love, I believe that nothing must be harder for you to bear than being so far from your loved ones and friends. Part of martyrdom consists in bearing Christ's cross also in compassion of your neighbors, as the mooing cows carry the Lord's Ark of the Covenant and the Lord's yoke.[80] The more you were wounded with love for your loved ones in Christ here on earth, the more joyfully will you gather them about you in the eternal mansion. And, finally, there is one who once was special to you, the only one against whom you seem to have had no trouble hardening your heart, whom you had removed so far from your heart and consigned to oblivion, as if he had died. Shall I try to cure your narrowed heart? Shall I bring consolation for rigor and soften the rock with oil? Or shall I add lead and weight and help fortify your hardness? Shall I aid the fugitive with valedictions, shall I add wings to her flight? May Christ's healing balm, the oil of gladness, console you in all things, and may Christ be merciful to the forsaken one, inconsolable, for now, in his misery. When your earlier love awakes and the storm of desiring emotions arises, it will be Christ to whom your very bones cry out, to whom our heart, sealed with his sign, calls: "Rise up, Lord, command our seas, and restore calm. You rule the power of the sea, you appease the motions of the waves thereof. Heal me, o Lord, and I shall be healed."[81]

Everything has its season: a time of war and a time of peace, a time of separation and a time of reunion, a time of weeping and a time of laughing. Going they went and wept, casting their seeds, but coming they shall come with joyfulness, carrying their sheaves.[82] We, too, had our times. Through God's mercy, we saw each other enough, we talked to each other enough, we had each other's company and ate together enough, we celebrated the holy rites together and rejoiced together enough – if anything could ever be enough for love. We owe much thanks to the giver of these gifts for his great generosity, who so kindly gave us leave, who satisfied our pure desires, as it pleased him, for a time; after separating us for a while,

[80] 1 Kings [KJV: 1 Sam] 6:10–15.
[81] Ps. 88:10; Jer. 17:14.
[82] Eccl. 3:1–8; Ps. 125:6.

he will finally call us to inseparable joy. But why does this wretch prate on about "inseparable joy," who is separated from you not only by physical distance but, much more importantly, in the conduct of his life? What business do I, a slave to worldly desires, have with one who is leaving all that behind? Alas, I blush at my indolence; and better still that I should so blush than that those should blush for me who seek you, O Lord.[83] Now indeed is the time to walk in tears, the time to sow, the time of war; and when all this runs its course, there will follow fruit, rejoicing, the triumph of eternal joy. Two souls stirred by a unanimous spirit are rarely allowed to remain together forever. Was anything dearer to David than Jonathan?[84] Most often sons turn against fathers and brothers against brothers and unleash parricidal wars out of naked lust for power. Jonathan, however, stood firm for David against his father's unleashed fury. His father feared and hated David, for threatening to supplant his son as heir to the kingdom; the son himself demonstrated that rather than rule, he would serve the one who was dearer to him than any kingdom, caring little which of the two of them would be king. And even they were not allowed to live together, who were one another's life and soul. And neither was Jonathan angry, nor did David despair, that they were not able to come together in the flesh.

To give you even higher examples: could there be any greater love than there was among the apostles? They had been sent out by the root of all love, and he left them this one prescription: "This is my commandment to you, that you love one another." From the sweetness of his own heart he had infused them with that spirit of loving one another even after his resurrection, that they might earn through mutual love the Holy Spirit from heaven, to love God with all their hearts. And they, too, merged though they were into one heart and one soul, were divided and dispersed through the whole earth, carrying about in their hearts and bodies the cross and the torments of Christ, and the wound of everlasting love. "I bear witness," said Paul, "before Jesus Christ, that I have a great sadness and continuing sorrow in my heart: for I wished to be an anathema from Christ, for my brothers the Israelites."[85] O great love! He calls them brothers, who together thirsted for his blood. How much do you think he must have loved his true brothers in Christ, who thus loved his enemies as if they were brothers? (Of course it is only in time that he wished to

---

[83]   Ps. 68:7.
[84]   1 Kings [KJV: 1 Sam] 19–20.
[85]   Romans 9:1–3.

be an anathema from Jesus, dying for the errant ones; he did not
mean to be perpetually separated from the Lord Jesus, which would
be extremely impious, for if someone loves his father or mother or
anyone else more, he is unworthy of God.) And John, the disciple the
Lord loved most, had been entrusted with the Lord's virgin mother,
for his virginal merits. Yet did he not leave the beloved lady behind
in Zion, at least in their sacred bodies? It is almost unimaginable,
and yet it was a saintly thing to do: he went all the way to Asia to
win a new kingdom and bride for the Lord. Only Peter and Paul, twin
apostles of the faith, remained in Rome together; and these two great
princes alone, as they loved each other in life, are also not separated
in death.[86] The blessed youths Sabinus and Sabina, brother and sister, similar in name and in piety, tied themselves together more
closely by the love of God than they already were tied by blood.
Their pagan father, Sabinian, pushed his children with threats and
punishments to sacrifice to the demons. Sabinus fled. After that,
Sabina, too, managed to escape with God's help, motivated by the
love of her brother as well as her father's cruelty. Sabinian begged
Christ, if he were the true God, to destroy the idols that took away
his children. Instantly, the temple with all its idols was destroyed by
lightning. Sabina stayed in Rome and shone through miracles, yet
wept many tears for love of her brother. Finally, she received word
from an angel to go to Troyes, where she would see her beloved
brother. She arrived there and found her brother already crowned a
martyr, already buried. In the same hour, as if she had come to hate
the light of this world, she said a prayer and gave up her soul to
Christ.[87] Now what has become of the angel's promise? What she
had sought she did not find, what she had hoped she did not attain:
she did not find her brother in his living presence; and she did not
even arrive in time to see him dead. Clearly, this heavenly promise
had to be not perishable but immortal, not temporal, not transitory,
but for all eternity. Without a doubt, she did see her beloved brother
and attained her desire in the place where no harm, no painful
separation could ever intervene again. For no pious desire can be
frustrated by the most merciful hand of our savior.

Should I add a non-Christian example of friendship? The pagans
cherish the memory of two very handsome young twins, so much
alike that they could be told apart only by their names and their

---

[86] An antiphon for the office of Sts. Peter and Paul.
[87] AASS, Aug. VI, 496–504; Jan III, 558–61.

dress, and so dear to each other that each preferred to be punished in place of the other. One of them was named Orestes.[88] Now a theft occurred in the temple of Diana, and the heathen oracles named Orestes as the culprit. So when one of the two, Orestes, was summoned to be executed, each of them gave himself up for the other, each of them insisted his name was Orestes, and the true Orestes among them could not be identified, for each of them was Orestes in looks and spirit and by his own admission. The only solution for the court would have been to kill both for the crime, and to besmirch itself with the execution of this ambiguous innocence. Therefore the judges, either moved by compassion or simply frustrated, let them both go. Who taught these youths the Lord's saying, "Greater love than this has no man, that a man lay down his life for his friends"?[89] There is no greater teacher than love. Happy is a friendship if Christ is in the middle of it, without whom all probity is improper, and all piety proves impious. Whatever grace the maker of all dispersed among the unbelievers, he prepared as an exemplum for his faithful. So if the faith is no good to the faithless, an example of faith, even among the faithless, can always help the faithful.

St. Gertrude is said to be resting near the monastery of St. Sergius. During her lifetime, a certain abbess named Modesta fervently loved her, only from the reports of her sanctity. At the moment when she gave back her soul to heaven, the glorious virgin Gertrude visibly appeared to Modesta as she was praying in church. Despite the great geographical distance of the place where she physically died, she showed herself present as if in the flesh; and she said, "I am Gertrude, whom you loved much, whom you knew better through your affection than you could have known her by sight; know that in this hour I have left the prison of my body and gone over to the Lord." Later, the visionary heard from those who knew the saint that she was identical in appearance and stature with the figure she had seen; and it was found that she had died in the same hour in which she had appeared to Modesta.[90] O Lord, for whom all things live, you make all pious and faithful desires better after death, you rejoin in all eternity all that died in the world! It also happens frequently that the spirits of saints who are still in the body appear in faraway places, visibly and as if corporeally, and speak to people. Thus, we read of

---

[88] A standard exemplum, cited frequently, for instance in Ambrose's *De Officiis* (PL 16:85).

[89] John 15:13.

[90] AASS, Nov. II.i: p. 310, n. 40.

St. Nicholas that he appeared to those who had invoked him in an emergency at sea, and said, "Here I am; why did you call me?" And the storm instantly subsided. When they gained the shore, the sailors recognized him by his appearance, even though they had never seen him before. We also read that St. Martin and St. Benedict wrought miracles in the spirit. St. Ambrose of Milan is said to have fallen asleep during Holy Mass and to have been present at the funeral of St. Martin in Tours.[91] Thus, they cannot be separated from a friend, no matter how great the physical distance, who trust in the Lord's power that makes all things ever present. Those who have a pure soul and may see God, can certainly see to all corners of the world.

Yet as I said above, impatience knows no bounds and cannot bear to wait for what it desires. How often I envied your friend Eadgyth, who not only loved you more intimately, but, since she shared your place and your sex, was able to warm herself in your presence![92] But now her rejoicing, too, has turned into mourning and solitude, though she was somewhat more fortunate in that she was able to say good-bye to you when you left. Thus, I know not by what divine dispensation, hearts that have coalesced into one are often torn away from the beloved presence as if from their own limbs – even though they would have been divided in death anyway, even if they had remained together in life. Yet the Lord, the weigher of hearts, will call back all beloved souls. Rebuilding Jerusalem the Lord will gather the dispersed of Israel, and will heal the broken of heart and will bind up their bruises and will tell by name the multitude of his stars and of his souls. "I will gather you together out of all the lands and will bring you again to your land."[93]

Consider carefully, my soul, how all these things exhort you to burn with all your heart for eternal love, and to be strong in all sufferings in this brief mortal interlude; and, finally, never to forget Goscelin, the womb that gave birth to you in Christ. And if you do indeed suffer at all from this bitter separation, may your wounded love be comforted with the hope of eternity. What my unworthy conduct does not deserve, may it be granted through the goodness of your love and your prayers. If you still care a little bit, perhaps, about the one who is so devoted to you: he is the same absent as he was

---

[91] Gregory of Tours, "De Miraculis S. Martini," 1.5, PL 71, 918–19. For Benedict, see Gregory the Great, *Dialogues*, trans. Odo John Zimmerman O.S.B. (New York: Fathers of the Church, 1959) dialogue 2.22.

[92] "Egida," apparently a friend and fellow nun of Eva's at Wilton.

[93] Ps. 146:2–4; Jer. 32:37.

present. His mind and his appearance, his energy and his habits, his purity of faith and devotion, his powerful and fervid love are all the same. But his pain is sharper now and more desolate; his sighs of desire are deeper and longer. If he lives to white hair and old age and decrepitude, he will always persevere in the same sincere desire to find the Lord. And whenever you should chance to think of me and wonder, perhaps, "he was once dear to me – what may he be doing now?" this page will always answer, with one verb, active rather than passive, "he is sighing."[94] Wherever you may seek him, you will find him here; you will see and hear him with you, whispering to you. There was a time when I presumed to think, if God were to have mercy on my sins, that in God's Paradise I might be able to hold you in my lap. But now, all I hope is that I may see you happy in the far nobler bosom of Father Abraham.

So why would you hesitate to run the racecourse that leads to what Christ has promised us? You are so well prepared, having excluded the turbulence of the world from your enclosure. What shall we do, my soul? If we renounce present joys but do not reach the eternal reward because we are too sluggish, we shall be the most wretched of humans. What good is it to have left Egypt and, dying in the desert, not to inherit the promised land? Therefore, my soul, turn unto your rest; for the Lord has been bountiful unto you. Turn to the Lord with your whole heart, faith, words, and works, saying, "With my whole heart have I sought you, Lord. Do not repel me from your commandments. My heart has said to you: my face has sought you," that is, the intention of my heart; "your most clement face, Lord, I shall seek; turn not your face away from me. Uphold me according to your word, and I shall live; let me not be confounded in my expectation. Help me, and I shall be saved; and I will meditate always on your justifications." Throw all your cares unto the Lord; empty your mind and see that the Lord himself is your God; taste and see how sweet the Lord is; persevere in him, and say, "It is good

---

[94] Goscelin is playing on the literal meaning of the grammatical terms *active* ("active, practical") and *passive* ("subject to emotion; liable to suffering; vulnerable"). The whole passage imitates Ovid's Tristia 1:17, where the poet is sending his poem home from his exile:

> Go then, and with my words greet those dear places;
> At least I'll reach them with what foot I may.
> Among so many, if some one there recalls me,
> If someone asks about me, you will say,
> I live, but you will add that I don't flourish. . . .

(Ovid, *Sorrows of an Exile*, trans. A. D. Melville [Oxford: Clarendon, 1992] 1.)

for me to adhere to the Lord, to put my hope in the Lord my God."
More than that, he himself invites us, and offers himself to us:
"Come to me, all you that labor and are burdened, and I will refresh
you." You have come to him; remain in him, saying, "He that abides
in me and I in him, bears much fruit; for without me you can do
nothing."[95]

Hurry away from your warring adversaries and enter into his
peace, that peace of the saints where sadness has no place, where no
joy can be lacking, that you have sought so intently fleeing from
hell. And when your Jesus walks before, and you walk right through
the army of your foes and beyond, obtain forgiveness for your inert
and non-combatant counselor, just as you yourself have followed the
mercy of God your Redeemer. Here, then, after we have shattered
Pharaoh's reign and have passed through the Red Sea, let us build
our tents and recover our strength; tomorrow the trumpets will blow
for the battle against Amalech, and tomorrow the Lord's fighters
shall prepare for battle, ready to triumph over his land.

HERE ENDS THE FIRST BOOK OF EXHORTATIONS.

---

[95] Ps. 114:7, 118:10, 26:8–9, 118:116–17, 72:28; Mt. 11:28; John 15:5.

Here Begins the Second Book

The Divine War Trumpet

The voice of the Lord in power, the voice of the Lord shaking the desert, the resounding trumpet of prophets and apostles rousing us from the torpor of sleep: Awake, o strong ones, for the Lord is coming with healing. Stand fast in faith, acquit yourselves like men, all you who trust in the Lord. Put on God's armor, the breastplate of faith and the helmet of hope, the arms and buckler of a mind that trusts in the Lord.[1] The Lord ordered Moses, the Lawbearer, to enlist those he had led from Egyptian servitude into the army of the Lord, all aged twenty or older and were capable of going to war.[2] This age, being full of fervor, is highly trainable, be it in spiritual or material weapons. All the youth of military age throngs eagerly to war, young manhood clamors for weapons. Therefore act with confidence and courage; carry the standard of the Lord's cross, and as you trust in the Lord, you will not weaken. "I," says the Lord, "take you by the hand and say to you: Do not fear, for I am with you, a strong warrior and helper."[3] The bigger the battles, the stronger the divine help that will support you; and the higher the honors and more ample the rewards that will follow. Through places of horror and vast solitude, through pathless and waterless deserts[4] beset with serpents, through hostile regions and harsh wars, yet also with refreshment and solace from above, with manna from heaven and water from a rock, with the column of fire for a guide and constant victory for a companion: thus did the Lord lead Israel to the land of milk and honey, teaching us that it is through similar labors that we will enter into his peace and joy. "Through many tribulations," says Paul, "we must enter into the kingdom of God."[5] Quite similar is what Virgil sings; but the torch of heaven calls us upward, and the pot on the fire boils with earthly hope:

> Through various fortunes and so many trials
> We hold our course for Latium, where the fates

---

[1] Ps. 28:4, 8; 1 Cor. 16:13; Ps. 30:25; 1 Thess. 5:8; Ps. 34:2.
[2] Numbers 26:1.
[3] Is. 41:13; Jer. 20:11.
[4] Ps. 62:3.
[5] Acts 14:21.

Hold out a settlement and rest for us,
Our haven after toil.
And our Boethius, telling the story of Hercules:
His dire labors celebrate Hercules.
His last labor is to hold up heaven
  On his unbowed shoulders.
Go forth now with strength, where the high
Path of the great example leads you; why do you idly
Bare your backs unguarded? Earth once conquered,
The stars are all yours.
And Prudentius:
And the stars are reached by way of suffering.
And Horace:
Life gives nothing to miserable mortals without great toil.[6]

Thus, joy is purchased with pain, glory with labor, victory with battles, and the crown with victories. Adversities are the merits that win prizes; we should embrace them like the prizes themselves, or like heavenly goods. After a stormy journey, rest will feel that much sweeter. Finally, if all earthly and transient matters go "through various fortunes and so many trials," if what was created over a long time can fall in an instant, why should we begrudge the brief struggle that will earn us eternal joy? Let these thoughts urge you heavenward. Direct your heart to the eternal years and perennial centuries. Concentrate your entire attention on reflecting what it will be like to live immortally for all the endless ages of eternity; how the glories of the saints and the sufferings of the rejected will last for one infinite immortality; how unimaginable the joy that the Lord will give, the rewards that will exceed all desires; how inescapable, by contrast, the anguish of the lost, as they will suffer forever intolerable tortures, and they will know that these will never end. How we fear in this mortal life every little jab of pain, even pain that is easily cured or will go away by itself! How would we bear an eternity of affliction, not eased by any hope? From Adam to today they count barely six thousand years, and to us that fleeting span appears endless. Even if our lives are good, we barely tolerate the tedium of one hundred, or even sixty years. How about a hundred thousand and a hundred times one hundred, or thousands of thousands of years or centuries? One day will last forever for the blessed dead, and one infinite night for the

---

[6] Virgil, *Aeneid* 1:204–206, 3:393; Boethius, *Consolation of Philosophy*, 4 metr. 7; Prudentius, *Cathemerinon* 10:92; Horace, *Satires* 1:9:59–60.

damned.[7] Rise up therefore, rise and assume your strength, assume the arm of the Lord, who is the strength of your weakness, who will lead you to the mountain of his sanctification, the mountain which he conquered with his own hand as he suffered on the cross. In love and contemplation, assume the inner strength of eternal joy, and every pain will appear minor and fleeting compared to eternity. "The sufferings of this time," says the Apostle, "are not worthy to be compared with the glory to come that shall be revealed in us."[8]

This is why you entered and stepped up to this single combat: to wrest with sacred zeal your crown from the hand of the Enemy. To one side are the prizes for the winners, to the other the torments for the losers. In the middle of the field, God has put everything at stake. You must either prevail or die. I often used to sail down the Thames to London with the bishop and had to pass those fish-rich narrows, where the water, straitened, boiled with violent force and the sailors shouted and struggled as if for their lives. Some would pull on long ropes from the shore, others would fight the waters with short and quick strokes of the oars to propel the boat forward; for if their arms had slackened and if they had not struggled with manly force, the river's might would have beaten the boat back and hurled it towards the bottom.[9] On those occasions, my heart's reasoning would say to me, thus it is with anyone traveling on the road to heaven: either he will forcefully break free, or he will fall.

At Peterbury,[10] where I am currently staying, there is a young Dane who just recently became a monk and is carefully concerned with the state of his soul. The other day, when I said something to him in passing about the wars of the spirit, how much more frightening any enemy seems when you battle him constantly, and how the weak warrior will fall to the stronger one, my listener responded

---

7   Taken together, these two sentences (the play of hundreds and thousands, plus the notion of one everlasting night) strongly suggest a reminiscence of Catullus's poem 5 ("Vivamus, mea Lesbia, atque amemus.") Catullus was known to most medieval readers only by name, his works having been lost, for all practical purposes. But bits and pieces survived as examples in grammar textbooks, excerpts in florilegia, or quotations in other writers. (See James A. S. McPeek, *Catullus in Strange and Distant Britain* [Cambridge: Harvard University Press, 1939], xv–xvi, 261 n. 11, 267–68 n. 24.) It is not inconceivable that Goscelin might have known Catullus's famous lines from some such source.

8   Romans 8:18.

9   No doubt a real-life memory, but also a reminiscence of Virgil, *Georgics* 1.201–203.

10   Or possibly Bury St. Edmunds ("Burgis"); see Talbot p. 8.

with this: "In my native Denmark, I once saw a judge in court pro-
claim a death sentence over a robber, leaning on his double-edged
axe. The robber jumped up, snatched the poleax from him, and cut
down the judge whose grip on both his judicial authority and his axe
was so weak. Wielding the axe, striking hither and thither, he forced
a broad path for himself as the thick throng of spectators gave way,
and escaped untouched." Thus audacity will prosper; thus fortitude
can break open out of dire straits. Thus you too, fortified with faith
and sheer audacity, will drive far away the enemy's tribulations.
Picture yourself as a calf shut in by demonic dogs. They are mad
with envy, but their teeth lack strength. You, by contrast, are armed
with the fearsome horns of the holy cross. With your forehead thus
armed, you will trample any hostile attack under your feet.
"Behold," says the Lord, "I gave you the power to tread upon serpents and scorpions, and upon all the power of the enemy, and nothing shall harm you."[11] The Lord stands by watching on high with the
angels and archangels and the great host of powers, and if he sees
you fight he will grind the enemies' savage teeth in their mouths with
the lance of his cross. And when the lion goes about roaring, seeing
whom he may devour,[12] the Lord will break the lion's teeth.

The Heavenly Palm
Likewise the Lord stands on high leaning on a ladder leading up to
heaven. From there he sees all the sons of men, looks upon all who
inhabit the earth;[13] he knows all their works for he fashioned all their
hearts. He receives those who climb up with humility and constancy,
and throws down those who slip for pride and negligence.

Exemplum[14]
When St. Perpetua was thrown into a dungeon for her faith in Christ,
together with her most fortunate sister Felicitas,[15] she first abhorred

---

[11] Luke 10:19.
[12] 1 Peter 5:8.
[13] Ps. 32:14; Rule of St. Benedict, 7.1.
[14] An abstract of the Passion of St. Perpetua. There are numerous editions and
translations of this famous third-century text, e.g., trans. and introd. Rosemary
Rader, in *A Lost Tradition: Women Writers of the Early Church*, ed. Patricia
Wilson-Kastner et al. (Washington: University Press of America, 1981), 1–32; or
in *Medieval Saints: A Reader*, ed. Mary-Ann Stouck (Peterborough, Ont.:
Broadview Press, 1999), 21–32.
[15] *Felicitas* means "fruitfulness, prosperity, good fortune."

the darkness she was unaccustomed to; but soon, once she became used to it, she considered her dungeon, in her own words, her palace. A little one hung from her breast – a tiny martyr himself, since he sucked in the martyrdom from his martyr mother. Her fellow prisoners and martyrs, knowing that she had God's ear, begged her to ask him to reveal whether they would be vouchsafed the trial of suffering. In response to her prayers, she was shown in her dreams a golden ladder culminating in heaven, so narrow that only one person at a time could climb it. Both sides of it, from the ground to the stars, were studded with all sorts of torments. Crosses, racks, lances, swords, grates, fires, hooks, whips, lead weights, scorpions, wild beasts, and the terrible sights of all known tortures frightened her. Across the foot of the ladder lay an immense, sleepless dragon, perpetually lying in wait for climbers. She called out to Christ, stepped over the dragon, who, scared rigid by her faith, did not dare to move, and she climbed up, preceded by St. Satyrus, who had triumphed before her. She also saw a Moor threatening to wrestle with her, and on the other side a distinguished man wearing a conspicuous crown, who held out a leafed branch with golden apples, like a sign of victory, saying, "If this Moor vanquishes you, he will kill you; if you vanquish him, you will receive this as an honor." Thus she went ahead, conquered, and received the honor of the palm branch.

And she also saw the soul of her deceased brother, the boy Dinocrates, if I remember the name correctly. His face was covered with ulcers and he was straining anxiously to drink from the living fountain, but he could not. She awoke and prayed for him, and immediately saw him completely cured from every strain and every ulcer, resplendent in bright light, rejoicing and playing happily. O Lord of all, who give to each his own! Cleansed of the stain of childish vanity, he was free to play in all innocence at the games holy children play. She also saw other secrets in her visions, as she describes at length in her book. Her pagan father, ruthlessly harsh and ruthlessly affectionate, almost scratched her eyes out in a fit of helpless rage, then sank to the floor to embrace her feet. His venerable white hair stained with dust, he broke out in such laments and entreaties that, as she writes herself, he could have moved the whole world. "Yet who can separate us," says the Apostle, "from the love of Christ?"[16] No matter how much she grieved for her father's unhappiness, she was founded on firm rock and could never be moved. In spurning her father she trampled the devil, raging and pleading by turns. Her father

---

[16] Romans 8:35.

tore her baby from her. Her mother's heart was torn up with anxiety, but God fashioned it so that the baby did not miss the breasts he was used to, and neither did she suffer a dangerous inflammation from the milk. Her sister Felicitas, on the other hand, was already eight months pregnant. Fearing that she would miss out on martyrdom, because it was against the law to execute a pregnant woman, she obtained through her prayers that she was freed from the birth.[17] Thus they offered themselves up to the glorious spectacle, to the wild beasts, to the martyr's crown. O Lord, how glorious and magnificent you are in your saints; o suffering that gives birth to the crown of saints! For thus says Father Benedict: "Self-will has its punishment, and constraint gives birth to the crown!"[18] It was an astonishing spectacle for the crowd around them how these two aristocratic young women vied to protect each other and take on the fury of the beasts for each other. Equally memorable is the remark with which Saint Perpetua, perpetually confident, had put to shame the throng of spectators the day before: "Note carefully what our faces look like," she said, "so you will recognize us on Judgment Day."

Here I am trying to encourage you, and I have done such a poor job of describing the passions of the martyrs to you. But what does it matter from where you derive your encouragement in words and examples of virtue? After all, we pray on the feasts of martyrs: "We celebrate his triumphs; let us be fired up by the examples."[19] It may not be a sword-wielding executioner, but a material cause for your victory, a persecutor, will not fail to arise: all that will live godly in Christ shall suffer persecution.[20] If your battles are not physical, they are spiritual. The former are external, the latter internal and visceral. The soul must be put in persecution's way. When we enjoy times of inner peace, your troops must be given war games to combat sluggishness. Carnal desires must be tamed; as soon as vices raise their heads, they must be crushed. Your army must butt their heads against the rocks of brooding thought and the forces of temptation. You must keep watch in the armor of prayer on the ramparts of your confinement. Against all the snares and hostile arguments, you must exert yourself on the steps of humility towards the heights of virtue.

---

[17] I.e., she gave birth prematurely. The child survived, as Perpetua's book tells us, and was adopted by Felicitas's sister.
[18] Rule of St. Benedict, ch. 7, second degree of humility.
[19] Collect from the mass "Salus autem iustorum."
[20] 2 Tim. 3:12.

The enemy fights more intensely when he keeps his attacks concealed than when he struggles against you openly. With peace, quiet, and flattery he sets snares to overwhelm the incautious; but he fears and avoids the circumspect and vigilant. He will not dare to unleash his full temptation against those whom he never finds idle. "The kingdom of heaven suffers violence," says the Lord, "and the violent bear it away."[21] It suffers violence: why? Because man having lost it through his sins, it will be removed longer and farther than it should be, unless it is wrested back by the violence of virtue. The forces of the air and the princes of darkness have closed off every region of heaven with dense battle lines, and they will not grant access to anyone unless they are conquered. Wherever you want to go, you must open yourself a path with the sword; you must break through the densely clustered ranks of the enemy. If it is not a literal battle sword, let the urgency of your fortitude be your sword. "The Lord has chosen new wars."[22] The old wars were to vanquish anger with the sword, to subject peoples like a tyrant, and submit their necks to vice. The new wars, by contrast, are to repay our adversaries with kindness and love; to submit to all suffering; and to vanquish all vice with all the aggression you can muster. You should be ashamed to sleep, when so many thousands of holy men and women are soaring to heaven amongst arrows, swords, fires, and other instruments of torture, or are struggling up the steep, spiked ladder. "And who," you will ask, "can survive all those trials?" Christ the king of glory, the Lord of hosts, strong and mighty in battle, has shattered all the might of the enemy's army; he has seized their king and laid him in chains in a never-ending prison; and with a great slaughter of the enemy forces will ensure access to his kingdom for all who follow him. Whoever follows this great victor in true faith and charity will always conquer and never be conquered. Steady use will make the narrow path that leads to virtue wider and wider. The sinister forces of darkness already have no real strength left after Christ's triumph. They can only threaten vainly, or mount a timid assault. The only thing that gives them strength is our indulgence: they are lifted up to the extent that they find something of themselves in us. But against those in whom the Prince of this World finds nothing, they quickly lose their nerve. "Be confident," says our leader, "be confident, for I have overcome the world.[23] I hold

---

[21] Mt. 11:12.
[22] Judges 5:8.
[23] John 16:33.

the prince of the world captive; I have taken all his weapons from him and I have distributed his spoils. I gave Rome to Peter, Achaia to Andrew, Asia to John, Africa to Matthew, Jerusalem to James, India to Thomas. Appointing my representative to each land, I have made the whole world my empire. If you want to be men, o my soldiers, I have given you not so much a war to fight against the already vanquished enemy as a ready-made victory. I had you pursue fleeing armies and smite the backs of the retreating enemy. I gave you your enemies with their backs already turned in flight. A thousand may fall at your side and ten thousand at your right hand, but it will not come near you. Take courage, you fearful ones, and do not be afraid; strengthen your feeble hands and confirm your weak knees. Fear me, for I come to break the yoke of your servitude, I come to lead the vanquished from their captivity. And behold, I am with you even unto the end of the world."[24]

A Theory of the Lord's Passion[25]
Pause here a little to consider with what rational love[26] the Lord has miraculously redeemed those whom he miraculously created. Man, created as his free child, had enslaved himself to the Deceiver through his own insolent will, that same deceiver to whose original place he would have ascended had he prevailed. Hence, since he had become a captive voluntarily, it was not right for divine justice to liberate him forcefully. To liberate mankind, it was necessary to give them a man who, pure and free from any contamination, could wrest the palm of victory from the enemy. But our earth was not able to provide such a man.[27] For in this captive nation that is the entire human race, where

---

[24] Ps. 90:7; Is. 35:3, 42:7; Mt. 27:20.

[25] The Latin word is *ratio* – a capacious word with numerous senses, many of which are in play here: "reason," "explanation," "account," "plan of action," "rationale," "purpose," "guiding principle," "logic," "reasonableness." "Theory," as used today, combines many of these semantic components.

[26] "Rationabili caritate."

[27] The reason why God became man was one of the major theological debates of the day. The old answer to the question, which Goscelin explains first, is known as the "devil's rights" argument: the devil had to be tricked into overstepping his rights and thereby forfeit his just claim to humankind. In his celebrated treatise "Cur Deus Homo" ("Why God became Man"), written about a decade after the *Liber Confortatorius*, St. Anselm rejected this explanation as too legalistic. The issue is not what rights the devil may have – he has none – but what would set the universe right again after the fall of man. Obviously, since humankind had failed, any satisfaction had to come from humans, so God could not simply intervene and redress the balance; on the other hand, having fallen, humans were in

no one could ever be born or live without guilt, who could fight to free the guilty captive? No, he had to shine forth from elsewhere, he who would be free from any sin and would take upon himself the penalty owed by the sinners for the sinners. The holy son of God came from his holy heaven, true God was made true man; he joined battle with our enemy, not in the majesty of his divinity but in the frailty of our flesh. In that frailty, the Lord clothed himself with strength and girded himself with virtue;[28] he made himself exceedingly strong to bear suffering, pain, and physical tortures, taunts, spitting, scourging, the cross, wounds, even unto the bitter death and the rites of burial. Impassible in his divinity, he subjected his soul and his passible body to suffering. And see how strong he is. "You have placed," he says, "my arms like a bow of steel,"[29] that is, stretched out on the cross. See what strength he has put on. When his enemies searched for him he did not retreat, he did not hide, he did not hesitate, but knowing all that was to happen to him, as he himself had decreed it from time immemorial, he went forth; he freely delivered himself into the hands of those whom he could have struck down by a mere nod of his head. Thus he displayed strength both potent and patient. Strong, he fought with undefeated patience; powerful, he felled the entire hostile army with one word. They could not withstand him when he was going to his judgment: how will they withstand him when he returns as judge? Just one word from the man doomed to be crucified: "It is I," and the armored force could not stand up. How will they stand when the judge proclaims his sentence: "Depart from me, you cursed, into everlasting fire!"[30] The enemy had vanquished Adam first, with gluttony, vainglory, and avarice: gluttony, when he handed him an apple that was fair to behold and pleasant to eat; vainglory: "You shall be as gods"; avarice: "knowing good and evil." With these three temptations the fiend had captured both him and all of us who are his progeny. Then, the puffed-up victor, yet to be stripped of his victory, attacked the second Adam in the same

no position to make such satisfaction. Ergo, God had to become man. Goscelin's exposition, especially in its second half, contains elements of this second argument; despite the timing, this is not too surprising, since Anselm's argument had been partially anticipated by several theologians, and, as G. R. Evans observes, was in the air throughout the eleventh century: G. R. Evans, *Anselm and a New Generation* (Oxford: Clarendon, 1980), 140–41; for an extended summary and discussion of Anselm's treatise, see ibid., pp. 154–92.

28   Ps. 92:1.
29   Ps. 17:35.
30   John 18:4–8; Mt. 25:41.

manner. Gluttony: "Command that these stones be made into bread"; vainglory: "Cast yourself down, for God has told his angels to watch over you"; avarice: "All these will I give you." But free from all the passions of sin and immune to temptation, he shattered the enemy with his replies. And by his replies he taught us, who are sorely tempted from within by our own passions of sin and cupidity, how to prevail. Gluttony: "Man shall not live by bread alone"; Vainglory, as in showing off one's virtues or usurping marks of distinction: "You shall not tempt the Lord your God"; Avarice, which is idol worship: "You shall worship the Lord your God and him only shall you serve," not the iniquity of Mammon. "The Earth is the Lord's, and all the fullness thereof." And: "The Lord is my shepherd, I shall not want."[31] Thus, a man conquered the conqueror of man. Suffering the penalty of death even though he was not guilty, he turned the just penalty of guilty men against the scourge of innocence, and redeemed the guilty.

The serpent has seduced man with its malign shrewdness, and God in his loving wisdom has toppled the seducer through a man. For when that greedy mouth snatched more human perdition than was his due, that is, when he unjustly punished with the pains of death the sacred one in whom he could find nothing of his own, he forfeited also all those whom he had obtained justly. Going after the innocent one, he lost the guilty ones. The irreproachable and unbindable one bound him, and he had to pay the penalty for his presumption. For even in human law, he who steals what is not his own forfeits even that which is his own.

A victim had to be sacrificed that we might be reconciled with God; but since everything was imprisoned under sin, no worthy victim could be found in the world. "Sacrifice and burnt offering thou wouldest not," said the Psalmist in the role of the Savior.[32] No sacrifice could be accepted in place of the human race, because none was flawless. So God's only-begotten, word-begotten son looked down on the earth from his holy eminence, from his father's throne, to see how he might redeem the children of the lost; and so he said, "Behold, I come."[33] Meek as a sacrificial lamb, conciliatory and mediating,

---

[31]   Gen. 2:9, 3:5; Mt. 4:3–11; Ps. 23:1, 22:1.

[32]   Ps. 39:7; Heb. 10:5 quotes this verse as spoken by Christ ("Wherefore when he comes into the world, he says, 'sacrifice and oblation thou wouldest not' "). Cf. Augustine, *Enarrationes in Psalmos* 39:5 and 39:12. The notion that the Psalms are spoken by Christ throughout is further explained in Book III, p. 98 (see Book III, n. 77).

[33]   Heb. 10:7.

weighed in the scales of the cross and suspended between heaven and earth, he reconciled humankind to god, earth to heaven.[34]

So much did God care to show his ineffable goodness to the world and the exceeding love with which he loved us, that he gave up to death in our stead not an angel, not an archangel, but his own beloved son, his own heart, and through his son he made us his sons and heirs, and coheirs to the son. What can I give back to God for all the good that he gave me in return for all the bad that I gave him? And it was not enough that he redeemed us with such a singular price, which exceeds everything in heaven and on earth in the same measure as the creator exceeds all his creation; in the same measure that the sea is larger than all receptacles in the world – it could fill them all without any diminution of itself. It was not enough that he transported us, who deserve eternal torment, into the kingdom of his light. It was not enough that he took us, children of wrath, and made us children of God's grace. No, he took upon himself our filth and our flesh and placed them at the right hand of the Father. That same creature to which he had said, "You are earth and to earth you shall return," he lifted up in triumph over all the heavens. Who shall declare the power of the Lord, who shall set forth all his praises?[35] Where the lying angel, who in his godless pride had tried to rise up, fell into the depth of Tartarus, in that same place the humility of our condition gained us a fortress in the Lord, and God fashioned one body and one spirit with himself as head and us as limbs. Hence the Apostle says: "You are not your own, but the body and members of Christ."[36] The universal church is the body and the only bride of all the elect; all individual believers are God's members.[37] How reverently must we care for

---

[34] Gregorius, *Moralia in Job*, 7.2.2.

[35] Gen. 3:19; Ps. 105:2.

[36] 1 Cor. 12:27.

[37] The imagery here is (deliberately) mind-boggling. Normally, in the traditional and widespread allegory of Christ marrying the Church, the Church, made up of individual believers, is the bride; i.e., if we are the Church and the Church is Christ's bride, we are encouraged to see ourselves as Christ's bride. This logic seems to be at work here, too, but at the same time the Church is seen as the bride of Christ, whose body is made up of all believers; i.e., if we are Christ's body and Christ is marrying the Church, we are encouraged to see ourselves as marrying the Church. Both ideas are simultaneously in play, and we are invited, above all, to spend some time pondering the complexities. The point, in the end, appears to be that all the terms of the various syllogisms are collapsed into one (all believers = the Church = the Bride = the body of Christ = the Groom); syllogisms are merely our human way of puzzling out what is one incomprehensible divine oneness.

these members of Christ (not our own), lest, God forbid, he should cut them off because of festering sin! And at the end of time, in the presence of all the powers of heaven and all peoples of the world, the prince of pride and inventor of all iniquity, will be vanquished and hurled down by our champion Michael. Then he will find out that he will never rise to the likeness of God through pride, as Saint Gregory proclaims.[38] "At that time," said the angel to Daniel, "Michael, your leader, shall rise, and a time shall come such as never was from the time that the nations began."[39] Never has any era seen such a war as will be seen then, when the heavens shall be on fire and the abyss shall burst open. And consider this also, that this battle between Michael and the dragon that will pull one third of the stars with its tail, will be fought on Christ's behalf and for Christ's birthright.[40] For the entire kingdom of the Just belongs more justly to him who redeemed us with his holy blood, than to him who deceived us with his malice: in the death of the innocent Christ, he lost the guilty ones he held. Consider, my beloved, how urgently we must live right and act well: for if we shall have been iniquitous (God forbid, who created us good and redeemed us from evil through His goodness), we shall not be among those for whom the invincible Michael shall fight. May the just God then justify us, so that our victorious champion, armed in the just cause of Christ, may carry the day for us.

Go then with all your desire and jubilant exultation to those triumphant feasts and dances which our great victorious king has given as a reward to all his soldiers. This single-handed victory has filled up the entire universe with triumphs and crowns above the stars. Uncountable are the troops of martyrs, inestimable the batallions of confessors, innumerable the cohorts of virgins following the Lord of hosts to the stars. No sex, no age, no class shall be denied the palm of victory in Christ. All earth-born children of man, rich and poor, kings and princes, young men and virgins, the old and the young, boys and girls, sucking and screaming infants, all together, will be crowned for their martyrdom, their virginity, or their self-discipline; and our Solomon, who could not dress so richly on earth for all his glory, will be covered in roses and lilies and violets.[41] The grain of wheat that fell to the ground has brought much fruit back from the dead, and lifted up from the earth has drawn everything to

[38] Gregory, Homilies on the Gospels, Homily 34.9 (PL 76:1251).
[39] Dan. 12:1.
[40] Apoc. 12:4.
[41] Ps. 148:12; Luke 12:27.

himself, to whom nobody will come unless drawn by the Father, who sent him.

Then are we drawn by God, says St. Augustine, when we delight in the justice, delight in the beatitude, delight in the eternal life, all of which is Christ.[42] And if you are not being drawn, pray that you may be, for the Savior in his goodness dearly loves to be called to, "Draw me to you";[43] he loves to be called with every fiber of the heart and the body and with long sighs: "Draw me." And the groom and the bride say, "Come," that he or she who hears it may also say, "Come." The road to heaven, opened up by all the victories of all the saints, is already wide open. For those who fight lazily and languidly, it is a narrow path; but for the brave, it is a wide street fit for a king.

The Slaughter of the Demons

And God's side grows constantly, as the devil's side diminishes, and Christ's gains are the enemy's losses. Jerome, heaven's champion, explicates the Book of Joshua in twenty-six homilies.[44] Joshua typologically anticipates both the name and the person of Jesus our Savior.[45] He completely destroyed the kings all around with his armies: that is, he completely extirpated the vices with their main subdivisions.[46] He submerged the horses and chariots: that is, he routed the demons, the instigators of evil, or else the passions of the flesh, lust, lewdness, pride, levity, all the false vanities and madnesses with which the unfortunate soul (to use the author's own words) careens along as if on horseback and is brought to the edge

---

[42]   Tractatus in Ioannem, XXVI. 4 (PL 76: 1251).

[43]   Song of Songs 1:3.

[44]   Actually the text excerpted here is Rufinus's translation of Origenes' Greek homilies, PG 12: 825–940. "Heaven's champion": the ms. has "ala coeli," "wing of heaven," which is puzzling; perhaps it means "ala" in a military sense, "wing of a formation," hence something like "a one-man army in the service of heaven." But perhaps one should read "ara," "champion." (See Book IV, n. 92, for another possible error involving the letters "l" and "r.")

[45]   PG 12:825–28. "Joshua" and "Jesus" are two forms of the same name; the Vulgate uses "Josua" but also mentions the name "Jesus." In this exegetical passage, Joshua is consistently referred to as "Jesus," to highlight the typological connections.

[46]   Cf. PG 12:900–901. On the classifications and subdivisions of the sins in Patristic and medieval literature, see Morton Bloomfield, The Seven Deadly Sins (Lansing: Michigan State College Press, 1952) and Siegfried Wenzel, The Sin of Sloth: Acedia in Medieval Thought and Literature (Chapel Hill: University of North Carolina Press, 1967).

of the abyss.[47] Once the enemy has been routed, Joshua/Jesus distributes the promised land among the victors: for once the demons and vices are extinct, he allots the land of the living as an eternal patrimony to those who have vanquished the flesh and the world, to each according to his labors. Note, however, that just as I said above that Solomon's glory prefigures Christ's sacraments, thus in every divine history external wars signify the internal ones of the soul. The fifteenth sermon begins thus: "If these physical wars did not bear the figurative meaning of spiritual wars, I believe that these books of Jewish history would never have been introduced into the church by the apostles and passed on to the disciples of Christ, who came to teach peace. The Apostle, like a military instructor, ordered the soldiers of Christ: 'Put on the armor of God, that you may stand firm against the wiles of the devil. Have your loins girt about with truth and your feet shod,'[48] that is, mortify your members on earth and cleanse them of fornication, uncleanness, luxury, etc. 'Our struggle is not against flesh and blood,' where one fights with physical swords and lances, 'but against the princes and powers, against the rulers of the darkness of this world':[49] that is, the instigators of worldly temptations, lascivious leaders who do not lead but mislead. Joshua/Jesus commanded us to kill all the enemies and leave not one alive: that is, not one vice, not one ghost of a vice. For if someone were to keep one of those alive in himself, sin would rule his mortal body, and he could not be in Jesus' army. 'And God hardened their hearts that they might go into battle against Israel and be destroyed': that is, he gives the demons who are eager to destroy us humans the power and the boldness to tempt us, that they may be fought by the saints of God, and that Christ's victorious soldiers may be crowned in him with glory and honor, and the vanquished may be hurled into the abyss forever, until the entire reign of the devil will be completely destroyed."[50]

Believe Jerome, that most learned of authors, that whenever any malign spirits are overcome by saints they are always thrown into the abyss by the Lord Jesus, and they can never again in all eternity regain the power to fight with any human: so much honor does our God bestow upon his victors. Thus, as I mentioned above, God's side always grows and Satan's always shrinks. Therefore a fighter for the

---

[47] PG 12:899.
[48] Eph. 6:11.
[49] Eph. 6:12.
[50] PG 12:897.

Lord should not think of the battle as a punishment but as a glorious victory. I hope you will bear with me and not find it too tedious if I insert here a most plausible explanation by that same Jerome, helping us understand these obscure and astonishing matters. Here is how he continues in that fifteenth sermon:

"It seems to me," he says, "that the number of those opposed to virtue is infinite, because in almost every human being there are some spirits who promote the various kinds of sin in them.[51] For instance, there is the spirit of fornication and also the spirit of wrath. Another is the spirit of avarice, yet another the spirit of pride. And if there were a man who is driven by all these evils, one would have to think of him as having all these and even more fiends inside him. Hence, we must believe that there are several spirits for each individual human, for each human does not have a single vice or commit a single sin, but it is evident that everyone hosts several. And moreover we cannot think that it is one single spirit of fornication that seduces, for instance, a man who fornicates in Britain and one who fornicates in India or elsewhere; nor that there is a single spirit of wrath that agitates different people in different places. Rather, I think that there is one chief spirit of fornication, but that there are uncounted ones who obey him and help him in his duties, and that there are diverse spirits who operate under him in different humans, thus inciting them to sin. And similarly I think there is a chief spirit of wrath, yet innumerable ones operating under his command, who effect the sin of that vice through many individual humans. And similarly, that there is a chief spirit of avarice, and thus also for pride and the other vices. And thus the Apostle says that there is not one but many powers militating against virtue, against whom he says he must fight and we all must fight.

"There is, however, one among these princes who is more eminent in evil and more outstanding in crime. He alone, as the leader of all the princes and the master of the entire evil-doing army, shakes up the whole world, which they individually try to recruit for the side of evil through all the different kinds of sin. And whom I have in mind – namely the one I would like to quash together with Jabin, who is his prefiguration – I have set out above, as far as my intelligence is capable.[52] I believe that all the saints who fight

---

[51] The text seems faulty in a few places; where I could not make sense of it I have followed the PG text of Rufinus.

[52] A coy and roundabout way of saying "Satan": Rufinus has indeed discussed earlier (PG 12:392–96) the various typological meanings of Jabin, a ringleader in an alliance of local kings against Joshua (Jos. 11); among other things (396B) he

against these corrupting spirits, and overcome each of them one at a time, greatly weaken the army of demons, and eliminate a great many of them. For instance, if someone through his chaste and decent life has overcome the spirit of fornication, it would not be unreasonable for that spirit, though he has been vanquished by that saint, to attack another human being. But we read that the evil spirits about to be cast out by Jesus asked him not to be thrown into the abyss. Even though the Lord on this particular occasion granted them a temporary reprieve, it would seem to follow that generally every spirit overcome by a saint would be taken to the abyss, or to the outer darkness, or to whatever place is appropriate for him, by Christ the just judge, protector of all humankind against the struggles of this life.[53] And it is precisely because the greater part of the demons is already vanquished, that the nations are now free to come to the faith; the legion of demons would never permit them to do so if it continued undiminished as it was before. If anyone finds it hard to accept my contention that numerous demons work within each sinner, or if anyone thinks this is a fairytale, let him go back to the authority of the gospel, and he will find the one who dwelled suffering among the graves, and when the Lord questioned him, 'What is your name?' he responded, 'Legion. We are many demons.'[54] Why should it be surprising that different demons be assigned to each kind of sin, if it is written that an entire legion of demons inhabited one man?"

"Let me note that I have said something similar also in those places where I interpreted the psalm verse that says, 'At dawn I put to death all the wicked the land, that I might purge from God's city all those who work iniquity.'[55] Finally, it is said that even the just hold double-edged swords in their hands, no doubt to kill all the contrary powers."[56]

---

equates Jabin with Satan. The allusion is lost, of course, in Goscelin's excerpt of Rufinus, which does not include the Jabin passage, even though the reference to it remains ("I have set out above"). One wonders if he expects Eva to be sufficiently familiar with Rufinus's homilies to understand. From the way he introduces the lengthy excerpts, it seems unlikely that she owns the text; but perhaps they had studied it together at Wilton.

[53] Luke 8:31. The idea is that the exception made here by Jesus (by allowing the unclean spirits to decamp into a herd of swine) proves the rule. *Normally*, as their request indicates, cast-out spirits would expect to go to "the abyss."

[54] Mk 5:9; Luke 8:30.

[55] PG 12:1558D.

[56] Ps. 100:8, 149:6–7.

Thus St. Jerome. And a little further on, he says, "I say all this because it is written: 'The Lord hardened their hearts to make them go into battle against Israel, so they might be destroyed.' Therefore, blessed is he who never ceases to carry his spiritual sword and will not turn it away from the necks of those enemies whom we discussed above. We even kill demons within us if we hear what they say and do not carry out their works."[57] Jerome said this and more on the subject, but we are confined by insufficient space. What we read in the Lives of the Fathers about Sara also seems noteworthy. She was beset for many years by the spirit of fornication, yet she did not ask God to rid her of it, but rather that he might strengthen her to virtue and that God's hand might save her from ruin; until finally that most unclean spirit himself, utterly confounded, appeared to her and confessed himself defeated: "You have vanquished me, Sara." But she, wanting to prevail through the true victor, responded: "Not I, but my Lord Jesus Christ."[58]

So where would that spirit go, if not straight to the abyss? Next, we read in Joshua: "The earth rested from the battles."[59] Our earth, that is our flesh, will rest from the battles if we have mortified the things of the flesh, if we have crucified our flesh together with all its vices and desires, if we kill off all passions and incitements of the flesh, if we are crucified to the world and it to us, if we have amputated fornication, uncleanness, licentiousness from our members, if we have eradicated wrath, greed, the joys and hopes, and fears and sadnesses of the world from our minds. And do not let that saying introduce any doubts into your mind, "Let me see it, and I will believe." For that is the essence of the academic discipline of the philosophers, that they do not arrogate to themselves the authority to pronounce categorically, but relinquish their judgment to the judgment of the learned. Most of all, St. Jerome himself, because of his many adversaries who were more ready to condemn everything up front than to discuss or understand, proposes rather than announces most of his proofs, and works out the truth more by reasoning than by decree. And he is to be believed the more insofar as I know of no one more learned in the sacred text from the wellspring of the original languages.[60]

---

[57] Joshua 11:20; PG 12:904–905.
[58] *Verba Seniorum* 5.10–11 (PL 73:876).
[59] Joshua 14:15.
[60] This appears to be a double apology: on the one hand, Goscelin acknowledges that the foregoing discussion may well seem outlandish, and admonishes Eva to

The Multitude of Sacred Virtues

But now that you have heard about the countless multitudes of the enemy's forces, I should reassure you that the forces of the heavenly virtues that come to our aid are even greater. For it is written "that more are on our side than are against us."[61] If a whole legion of demons, that is six thousand, was able to live in one man, surely a much larger army of the heavenly host can set up camp in a heart where Christ, the Father and the Holy Spirit have made a dwelling for themselves, and vanquish any foe of any believer in the cross and the faith of Christ. It is plausible that at the hour of its parting every soul will have those spirits as its companions whom it gathered about itself while in the body. Evil spirits inhabit and then accompany the evil soul, and good spirits the good soul. For instance, the divine majesty with all the saints rested in the humble, quiet, poor soul of St. Martin; thus, when it traveled to the stars an entourage of all the powers of heaven received and accompanied him. It is through praying, chanting, and embracing our sacred readings that we acquire these holy escorts to bring us victoriously to the land of the living. Learn more about this subject from the twentieth homily of St. Jerome:

"If," he writes, "someone were able to reach that holy and good land of the living in which there is no more dying, if someone were to merit through the grace of the holy spirit to ascend to see all that, that man can truly know the fine points of the hereditary lands and the place names written about here.[62] Yet because it is difficult to find a soul so learned and so full of the Holy Spirit, I will try meanwhile, for everyone's spiritual comfort, to discuss these matters briefly in our lessons. At any rate, it will be best for me to attempt to grasp these matters while I am still alive and reap the just reward for my efforts. Or if not, after I die, these matters may become clear to others more

bow to Jerome's authority (because he has so carefully worked out his arguments, and because he was such an experienced linguist). On the other hand he may be forestalling objections to Jerome's overly scholastic method (prescholastic thinkers were somewhat on the defensive about trying to reason out matters of faith; hence St. Anselm's insistence that faith comes first, understanding second [credo ut intellegam]): Jerome had to argue so carefully because he was under constant attack.

[61] 4 Kings (KJV: 2 Kings) 6:16.

[62] I.e., Joshua 13–22, which describes in detail the land distribution made by Joshua among the tribes of Israel. Again, Goscelin's method of excerpting removes so much of the context, and even omits so much of the passage he selects, that the result is just barely intelligible without recourse to the original.

deserving than myself. Indeed, I should point out that the soul benefits greatly from the reading of God's words, even if it appears obscure to us, and merely washes against our ears. The pagans believe that there are certain songs they call 'magical,' which those who possess the skill need only pronounce in a whisper; and through certain names, known not even to those who perform the invocation, through the sound of the word alone, serpents can be put to sleep or else raised from the most hidden caverns. Often such chants are said to suppress tumors or fevers and other such ills in human bodies, by the sound alone; and sometimes they can inflict a stupor on the soul and make it unconscious – at least if there is no Christian faith to resist them. If pagan incantations and chants can do all that, should we not hold a recital of the words and names of Holy Scripture to be far stronger and more potent? According to the infidels, when the harmful powers hear such and such a name spoken in these charms or incantations, they come and offer their services and endeavor to do that which they heard themselves invoked to do in the naming, performing the services to which they have pledged themselves. Heavenly powers and angels of God are always with us; God said of the little ones of the church that their angels always stand before the eyes of God and see his face.[63] If the pagan spirits are eager to help, our angels will even more willingly and graciously accept the words of Scripture and the naming of those good names that always proceed from our mouths, like so many chants and invocations. For even if we do not understand what comes from our mouths, these powers who assist us do understand, and will delight in being with us at the utterance of a song, and to give us help. The Psalmist says that countless divine powers are not only around us but also inside us: 'Bless the Lord, o my soul, and all my insides praise his holy name,' that is: all that is within me.[64] Therefore it is clear that there are many powers within us who are charged with the protection of our souls and our bodies. They will be gladdened when we read Holy Scripture and grow stronger through our diligence, even if our mind is barren, as it is written: 'If I speak with tongues' and my spirit prays, yet our understanding bears no fruit. For the holy apostle said this too and put a great mystery before human ears: it can sometimes happen that our spirit may pray and our mind bear no fruit.[65]

---

[63] Mt. 18:10.

[64] Ps. 102:1.

[65] 1 Cor. 14:14, with an echo of 13:1. St. Paul here is being *critical* of those who pray "in tongues" but without understanding: their spirit bears no fruit, and they

"Understand from this that sometimes our mind can be without fruit but our spirits, that is, the powers which were given us to assist our soul, will be nourished and refreshed from hearing the holy scriptures, a divine food appropriate to them. But when we voice the words of Holy Scripture, we feed not only the divine powers in us. Our Lord himself, Jesus Christ, when he finds us occupied in this manner and applying ourselves to such studies and exercises, will deign to eat and be refreshed in us. Indeed, seeing such food prepared in us, he will also bring the Father with him. If that seems too much, beyond the capacity of a human being, take as proof not my words but the salvific words of the Lord himself: 'Amen, I say to you, that I and the Father will come to him and make our abode with him and eat in his house.'[66] Whom does he mean? Him, of course, who keeps his commandments.

"Now, just as we can enlist the assistance and services of these divine powers by using incantations of this sort, so by contrast can we dispel the ambushes of malignant powers and the attacks of evil demons by naming holy words and names. You may have seen a snake-charmer holding a stunned serpent in his hands or extract it from its burrow, powerless and unable to harm him with its venom, as though put to sleep by the power of the chanting. Thus, too, if there is any serpent inside us that is contrary to virtue, if any snake is lying in ambush, you would do well to remove it; unless, tired by boredom, you avert your attention, it can be dispelled by the charms of Scripture and the persistent force of the divine word. If, therefore, my listener, you ever find a Scripture read to you that you do not understand, and its sense appears obscure to you, you can, for the time being, accept its first usefulness: by the hearing alone, as by incantation, the venom of those noxious powers that besiege you and ambush you will be dispelled and expelled. Only take care lest you become like the deaf asps, which stop their ears and will not hear the voice of the charmer nor of the wizard that charms wisely,[67] for instance, the song that is chanted and sung by all the wise prophets. I say this lest we become bored when we listen to Scripture, even if we do not understand it. If we believe that all Scripture is useful, because it is divinely inspired, it will be done to us according to our faith. Even if we do not feel its usefulness, we nonetheless must believe that it is useful.

---

should pray for the grace to interpret the words they speak. Rufinus takes the passage out of context to suit his own homiletic purpose.

[66] John 14:23.
[67] Ps. 57:11.

"Doctors sometimes prescribe certain foods, or give a potion, say for example to cure a blurred vision. In eating that food or drinking that potion, we may not feel that it is beneficial and good for the eye. But as a day passes, and another, and a third, that food or potion will, in its own good time and by its own hidden paths, be carried to our eyes. It will slowly clear our vision, and then we first begin to feel that this food or potion is indeed beneficial to our eyes. And it is the same with other parts of our bodies. In the same way, we have to believe that it is thus with sacred scripture, that it is useful for the soul and benefits it, even if our mind cannot grasp its sense. For, as I have said, the good powers that reside in us will be refreshed and nourished by these words, and the contrary powers will be weakened and dispelled by such meditations."

Thus, in your solitude, armed with the erudition of the famous Jerome, with the charms of the Psalter and divine reading, pacify the snakes that lurk in the way of justice, and trample the lion and the dragon. Hurry, desiring soul, to the promised land of eternal immortality. Go to that mountain where those will reside who walk without blemish and speak the truth in their hearts, and reduce the evil one to nothing, victorious in the Lord. Those who are strong in faith and released from their weak worries assail that mountain, and the violent bear it away.[68] Thus, the brave Caleb, who alone of the six hundred thousand armed men freed from Egypt entered the Promised Land with Joshua, demanded of Joshua an inheritance, to be wrested from the hand of the strongest enemy, commensurate to his great courage. There was a rich mountain, standing tall among the cities and strong in fortifications. On this mountain stood the turreted city of Hebron, which received tribute from a hundred cities in the tribes of Judah. "Give me," said the Lord's warrior, "that mountain." And Joshua gave it to him, congratulating him and thanking him for his great courage. Caleb did away with the king and a strong enemy army, and occupied the town and all the regions surrounding it in a wide swath.[69] Thus every soul that has vanquished any kind of spiritual enemy will inherit that enemy's former good fortune. Therefore, if we want greater glory, we must be persistent in our struggle; for we know that glory will not be given without supreme effort. While the crowd stayed below, weighed down by its earthly desires, Moses, cleansed and lightened after a forty days' fast, ascended the mountain towards

---

[68] Mt. 11:12.
[69] Joshua 14:6–14.

God's glory. Elijah also, having suffered persecution for justice, arrived at the holy Mount Horeb after the same number of days of travel and abstinence. Our Redeemer himself ascended the mountain with his disciples, while the common people stayed below in the fields of heavy cupidity. Thus the Most High summons the most high towards high heaven, to give them in that exalted location the highest signs of his blessings. Elsewhere, he says to them, "To you it is given to know the mystery of the kingdom of God; but to the rest in parables."[70] He who wishes to ascend the true mountain with the Lord and to build a tower to heaven must outfit himself in strength, not in the pride of Babylon but from the valley of humility, and must prepare the necessary provisions of complete patience and long-suffering. Hence St. Gregory, exhorting us to desire higher things and despise the transitory, speaks to us of the Gospel passage, "If anyone come to me, and hate not his father and mother . . ." etc., with the following teaching:[71]

"If we consider, dearest brethren, how much is promised to us in heaven, all that is contained in this world must seem vile to our mind. For all earthly substance, compared to the happiness on high, is a burden, not a support. Temporal life, compared to eternal life, should be called death rather than life. For what is our daily slide towards corruption, if not a prolonged death? What tongue can speak, what mind can comprehend, how great are the joys of that city on high: to mingle with the angelic choirs, stand in the presence of the Creator's glory with all the blessed spirits, see the uncircumscribed light, be afflicted by no fear of death, and rejoice in the gift of perpetual incorruption. On hearing this, our mind catches on fire, and wishes it were already there, rejoicing without end. But one cannot come to that great joy without great labors. Hence, the famous preacher says: 'no one will be crowned except if he has striven lawfully.' "[72] That is, no one can take the laurel wreath unless he has run the race to attain it, forgetting all else and fighting as if for his life. "The greatness of the prize delights us, but let not the struggle and the labors deter us. We are told to hate those closest to us, and to hate even our own soul. For then do we well hate our soul when we do not give in to its carnal desires, when we break its appetites, when

---

[70] Luke 18:10.
[71] Luke 14:26; Gregory, Homilies on the Gospel 37, PL 76:1275–76; *Forty Gospel Homilies*, trans. Dom David Hurst (Kalamazoo: Cistercian Publications, 1990), 327–29.
[72] 2 Tim. 2:5.

we resist its will. We must hate our soul, and lose it for the savior's sake; that is, we must hate our self-will and lose it in this world, so that our soul may be saved forever in the eternal life. Such is also the hate of those close to us, which does not arise from hatred but from love: he loves his neighbor well who hates him as he does himself, as he hates his own soul."

God forbid, my soul burning in God, that you should be deterred by this long, confusing and noisy war. Rather, I pray you may be encouraged, and ever more confidently expect your final glory. Fear reveals a weak mind, and I am afraid I may be one when I read how Abraham offered up his only son; how Jeptha sacrificed his only daughter; how David, by spilling water in sacrifice to God, tamed his appetite[73]; how Stephen acknowledged Christ amid the stones;[74] how your own St Lawrence, roasted on a grate, made fun of the men who stoked the glowing coals;[75] how the young girl Agnes, with similar fortitude, derided the prefect who both flattered and intimidated her, and welcomed the sword plunged into her throat rather than submit to the rapist;[76] how Daniel, in constant converse with angelic visions, "ate no desirable bread, and neither flesh;"[77] how our patron saint Silvinus, bishop of the city of Toulouse, who lies next to St. Bertin, completely abstained from bread and wine for forty years, the length of time God rained manna for the children of Israel, and contented himself with herbs and water; how Germaine of Auxerre lived on bread made with urine; how the most holy virgin Genoveva from her fifteenth to her fiftieth year never ate or drank anything except on Sundays and Thursdays, and then her food was peas or beans left standing for about two weeks after cooking.[78] Whenever I am told about these and innumerable other struggles of the saints, I shy away from my signal trumpet as I would from an arrow, and a cold shiver runs through my innermost bones. But I would think that you are stronger of courage than this unwarlike trumpeter, and that all my

---

[73] 1 Chronicles 11:16–19. David, under siege from the Philistines and weak from dehydration, heroically refused a drink of water which his men had risked their lives to obtain for him, saying that he could not "drink the blood of these men."
[74] Acts 7:55.
[75] Ambrose, De officiis 1.41 (PL 16:85–86); Augustine, Sermon 303. The famous story is that Lawrence said, in the middle of the torture, "I am done on this side, turn me over."
[76] Ambrose, De Virginitate 1:2:9 (PL 16:191).
[77] Dan. 10:3.
[78] AASS Feb. III, p. 31; AASS Julii VII, 215; AASS Jan. I, p. 139.

exhortations fall far short of your fervor. Yet even if my effort seems less than adequate to your spiritual proficiency, it will still make it clear that I am pouring out my affection for you: if it is of no use to you in your abundance and your satiety, may it be useful insofar as I can do justice to my love, and speak to you for as long as this letter lasts. You, meanwhile, take this letter like one who eats as much as she needs from a full table. From among these reflections, and whatever else you may read by way of exhortations and examples, take according to your courage and your strength, as the Lord inspires you to follow them. And with all your desire strive to win the high prize promised, with the modesty and earnestness that come of the fear of God, and with such consonance of fortitude and humility that you will neither fall nor faint along the way. You need not fear the enemy, as long as you fear the Lord and put your trust in the protection of his wings. For the enemy can never tempt you any further than he is permitted by the Lord, in whose hand you are. Not a fly will die, not a leaf will fall, not one hair of our heads can perish without his consent. God, says the Apostle, will not suffer you to be tempted above that which you are able to bear, but will make also with the temptation an escape, so that you may be able to bear it.[78a] The greater our trials and tribulations, the greater the powers our helper in every need will supply. Let me support this idea with a little exemplum.

Saint Blandina[79]

At the time when the holy martyrs were being tested by all sorts of ordeals, as Eusebius of Caesarea recalls in his *History of the Church*, one lady, together with the entire army of martyrs, was afraid for her slave Blandina, that she might fall from the faith amid the torture; and they prayed together that God might show his greatness. And Blandina turned out to surpass men, even Christ's strongest soldiers, in her fortitude, endurance, and constancy. The torturers' mad ferocity and contempt fell on her with full force; the crowd's jeers, furor, violence, and madness raged against her. She was cut and torn, gored, stoned, and thrown among the wild beasts like so many chunks of meat. All day, she was tormented with all the cruelties the butchers' inhumanity could devise. The torturers tired, but she did not. New torturers and new wounds were inflicted on her, but as the

---

[78a] I Cor. 10:13.
[79] Eusebius, *The History of the Church*, 5.1 (trans. G. A. Williamson [Baltimore: Penguin, 1965], 196–200).

torturers exhausted themselves almost to death, she just grew stronger and stronger. They fell; she persisted. They foamed with rage; she laughed. The victim was stronger than the tormenter, the wounded stronger than the inflicter of the wounds. The torture that had terrorized all the people was trampled by the weaker sex. Amid all the torments, she repeated only one sentence: "I am a Christian." She told the astonished Christians that every time she called out, "I am a Christian," she felt herself restored with new strength. Finally, the sword won her the palm. Thus almighty God triumphs not only through royal heroes and soldiers, but even through the lowliest slaves among humans. What to the world is weak, base, and contemptible, God singles out to confound the strong. The greatest among the great performs miracles through the least. Through the women Deborah, Jael, and Judith, he crushed proud rulers and hostile armies.

Along the lines of this story, let me further instruct you in the exercise of your faith, and tell you how the Lord Jesus, the morning star who chose to rise in the world through a woman, also allowed himself be proclaimed by a captive woman in a nation not yet reached by the rays of the apostolic mission. Through that captive he captured the kingdom which held her prisoner. To strengthen you further in faith, I will insert this narrative, not my own but the Historiographer's.[80]

The power of the captive woman[81]
"At that same time," he says, "the people of the Georgians, who dwell in the region of the Black Sea, received the covenants of the word of God and the faith in the world to come. The cause of this great good was a captive woman living among them, who led a faithful, sober, and chaste life. Every day and night she stayed awake to pray to God. The barbarians, who had never seen such a thing before, were astonished, and with mounting curiosity they demanded to know the purpose of her actions. She answered simply just as it was: that with this rite she worshipped Christ, her God. This in itself did

---

[80] I.e., in Rufinus of Aquileia's continuation of Eusebius, Book 10:11. *The Church History of Rufinus of Aquileia*, trans. Philip R. Amidon, S. J. (New York: Oxford University Press, 1997), 20–23.

[81] The word is "virtus," which, especially in medieval usage, can correspond to our "virtue"; but it also carries meanings of "strength, power," especially in Classical usage. No one English word renders it perfectly; I have decided case by case.

not surprise the barbarians, except for the newness of the name. But, as often happens, the woman's very persistence aroused their curiosity, and they wanted to see if all this devotion gained her some advantage. They apparently have this custom: when a small child is ill, the mother carries it around from house to house, and if anyone happens to know of a proven remedy, it is given to the sick child. One day some woman carried her baby around according to this custom, but had not yet received any medicine, even though she had gone to every house. Finally she came to the captive woman to have her disclose what she knew. She said that she knew of no human remedy, but claimed that Christ, her God, whom she worshipped, had once cured her when everyone else despaired of her health. So she placed the infant on her hair shirt, and prayed fervently over it to her God, and returned it to its mother all cured. Word of this miracle spread, and the news reached the queen, who was suffering from a grave, painful illness and was in great despair. She asked that the captive be brought to her. But the captive declined to go, lest she seem to be presuming more than her sex allowed. So the queen had herself carried to the captive's hut. Again, the captive woman had the patient placed upon her hair shirt and invoked Christ's name; and again, after her prayer she had her get up, healthy and in good spirits. She instructed the queen that it was Christ, the son of the highest God, who had given her health. She counseled her to call to him whom she knew to be the author of her health and her life, because it was he who bestowed realms on kings and life on mortals. The queen joyfully returned home and disclosed to her hesitant husband the cause of her sudden cure. The king, happy of his wife's cure, wanted to honor the woman. The queen said, 'this captive does not care at all about that, sir. She despises gold, rejects silver, and seems to thrive on fasting as if on food. We owe her only one gift: that we worship the one who saved me at her request – Christ, her God.' But the king was slow to act on this advice, and delayed it several times, even though his wife admonished him. One day it happened when he was hunting in the woods with his companions, that the day suddenly darkened with the densest darkness, and the horror of the dark night made it impossible for them to walk on. The companions lost each other and went off one by one. The king, alone and surrounded by thick darkness, did not know what to do or where to turn. Finally, as he feared more and more for his safety, this thought arose in his troubled mind: if that Christ, of whom the captive woman has told my wife, is indeed God, let him deliver me now from this darkness, and then I will worship him, forgetting all others. He had not even spoken this but simply vowed it in his thoughts, when daylight was restored to the world and led the king safely back to the city, where he told the queen everything that had happened. He had the captive woman called before him and demanded that she instruct him in the rites of worship, confirming that he would worship no god besides Christ. The captive woman came, taught him that Christ is God, instructed him in the prayers and rites, insofar as it is right for a woman to explicate these things, urged him to build a church and described for him what it should look like. The king assembled his people, told them everything that had happened to him and the queen from the beginning, taught them about the faith, and even though he himself was not yet initiated into the sacred rites, became the apostle of his people. The men believed through the king, the women through the queen, and by general consensus a church was built instantly. The outer walls were quickly built; then came the time to put in the columns. The first was erected, then the second. But when it came to the third column, despite the use of all machines and the labor of strong men, when it was already raised halfway, at an oblique angle, it could not be raised the rest of the way with any contraption. They tried a second and a third time, yet even though they exhausted all forces, they were not able to move it. The people were astonished, the king's resolve waned, and no one knew what to do. Night fell, and all went away; all mortals and all labors ceased; only the captive woman remained inside, waking in prayer. The king returned early in the morning, anxious, with all his people: he saw the column, which so many machines and so many people had not been able to move, all erect and suspended above its base, not resting on it but hanging in the air about one foot above the base. Now the entire people rejoiced and praised God, and acknowledged that the king's faith and the captive woman's religion were true, as testified by this evident miracle. And as they were still marveling and puzzling, the column, untouched by anyone, lowered itself down before their very eyes and settled on its base perfectly balanced. After that, the remaining columns went up so easily that all the rest were put in place that same day. Now the magnificent building was completed, and the people thirsted even more ardently for the faith. At the suggestion of the captive woman a delegation was sent from the whole people to the emperor Constantine. They told him all that had happened and asked that priests be sent to complete the gift that God had begun among them. Constantine joyfully sent priests; he was especially happy that they would be reaching people and realms unknown to the Roman Empire. This was told to us by the honorable

Bacurius, the king of that people and garrison commander in our parts, and a man of the highest integrity and respect for the faith, when he commanded the border troops in Palestine and resided among us as a friend in Jerusalem."

The power of the anchorite
Finally, let me give you a recent example of virtue from your own England. The matter is well known, being quite recent. My witness is Dom Aelsi, a monk from boyhood and now my good friend.[82] Being detained not long ago at a royal whim in some fortified town about fifteen miles from Bury St. Edmunds, he made it his business to befriend an anchorite in a wooden cell attached to the church. The anchorite was a simple, upright man, claiming to know nothing save Jesus, and him crucified;[83] so he constantly repeated the prayers he had learned in the simple way of laymen, namely the Lord's Prayer and the first verse of the fiftieth psalm, with the Gloria Patri. This irritated the Enemy of human salvation beyond toleration. One night he called him by name: "Brithric, won't you ever allow God or your fellow humans some rest? Do you think God is hard of hearing, or stupid, that you deafen him so incessantly with this one, same, illiterate prayer? Do you think he is daft, that he won't know what to do unless asked? Don't you know, you dunce, that you are provoking rather than pleasing him with your importunity, as Scripture says, 'Do not repeat a word in your prayers'? So be quiet and settle down, or else God will get angry with you for your restlessness instead of having mercy on you." Pressured by these attacks, the simple man imposed silence on his mouth for a while. But the next day, he explained to Aelsi why he had stopped praying, and Aelsi instructed him about the fallacious illusions of the demons. Like a soldier, the more determined for having been wounded, Brithric rose up and repeated his perpetual prayer with even more ardor. The next night, the enemy attacked him again and berated him even more sharply. Unless he toned down his reckless prayers, he threatened, the wrath of God would descend not only on him but also on that monk of his, who was deceiving him. Yet Brithric, in his own simple way a lover

---

[82] Talbot surmises that this "Eilsius" may be Aelsi (also spelled "Aethelsige"), abbot of Ramsey from 1080–87, but found no written source for this story, and no mention in any document of Brithric the anchorite, the pirate raid, or the fire. There may indeed be no written source: Goscelin's introduction suggests oral transmission.

[83] 1 Cor. 2:2.

of light, not darkness, renounced the tempter of sloth with fervid zeal, and making the sign of the cross at him drove him far away.

Then one day, pirates attacked the fortress with fire and sword, and his confidant Aelsi was begging the anchorite to flee the danger. But Brithric called out, "my brother, Christ went so far as to suffer an undeserved death, and I should flee from a death I deserve? What he suffered voluntarily, although innocent, I, being guilty, should not suffer from necessity? There was no condition when I entered here that I could leave in an emergency.[84] Know then, brother, that I will not be frightened away from here but will die here as a burnt offering to God. I will spread myself out in the shape of the cross and prayerfully accept the hand of God that is coming upon me, and you will find me in that position. I know that the melting lead from the roof of the church will whip my back like a torrid rain, but though the torment be violent, it will hasten my end. You go ahead and save yourselves by fleeing; leave me behind; thus you can escape inescapable death for the time being."

To cut a long story short, the castle, the church, and the cell burned down, and a week later, when the fire had barely died down, the warrior of God was found lying there with his arms spread out, as he had predicted. He was burned, and his back was shot through with a great deal of lead, which had both charred and filled out his emaciated body accustomed to fasting. Aelsi, who bears witness to all this, swears that he and the others who rushed in were enveloped by such a sweet fragrance, as if a great deal of incense had been burned there; and very fitting it was, for Brithric, as God's sacrificial lamb, had burnt in this place like incense. His blessed soul enjoys the rest and quiet of the martyrs, and his body is buried in peace.

On the other hand, as I learned just recently, she who had been fighting the fight at your church before you, my sweetest, survived unharmed amid the flames when the church burned down.[85]

How many saints were devoured by wild beasts, fires, and floods; and how many did God preserve unharmed, such as Daniel, such as the hymn-singing youths, such as Peter.[86] When they escaped from dangers untouched, they had the miraculous gift of divine grace. When they fought to the end in agony, they had the great trophy of divine power. It is a beautiful story how the captive woman, by the

---

[84] An anchorite had himself enclosed in a cell and vowed never to leave it.
[85] See Book IV, n. 10.
[86] Daniel 6, 3; Acts 5:18–23.

wings of prayer alone, erected the column whose weight no power in the kingdom had been able to move, and even balanced it suspended and only then set it down firmly on its base. But even greater strength was shown when Stephen succumbed to the stones, and turned Saul into Paul. Nor is that man who was tried by fire any less proof of the power of miracles.

Therefore, armed with these examples of fortitude or grace, wipe out Amalech and his army, and cut down every obstacle the Enemy puts before you; go forth, my beloved, towards your destiny and your eternal birthright. As the soul which longs for God the living spring, and thirsts like the stag for the water fountains, pass across the Jordan of tears as your soul flows freely within you. Walk with desire to the miraculous tabernacle and advance as far as the house of God, in a voice of exultation and confession and the rejoicing of one invited to the feast. And when you question yourself as you are wounded by love, "why are you sad, my soul, and why do you trouble me?" answer yourself with the only remedy: "Hope then in God, for I will still give praise to him: the salvation of my countenance and my God."[87]

HERE ENDS THE SECOND BOOK OF EXHORTATIONS.

---

[87]   Ps. 41.6, 12.

Here Begins the Third Book

Against Depression[1]

Moses, the archetype, made a tabernacle at the command and the specifications of the Lord's majesty, where God gave him commandments for the people and conversed with him as a friend.[2] This tent was like a very large temple with purple walls, stretched widely over golden columns and posts. The world had seen nothing more beautiful, nothing more laboriously made, nothing more artful until that time. I do not think that even today any king could match this dignified structure. As the sky is decorated with stars, the ground with flowers, the world with various kinds of ornaments, thus this mobile palace shone with every imaginable splendor. The entire structure consisted of the whitest linen, and was adorned with twice-tinted purple cloth and golden fabric. Superb painting of every color and every shape added to the decoration. All the lands and all the seas and all the beauty of the world – you would have thought that it had all been gathered there. And the golden cheer of the sun would shine its rays through this most translucent structure, like a temple of solid glass in every color, and with its light would beautify the abundant gold and the manifold painted figures, and reflect from the light-flooded roof as if from a second sky, and it would paint the

---

[1] Goscelin's term is "taedia" (weariness, ennui, disgust); other writers called it "tristitia" (sadness) or, with a Greek term, "acedia." Monks, nuns, and hermits were, not surprisingly, familiar with depressed mental states, and there is a considerable literature, from the Desert Fathers onwards, devoted to describing, theorizing, and combating it. (It would not be much of an exaggeration to say that the ascetic discipline of the Desert Fathers consisted in provoking, then overcoming "acedia".) For a comprehensive treatment of the topic, see Siegfried Wenzel, *The Sin of Sloth: Acedia in Medieval Thought and Literature* (Chapel Hill: University of North Carolina Press, 1967). The phenomenon is, to us, clearly recognizable as depression, and despite some misgivings I have translated it as such. ("Acedia," the best-known and most specific term for monastic melancholia, is a good option but sounds awkward in English prose.) It must be remembered that the cultural connotations are quite different: to begin with, modern depression is thought of as an illness, or (in less serious cases) an everyday mood disturbance; medieval "acedia" is a sin, albeit a common and understandable one.

[2] Exodus 33:11.

inside of the entire tabernacle and all the sacred utensils golden. So much dignity and so much beauty surely prefigured the majesty of the Church's Holy Sacraments. But it also afforded much solace at that time to the Hebrew people in the desert, and lightened the labors and the tedium of their long solitude. They were blessed with a column of light from the sky, and with artful beauty from the floor of the desert.

Thus you, too, my sweet child, if the power of your mind has not yet allowed you to enter the land of the living; if you sometimes forget the homeland that you are seeking and are depressed by your solitude, your imprisonment and your enclosure; build yourself a column of faith and a tent of hope, and as in a tabernacle painted in every color rejoice in the law of the Lord, practicing and meditating in it day and night, with the manifold decorations of the examples of the saints. Measure in your mind the eternal brightness and the eternal night, and with that much hope and that much fear dispel depression. Delight in the Lord, and you will no longer be dejected. Be with the Lord, and you will not be alone. Liberated from the slavery of sin be a freedwoman among the adopted children of God, and you will no longer be imprisoned. We are shifting, inconstant creatures. Now hope lifts us up, now hope slips away, and we break. Peter walked steadily on the water, but soon his faith weakened and he sank. While God supports us we think we will stand forever, but if he leaves us for just a moment we lose the very ground under our feet. And we cannot get up unless the hand of the Lord raises us up, we cannot stand unless his hand holds us. "In my abundance I said: I shall never be moved. Lord, by your favor you gave strength to my beauty." That is standing forever. And what comes next? "You turned away your face from me, and I became troubled."[3] I shall never be moved: what could be more stable? I became troubled: what could be more prone to fall? Night pushes out day and day pushes out night, and we change constantly between serenity and storminess. Our road is sometimes smooth, sometimes rough. And man changes with the world, unless he is steadied in God. Therefore if your constancy weakens and your lantern darkens, breathe in him who is your strength, your light and your salvation. The serpent-seductor of the old Eva whispers with a pleasing voice, which, as God said to Job, is like a pipe of brass.[4] With that sweet-sounding persuasion he solicits you: "What have you done? Why have you deprived yourself,

---

[3]   Ps. 29:7–8.
[4]   Job 40:13.

so young, so promising, of so many splendid things? Ah, verdant branch, transplanted from the pleasant springtime, you have withered before your time. You are just a girl, an adolescent, the flower of life itself, and you have suddenly died. From your tender age of twenty, are you going to sit here until your fiftieth or even hundredth year, into old age and decrepitude, into a long, drawn-out end, all the long days, the profound nights, the endless labors, the perpetual prison, the continual deaths of desolation?"

To combat these whisperings of the coiled dragon, think that you might die any day; always think that today's dawn might be your last – not tomorrow's, not one a long time away. As Horace says, "think of every day as the last one that shines upon you."[5] But he who gives and receives our life urges you even more strongly: "Watch you therefore, for you know not the day nor the hour of God's coming";[6] that is, everyone should fear that hour, for no one knows the hour. For to every mortal, "death is certain but the hour is uncertain."[7] Why, you unquiet voice, you author of death, are you promising long days? Death spares no age; it sweeps away the old with the young, it cuts down the vigorous and the decrepit with the same scythe. Let me die, Lord, lest I die, said the great Augustine;[8] meaning, let me die to the world and to sin, and I shall live for the Lord of life. And Paul said, "For you are dead, and your life is hid with Christ in God." And "I live, now not I; but Christ lives in me."[9] From the moment of my death, I shall begin to live for my God, and when life fails me I shall begin to last unfailingly. In childhood and youth, man is a flower, which lives for a short time, then is destroyed in much misery; he flees like a shadow, and his days go by like a shadow. But I trust in the Lord and I shall not weaken; dying in God I shall not die but live. Blessed are the dead who die in the Lord, with whom to die is to live, without whom to live is to die. Yet the dead shall not praise you, Lord, nor all those who go down to hell, but we who live for the Lord, bless the Lord, we whose life is hid with Christ in God, who says, "He who believes in me will not die forever," and "He who preserves my words will not taste death forever, but will pass from death into life."[10] Only those will die forever, separated from all

---

5   Epist. 1.3.13.
6   Mt. 25:13.
7   Cicero, *De Senectute* 20:74.
8   Augustine, *Confessions* 1:5.
9   Colossians 3:3; Gal. 2:20.
10   Job 14:2; Ps. 25:1; Apoc. 14:13; Ps. 113:17; John 11:26, 8:52.

good, only those will be swallowed by the sad chaos of hell who believed your flatteries, oh enemy of humankind, those whom you inebriate with the honey-sweet venom of your temptations, and whom you delight, drunken and blinded, with untold bitterness, until you hurl them into the sulphureous mouth of the abyss, where they will never see light again in all eternity. But I shall delight in the Lord, and I rejoice in Jesus my God, who saved me from the lion's mouth, who redeemed my life from destruction and snatched my soul from hell. I shall expect that Lord, my savior, and if he make delay I shall wait for him. All my life until the end I shall await him, for he will come, and those who stand ready to receive him he will never leave again. I will sing to God as long as I live.[11] In his hands my days rest, and he will stand at my right so I shall not be moved. He is with me as a strong warrior, and will not leave me for the length of my days, and will be with me until old age and decrepitude and until the end of time.[12] For whether we live, we live unto the Lord; or whether we die, we die unto the Lord; and whether we live or die, we are the Lord's.[13] Burning with the faith and heat of such words, where the king lies at midday, reject the cold and the indolence and the depression that the evil angel sends you who is seated on the sides of the North; and if your soul sleeps for sadness, call out, "Strengthen me, Lord, in your words, and revive me."[14] But if he tries to attack you outright and openly, which he can never succeed in doing against God's command, you hold up the lantern of faith and the cross and intone: "The Lord is my light and my salvation; whom shall I fear? The Lord is the protector of my life; before whom should I tremble? If armies in camp should stand together, my heart shall not fear. If a battle should surge against me, I shall be confident in this sign of the cross. One thing have I asked of the Lord – this one request I shall pursue – that I shall dwell in the house of the Lord all the days of my life. If I walk in the valley of the shadow of death, I shall fear no evil, for you are with me."[15] And when you are of little faith – as the faithful Lord reproached Peter when, doubting, he sank, for the Lord is close to all who call on him in truth; and when the eyes of your faith darken and you fear that you have been left behind alone, and you do not see God present, who has said,

---

[11]   Habac. 3:18; Ps. 21:22, 102:4; Habac. 2:3; Ps. 103:33.
[12]   Jer. 20:11, Ps. 70:18.
[13]   Rom. 14:8.
[14]   Song of Songs 1:6; Isaiah 14:13; Ps. 40:11.
[15]   Ps. 26:1–4, 22:4.

"Am I become a wilderness to Israel?"[16]; in short, when the peace of Christ cannot cure your depression, then, finally, recall what you read in the Lives of the Fathers, where someone asked a hermit whether he did not suffer depression in his cell, and the experienced warrior answered thus: "You do not know the sufferings of hell. For if you knew them, the cell would not depress you, even if it were full of snakes and you were immersed in them up to your neck."[17]

The Happiness of Scarcity

Consider carefully, my dearest, how happy is your portion. The Lord, your God, has led you here to a safe place, where you find "your haven after toil."[18] One's "portion" is what one desires, what one loves, what one possesses. One man strives for lands, another for a house, another for friendship; some crave money, others fame. Everyone is led by his desires.[19] Your portion is the Lord in the land of the living;[20] your portion is to follow the law of the Lord, which is all love, and is completely fulfilled by loving God and your neighbor. Your portion is also this, your little cell, your shelter on your pilgrimage and your pasture, that little eight-foot house, like Noah's ark, which sheltered eight souls from the attacks of the world. So you can rest in your ark from the high seas of the world, where you can grow big in sacrificing to God, like a fowl being fattened in a cage, but not in the flesh but in the soul, not with tempting food but with sacred readings.

You need not fear the human masses that throw themselves into the bitter salt swamps of desires. In any community, people oppose each other with their contrary wills. Anger, fighting, disagreements, strife, rivalries, envies, jealousies, scandals, murders, the maelstrom of lust and the furies of war, right and wrong are mixed up together. If seeking out these evils would be madness, then surely escaping them as you did is prudence. "Arsenius, flee from humans, and you will be safe."[21] Jesus stole away from the crowd and was found in the temple.[22] A true solitary becomes a familiar of God and companion of the angels. The book of the Lives of the Fathers and the various

---

[16] Jer. 2:31.
[17] *Verba Seniorum*, 7.28 (PL 73:900).
[18] Virgil, Aen. 3:393.
[19] Virgil, Ecl. 2:65.
[20] Ps. 141:6.
[21] *Verba Seniorum* 1.190 (PL 73:801).
[22] Luke 2:42–49.

endeavors of the saints, a storehouse fragrant with an array of aromatic herbs, includes among others a story about three seekers of different lives. One chose to serve the sick and the strangers, another chose to reconcile the discordant, and a third chose the peace of the contemplative life, that "best part" elected by Mary.[23] The other two, losing strength from the hubbub of the world as they did the work of Martha, together decided to consult the peace-seeker. He put a small dish of water before them. When the liquid was agitated, they saw nothing; when it was calm, they recognized their own faces. "Just so," said the one who had put it there, "did I not know myself in the tumultuous crowds. But now I see clearly my own weakness in this mirror of divine peace, and in this sweetness I recognize how miserable I am."[24] As one clears one's mind of things, the purer one becomes and the closer one gets to God, the more one mirrors oneself in God's purity, and the more unworthy one seems to oneself.

When our blessed father Benedict had become so great that he could bring the dead back to life, he still ranked a simple man's faith above his own merits. "Lord," he said, "do not look upon my sins, but upon the faith of this man, who asks that his son be resuscitated."[25]

The Philosophy of the Pagans

Even the wise men of this world, who do not know that the Lord governs virtue and repays all men's merit, simply out of desire for quiet and love of philosophy flee the crowd, condemn luxury, strive for chastity, and find in balance and measuredness a blessed and secure life. Thus, Horace:

> Happy is he who far from all business,
> Like the most ancient human generations,
> Works his ancestral lands with his oxen,
> Free from all money and debt,
> And is not roused by the warlike bugle
> Or terrified by the furious sea,
> Who avoids the forum and stays away
> From the threshold of mighty people.[26]

---

[23] Luke 10:38–42. The distinction between Martha, standing for the "active life," and Mary, standing for the "contemplative life," was a commonplace of medieval religious literature.

[24] *Verba Seniorum* 2.16 (PL 73:860).

[25] Gregory, *Dialogues* 2:32.

[26] Horace, *Epodes* 2:1–8.

According to these philosophers, what are the rewards of fleeing the pleasures of Babylon? Peace of body and mind, at least in this life. Thus our Boethius, too, follows the opinion of previous thinkers:

> How fortunate was the earlier age, which
> Content with its faithful fields,
> Not lost to needless luxury,
> Would break its fast in the evening
> With easily available acorns;
> Herbs gave them healthy sleep,
> And they drank from the smooth-flowing stream.[27]

Many chose such a life, such as the Brahmans and other peoples, not for the sake of the Kingdom of God, of which they knew nothing, but for the sake of peace in the present life, which they considered more blessed than anything else.[28] With nothing but that natural goodness the Creator has generously instilled in all humans, they freed their minds from all the worries about riches that tear at us, and devoted themselves to the liberal arts. They disciplined their bodies and weaned them from luxury, lest the weight of fatness weigh down the mind that tends towards higher things. The Romans were able to subjugate the entire world to their rule – by divine disposition, of course, but also because they had trained their bodies to hardships and abstinence. They took pride in enduring the heat of summer and the ice of winter half-naked, and their hardiness became second nature through long habit. Socrates noticed with dismay that the care of riches was eating away at him and hindered him from his philosophy; so he threw a huge lump of gold – the proceeds from his lands and all his personal wealth – into the sea, saying, "Go down to the depths, you evil desires! I am drowning you, lest I be drowned in you."[29] Pythagoras, despising superfluity, praised beans. Likewise St. Jerome: "Why convert costly food into dung? I will fill my stomach

---

[27] *Consolation of Philosophy*, 2 metr. 5.
[28] The Brahmans, or "gymnosophists," or "wise men of India," are mentioned in various Classical texts, such as Quintus Curtius's *History of Alexander*, 8.9. The longest description is in the Greek *Geography* by Strabo (15.1). There is a Latin treatise, "De moribus Brachmannorum," attributed to Ambrose in some manuscripts (PL 17:1167–84). According to these sources, the Brahmans despise the world and live extremely ascetic lives; they welcome death and sometimes even commit suicide.
[29] Jerome, *Adversus Jovinianum* 2:9 (PL 23:298) (though he has "Crates," not "Socrates").

with beans."[30] Diogenes, for whom a satchel served for a pantry and a barrel for a house, Diogenes the Cynic, was celebrated by this epitaph: "Gruel, a tripod, a staff, a beaker, such scanty houseware/ was what the cynic possessed; yet he thought it too much." Someone, on seeing another drinking water from his cupped hands, broke the beaker he was carrying and said, "For one need of my body, should I carry three receptacles, when I already have two in my very own hands?"[31] Others, cursing the need to serve their lust, amputated the very instruments of crime.[32] Some, going farther and indeed beyond sanity, even plucked out their eyes, thinking they could protect the sharp vision of their hearts from external distractions, and thus inwardly attend to philosophy with greater purity. So miserable, so bitter are the joys of this life that many have thought it the greatest blessing to do without them; and as they freed themselves of material things, they came to rejoice in having avoided them as if they were poison. So why would a Christian, who is invited to the heavenly banquet, waste time on those things which a pagan, without any better hope, is able to despise? What are the adopted children of God going to do, the children of the kingdom, the heirs of God and joint heirs with Christ,[33] when the children of darkness set such strong examples, even though their reward is nothing but the eternal fires? For they arrogantly took credit for the wisdom and insight the Creator had given them, and ascribed God's free gifts to their own strength, trying to do without God, without whom nothing can be. They paid the price for their theft: the more learned and just they attempted to be out of their own capacity, the more insane and abject they became. They boasted of practicing virtues without Christ: should not we Christians emulate those virtues in Christ's glory? For he who glories in the Lord will be glorified. They sought quiet by fleeing the world in worldly ways: why should we not seek that quiet in Christ, and keep his sabbaths? He himself told us, "Learn that I am meek and humble of heart, and you shall find rest for your souls; my yoke is easy."[34] As one begins to love divine quiet and stops craving worldly

---

[30] Letter 45.5 (CSEL 54, p. 326).

[31] *Adversus Jovinianum* 2.14 (PL 23:304). The entire section on pagan philosophy owes much to this source.

[32] The early Christian theologian Origen was said to have castrated himself in order to avoid all lust; contemporary and later commentators had mixed feelings about it. See Eusebius, *Ecclesiastical History* 6.3.3; Jerome, Letter 84.8.

[33] Romans 8:17.

[34] Mt. 11:29–30.

companionship, solitude will cease to be depressing. Nor is Christ's law so severe that we must tear out our eyes: we must only avert them to avoid seeing vanity. Nor does he command us to mutilate our members or amputate our vices, or to be castrated of vices and desires, or to be circumcised, or crucified. His law is richer than human philosophy is; his poor are poor in spirit; they suffer worldly injustice with a humble and devout mind, ready to bear anything with the aid of His mercy in whom we live, move, and have our being, as he asks of us: "On whom shall I rely," he says, "if not on him who is humble and quiet and trembles at my word?"[35] Riding on such a donkey foal, that is, a simple, submissive, meek soul, the Lord reaches Jerusalem. "Like a beast of burden," says David, "have I become before you, and I will always be with you."[36]

The Patience of the Saints

John, the precursor of the Lord, was a burning and glowing lamp, crying in the wilderness as the voice that preceded the Word of God: "Make straight the way of the Lord."[37] In becoming an anchoress, you have joined his family, whom the Church celebrates with this hymn:

> Tender in years, you sought out the caves of the desert,
> Fleeing the busy throng of the cities,
> Lest with just one thoughtless word you might
>   Stain your life.
> A camel furnished your hairy clothing,
> And oxen a belt for your sacred limbs,
> Water you drink, and for your repast
>   Honey and locusts.
> O happy you are, and your merits outstanding:
> You know not the ice-cold snowfall of shame;
> Eminent martyr who sought out solitude,
>   Greatest of prophets.
> Some get a crown for their thirty-fold harvest;
> Others, a double crown for sixtyfold harvest;
> You, for your hundredfold increase, with triple garland,
>   They crown as a saint.[38]

---

[35] Isaiah 66:2.
[36] Ps. 72:23.
[37] John 1:23.
[38] From a hymn for the Office for John the Baptist (*The Hours of the Divine Office in English and Latin* [Collegeville, Mn: The Liturgical Press, 1963] 2:1883, 94).

Next after him, Paul the Hermit, taking up the divine banner, endured sixty years of solitude as if he were the only human being in the world, completely sequestered from all of humankind. The palm-tree clothed and fed him, and he drank from a spring with hollowed hands. His righteousness did not abhor camelhair clothing, and yet the heir of the heavenly kingdom was not poor.[39]

Mary of Egypt, a matron whom virgins should venerate and a woman men should admire, spent almost forty-six winters and summers alone under the open sky. No house, no tree, no shirt, no cave sheltered her. All the darts of the burning sun, all the shafts of winter fogs, all the winds of the air, the heat of the long days and the storms of the darkest nights she took upon her naked body and uncovered head. All the long years of her life she patiently awaited the Lord;[40] and she gathered her fruits in patience, never seeing a human, an animal, a bird, or anything alive of all the earth's creatures, only her vast solitude. Her food was abstinence, her clothing was nakedness, her covering was her own skin, blackened by sun and frost, and her roof was the sky. She crushed the head of the serpent, wrestling naked with the naked, and she carried the palm over the one who had vanquished Eve.[41]

But the stars of the saints lit up the world not only after the Lord's ascension; even before his advent, many came before his face, and of these the Apostle says: "Holy men have conquered kingdoms by faith, such as Moses, Samuel, and Elijah, and others who stood up to kings. They wandered about in sheepskins, in goatskins, destitute, distressed, afflicted, of whom the world was not worthy: wandering in the deserts, in the mountains and glens, and caves of the earth.[42] The Lord is long-suffering, patient, and compassionate; he will never be angry forever; "in long-suffering and in hope shall your strength be," and "in your patience you shall possess your souls." And the Apostle: "in much patience" and "in all patience."[43] Be patient even in sorrow, and train your mind to bear anything. Be patient until the coming of the Lord. "Behold, the husbandman waits for the precious fruit of the earth, and has long patience for it, until he receive the

---

[39] Jerome, *Life of St. Paul*, PL 23:17–28; translation in *Early Christian Biographies*, ed. Roy J. Deferrari ([New York]: Fathers of the Church, 1952), 225–44.

[40] Reading "patienter" for Talbot's "patientem."

[41] The Life of Mary of Egypt, PL 73:684–5.

[42] Heb. 11:33, 37, 38.

[43] Isaiah 30:15; Luke 21:19; 2 Cor. 6:4; Col 1:11.

early and latter rain."[44] And for another example of patient labor take the prophets, who desired with unbearable desire the coming of the savior, as for example: "O that you would rend the heavens and come down," and, "Lord, bow down your heavens and descend." And, "Come, Lord, do not delay." And, "Hurry and do not delay." And, "let your tender mercy speedily prevent us." And, "O Lord, save me and make me prosper; blessed is he who comes in the name of the Lord."[45] And how could he be patient against all the impatient desire of the saints? The holy patriarchs, knowing they would go down to the nether regions, lived patiently among the evils of the world. Hoping for the distant arrival of the savior, they died patiently. From the time of Adam until the death of Christ, for a whole era of about five thousand years, they sat in the darkness and the shadow of death and waited to greet the Lord their savior, and finally called out to him with tearful voices: "You have come, desired one, whom we have so long awaited in the darkness!" But now, Christ's blood has reopened heaven for those who follow him; now every saint who walked the earth in perfection and put nothing before the love of Christ certainly ascends to heaven and to Christ the minute he passes from this life – provided he left the world so pure that the cleansing fire finds nothing to burn away. For Christ said, "Where I am, there also shall my servant be."[46] If such a great prize goes to the victors, who in his right mind would not bear these brief sufferings bravely, nay seek them out joyously, if through them he may attain such immense and infinite glory?

Peace for the Weak
But my cell is so narrow, you will say: the royal hall of heaven is huge. Why would you fear going to the eternal kingdom by a narrow path? How many thousands have suffered worse! The sons of kings and dukes and nobles, the glorious of this world have had their feet shackled, their wrists cuffed in irons, have been held in dungeons and prisons. Many of them lose limbs by sword or illness, or have their eyesight extinguished before they are released from the dungeon: all the daylight of the world will still be a dungeon to them, and they live a living death, because the sun, the greatest joy of human life, has set for them. Happy are those who are consoled by eternal hope; miserable those who do not believe and thus are

---

[44] James 5:7.
[45] Is. 64:1; Ps. 143:5; gradual for the 4th Sunday of advent; Ps. 69:6, 78:8, 117:25–26.
[46] John 12:16.

deprived of these goods and do not strive for the higher ones: their punishment begins here. The sun in this life shines for everyone, but is seen only by those who have their eyesight. The true sun of justice, Jesus Christ, never sets, it is always there for all; but it can be seen only by those who are pure of heart, those who perceive him with pure faith. We sing this sweet responsorium for our holy father Omer, to whose family I belong:[47] "Saint Omer gathered treasures of merit, for he lacked sight in his bodily eyes for many years before he died; but with the purity of his inner sight he beheld the Lord." And the verse: "Thus, outwardly blind but inwardly illuminated by grace, he beheld the Lord."[48]

When St. Vedastus, the glory of Artois, was translated here, he came before our generous, loving father Bertin. But he, giving thanks before the eyes of the Lord, and sighing with endless desire, said: "Lord Jesus, I did not ask you for that inane eyesight that we have in common with brute beasts, which entices many away from you. It would be better if you averted that light from me, lest it avert me from you. Avert my eyes that they may not see the world's vanity, for even its light is like darkness; let not death, as another prophet said, enter through our windows. Rather, I ask you to illuminate those eyes of mine with which I will see you, my light, in pure and intense radiance, the light which nourishes the entire family of angels." Thus he prayed; and as he had asked, his outward eyes received rest from the darkness of this world. He lifted his inward eyes to the source of light, and stricken with love, he received that unseen light.[49]

Are you more tightly confined that those to whom, because of their physical blindness, the whole world is a dungeon? Compare now this cavern of yours with Octavianus Augustus's dominion over the whole world. It is your ship against the ocean of this wasteland, your shelter from the storms of the world, your refuge from the

---

[47] Goscelin's home monastery, St. Bertin, is in the town of St. Omer.

[48] Talbot identifies this as one of the responsories in an office for St. Omer in the Breviary of St. Bertin, BM Add. 36672.

[49] "Vita Vedasti Atrebatensis Duplex," Appendix, *MGH Scriptorum rerum merovingiacarum*, vol. 3 (1896), 426 and editor's note p. 403. In ninth-century sources, Vedastus' relics were said to have been translated (i.e., solemnly transferred) to the monastery outside Arras that bears his name, under the seventh-century abbot Aubert – not "Bertin." This would be an odd mistake for Goscelin of St. Bertin, so fond of the saints of his *familia*; possibly a scribe copying the manuscript had trouble with the name "Aubertus" and rationalized it to the repeatedly mentioned "Bertinus."

whirlwind of evil. For Augustus, the grandeur of his circumstances meant captivity; for you, the smallness of your circumstances is your liberty. He, in striving for a kingdom, endured the servitude of hard effort; you, who despise those things, have the kingdom. He served the passions of his mind and surrendered to his appetites; the lord of the world was unable to govern himself. You just govern your desires, and you will be more august than Augustus. Every privilege he had of his kingship was a shackle of care that constrained him; you, stripped of everything, can spread out and be more regal than a king. In all his vast spaces, he was confined; you luxuriate in the security of a narrow space. The whole world was not enough to satisfy his desires; let this little cave be enough for you, and strive for nothing more. He moved from house to house, from kingdom to kingdom, and found only the torment of restlessness; you, to find peace of mind, possess a single space for yourself alone. Seneca said, "Why would you need more than one chamber? You can lie in only one." Horace said,

> Thus, since no one is granted perpetual use, and heir
> Follows heir like wave follows wave,
> What use are your vills and your granges?
>   Your Calabrian pastures
> And summer drifts in Lucania, if the nether world
>   measures

Great things with small, and does not yield to your gold?[50] Thus, even Caesar, with the entire size of his body, could not have occupied a space in the whole wide world larger than this little hut of yours; and of all his immeasurable wealth he did not use more than the dimensions of his body permitted. Indeed you are more blessed, having the spaces for all your activities combined in a single room. Here is your sanctuary, your oratory, your dining hall, your dormitory, your hall, your bedroom, your vestibule, your cellar, your office – you have merged all those living spaces into one. You have all your treasures, all your furnishings with you. A stone is your armchair, the ground your bed, a hair shirt your dress, the fat under your skin protects you from cold; your bread is healthy, your vegetables pure, your water crystal-clear to match your pure conscience and Christ's pure grace. Those are your assets, safer than the emperor's. Purple bedding and several layers of soft mattresses pamper the bodies of the rich, but the prickly thorns of their riches disturb their sleep and their rest, for even if their possessions are safe they always

---

[50]   Epist. 2:2:175–79. The Seneca quotation preceding this has not been identified.

seem threatened by dangers and vulnerable to thieves. But the earth, our mother, softly lulls to sleep in her loving lap a body wearied by vigils, and refreshes a mind freed from the worms of care with a gentle sleep. If your life seems harsh, is the life of shepherds and rustics any gentler, who bear the rains, snows, hails, ice, and storms of winter on their naked backs and unprotected heads? As Virgil tells us, "Naked they plough, naked they sow."[51] Laughing, they brave the attacks of heat and frost; they are content with their barley gruel and their fresh water. Is it really harder for the soldiers of Christ to bear these hardships, not for the exigencies of this life but for eternal reward? Anyone who suffers exhaustion, hunger, and thirst will be refreshed by beans, water, the bare ground more delectably than by all the delicacies of the kings. Seneca tells how he came home late one evening, and his baker had no bread – but the cook had some, the kind that is considered bad by the spoiled rich. What should a man accustomed to good food do with bad food? "Wait," he says. "It will be good." Hunger will make good what satiety thought bad.[52]

The Banquet of the Scriptures

You think of yourself as buried here, and consider your cell a tomb?[53] If you carry your cross after Christ, you will rise from the tomb. Burial does no harm to those who will rise again. I have seen how an ancient vine, mossy, spent and exhausted, is revived and made to bear fruit again by this trick: it is torn out with its roots, but not transplanted like a tree. It is buried whole, the stock with its long branches and shoots; only its fingers, that is the buds and tips of the shoots, poke out towards the sky. And very quickly, strange to behold, new shoots and new branches break out, and the tree which was already dying and infertile in its root, revives and bears numerous offspring from its grave. Thus the grain of wheat, by which the Savior signifies himself, falls into the ground and brings forth much fruit if it dies to the world.[54] "As dying," says Paul, "and behold, we live; as chastened but not killed, as having nothing and yet possessing all things."[55] Thus you are buried in humility and the mortification

---

[51] *Georgica* 1:299.
[52] Seneca, *Epistulae Morales* 20.6.2 (letter 123).
[53] The rite for the enclosure of anchoresses contained language from the ritual of burial. See Ann K. Warren, *Anchorites and their Patrons in Medieval England* (Berkeley: University of California Press, 1985), 97–100.
[54] John 12:24.
[55] 2 Cor. 6:9–10.

of desires; but you constantly stretch the shoots of hope towards heaven. In pain, sadness, and tears you give birth to eternal songs of joy, and you bear fruit in patience. A humble mind makes hope its ally, says Prudentius.[56] You must free yourself from both hope and fear, lest a crushed mind succumb, lest an elated mind fall down.[57] Avoid idleness, for idleness gives rise to depression, and, as St. Benedict testifies, "Idleness is an enemy of the soul"; and "The idler always wants for something," and "Long leisure gives nourishment to vices."[58]

It is a gift from God that prayers and sighs and tears, directed to God without ceasing, will keep the soul from being depressed. But can we pray all the time? asks our teacher Augustine. Can we read all the time? Wake all the time? In truth, prayer should come before all else, and the face of the Lord should be sought above all else. The Lord should have first place in all things; and whatever you do, do it all in his name, and dedicate everything to the Lord. That is what it means to pray at all times.[59]

After you have given the requisite offerings of prayer, when you are tired and exhausted, refresh yourself with sacred reading. Sharpen your dulled mind with the whetstone of books, and stoke the failing flame with some wood. "The fire of my altar," says the Lord, "shall always burn, and the priest shall feed it by putting wood on it" and other fuel.[60] You must be your own priest before God,

---

[56] *Psychomachia* 199, 201.

[57] Hymn, "Magnae Deus potentia," Friday vespers (see Inge B. Milfull, *The Hymns of the Anglo-Saxon Church* [Cambridge: Cambridge University Press, 1998], 163–64).

[58] Rule of St. Benedict, Ch. 48; Proverbs 21:25–26; Disticha Catonis 1.2.

[59] Augustine, *Enarrationes in Psalmos* 37:13 (CCSL 37, p. 392). On this section, see Gopa Roy, "Sharpen Your Mind with the Whetstone of Books: The Female Recluse as Reader in Goscelin's *Liber Confortatorius*, Aelred of Rievaulx's *De Institutione Inclusarum* and the *Ancrene Wisse*," in *Women, the Book and the Godly: Selected Proceedings of the St. Hilda's Conference, 1993*, Vol. 1, eds. Lesley Smith and Jane H. M. Taylor (Cambridge: Brewer, 1995), 113–22; Linda Olson, "Did Medieval English Women Read Augustine's *Confessiones*? Constructing Feminine Interiority and Literacy in the Eleventh and Twelfth Centuries," in *Learning and Literacy in Medieval England and Abroad*, ed. Sarah Rees Jones (Turnhout: Brépols, 2003), 69–80; Bella Millett, "Women in No Man's Land: English Recluses and the Development of Vernacular Literature in the Twelfth and Thirteenth Centuries," in *Women and Literature in Britain, 1150–1500*, ed. Carol M. Meale (Cambridge: Cambridge University Press, 1993), 88.

[60] Levit. 6:12.

sacrificing yourself, and the fire of divine love will always burn in the altar of your heart. You will feed it with the examples and deeds of the saints, and you will waft before God the fragrant fumes of holy desires. Hence the seraphim are properly said to be on fire, because they burn more and more intensely with the love of God the closer they get to him. Let not the judgments of the detractors come to you; build a hedge of thorns around your ears and guard them anxiously. Let the windows of your cell, your tongue and your ears be locked to false tales and idle talk, which is better named malicious talk.[61] No cat, no chicken, no irrational animal of any sort should be your companion, lest your fleeting time be frittered away.[62] Be solitary, alone with the Lord. Speak to God in your prayers, and in your reading hear God speaking to you. Therefore I urge, even implore you that you raid the holy banquet of the sacred volumes with eagerness, with a virtuous sort of gluttony; that you hunger and thirst for it as the bread and fountain of life. Let it sharpen your little mind,[63] feed it with nectar, fatten your lamp with oil, and light it more and more with heavenly love. There you will find the life of your soul, for man lives not by bread alone, but in every word that proceeds from the mouth of God, and whatever is written is written for our learning, that through the comfort of Scripture we may patiently hope.[64] This, as you may recall, is something I have always impressed on you, handing you the key to understanding, in words when I was present, and in letters when I was away. In Scripture you will find the treasure and the pearl which you will purchase by selling all your worldly desires. Read the commentaries of the holy fathers Jerome, Augustine, and Gregory and the other men learned in virtue. Set your heart on the understanding of Scripture, which among other things will teach you in symbolic words about the mystery of the Church and of the soul's spiritual struggles. I would like

---

[61] For a full and graphic elaboration of this theme, see Aelred of Rievaulx's *De Institutione Reclusarum* (*La Vie de Recluse; La Prière Pastorale*, ed. and trans. Charles Dumont [Paris: Cerf, 1961], 44–46).

[62] *The Ancrene Wisse*, by contrast, specifically permits anchoresses to keep a cat if they wish, though it too cautions against other domestic animals. (Ancrene Wisse: *The English Text of the Ancrene Rule*, ed. J. R. R. Tolkien [Oxford: EETS, 1962], 213; Anne Savage and Nicholas Watson, eds. and trans., *Anchoritic Spirituality: Ancrene Wisse and Associated Works* [New York: Paulist Press, 1991], 201).

[63] "Ingeniolum." The diminutive is not necessarily condescending; Goscelin refers to its own "ingeniolum" in Book I. The implication is that one person's mind is a small thing compared to the "banquet" of scripture.

[64] Mt. 4:4; Romans 15:4.

the window of your cell to be wide enough to admit a library of this size, or wide enough that you could read the books through the window if they are propped up for you there from outside. Read aloud[65] the lives and teachings of the Fathers, especially the life of St. Anthony, which can fortify you against the devil's attacks, and will teach you how weak his entire army is against those who believe in Christ.

Among all the others, do not neglect the Confessions of Augustine, which will instill in you a higher love for the divine. You should also cherish the three-part ecclesiastical history, together with the history of Eusebius, which will sing you of the struggles of the saints and of the victories of faith founded in Christ, unvanquished by any storm.[66] Read Augustine's *De Civitate Dei*, Orosius's *De Ormesta Mundi*, Boethius's *Consolation of Philosophy*, and you will understand that nothing is more miserable than worldly appetites, and nothing happier than the peace of Christ. Amid these exercises, depression will flee, time will seem short, and your solitude will delight you; these insipid exhortations of mine will even nauseate you, already well nourished on better food. And do not hurry on if you are stuck on the meaning of something, but pause, think it over, reread it, until you grasp it sufficiently; for nothing is so difficult that it cannot be found by seeking, and unrelenting toil overcomes everything; if you seek and knock, God will open the door, and the gentle spirit of wisdom will enter.[67] St. Gregory of Nazianz once saw in a dream the pure and beautiful house of wisdom, with twin girls sitting on either side of it and guarding the middle with their chaste love. The saint, a zealot for chastity, was indignant that women had

---

[65] The word is "recita"; it is likely that Goscelin and Eva would routinely have done most or all of their reading out loud. On reading aloud, and on monastic reading in particular, see Jean Leclercq, *The Love of Learning and the Desire for God* (New York: Fordham University Press, 1961), 72–75; Ivan Ilich, *In the Vineyard of the Text* (Chicago: U. of Chicago P., 1993), ch. 3; Paul Saenger, "Silent Reading: Its Impact on Late Medieval Script and Society," *Viator* 13 (1982):367–414.

[66] Eusebius's *History of the Church*, a fundamental work and one of the major sources of Goscelin's book, was known to the West in a Latin translation by Rufinus. The "Tripartite History" is a sixth-century continuation of Eusebius's *History* (from the year 324 onwards), compiled from three Greek chronicles, and translated into Latin by Cassiodorus. (Cassiodorus, *Historia Ecclesiastica Tripartita*, ed. Walter Jacob, CSEL vol. 71 [Vienna: Hoelder-Pichler-Tempsky, 1952].

[67] Virgil, *Georgica*, 1:145; Mt. 7:8; Wisdom 1:6.

entered, but he heard them say very sweetly, "We are two of your dearest friends, your inseparable companions, always at your side. We are Wisdom and Chastity, your sisters, your lovers whom you love above all others."[68] "Above health and beauty," said a wise man, "have I loved Wisdom, and I have said to Wisdom, 'you are my sister.' "[69] Follow the example of blessed Paula and St. Eustochium and also Blesilla, whom their teacher and affectionate friend Jerome called "Christ's library."[70] Mindful of Daniel's prophecy that the learned will shine like stars in the sky, listen and learn from Jerome about the difference between holy simplicity and learned sanctity.[71] St. Peter praises studious readers: "You have the more firm prophetical word," he says, "whereunto you do well to attend, until the day dawn and the day star arise in your hearts."[72] The Lord, too, attacks the unlearned in the Gospel: "You err," he says, "not knowing the Scriptures."[73] Even the holy Apostles were unable to understand the resurrection of the Lord until he opened their senses that they might understand Scripture. But the first thing is to fear God and obey God. "The fear of the Lord is the beginning of wisdom." And: "If you seek wisdom, obey the commandments, and God will give it to you." "Wisdom seeks out the humble and quiet, those who fear the word of God."[74] Arrogant knowledge puffs up; knowledge in charity builds up. Wisdom, the mother of the humble, steps on the neck of the proud and the haughty.[75] It is a mistake to forbid learning because of the danger of arrogance, for the more learned one is, the more humble one can be. As Solomon says, he who increases knowledge increases sorrow: he learns what he must fear, and therefore can better rebuff the archetype of arrogance.[76] It is just as insane to condemn chastity, abstinence, keeping vigils or any other virtue because they may give cause for arrogance. Rather, people may learn through their education how to guard their humility, the guardian of all virtues, and how to stamp out the barbarism of arrogance and the boasting of the unschooled. The unlearned often ridicule and despise

---

[68] Aldhelm, "De laudibus virginum," PL 89:25.

[69] Prov. 7:4.

[70] Cf. Epist. 39.7 (CSEL 54, p. 308).

[71] Epist. 27.1 (CSEL 54, pp. 223–24); Epist. 53, esp. 3–4 (CSEL 54, pp. 446–50).

[72] 2 Peter 1:19.

[73] Mt. 22:29.

[74] Ps. 110:10; Ecclus. 1:33; Isaiah 66:2.

[75] A liturgical antiphon; cf. Ecclus. 24:11.

[76] Eccl. 1:18. The "archetype of arrogance" is of course the devil.

the learned; they believe worldly ignorance to be prudence and holiness of life. Is it surprising if they belittle what they do not know, if they prefer what they do know, if the blind despise the seeing and the ignorant think themselves above the cultivation of humility?

Therefore, set aside periods of time for prayer and reading; but concentrate first and foremost on prayer, always seeking the face of God. In the dark and when light is scarce, bring on Christ's true light through prayer; when a trickle of light enters your cell, look for God's word by reading, as a lantern to guide your feet. When you reweave the cloth of the psalms, sing them knowing that you are singing the Savior's own words under the eyes of the angels and before God's own majesty. The Lord our Redeemer himself, exercising his human nature, intercedes for us in the sacrament of psalmody. Because our voice is not worthy to be heard by God except through this same intermediary, we have him as our advocate before the Father, praying for us, his members, as if for himself: "Deliver, o God, my soul from the sword," that is, my church, "my only one from the hands of the dog," that is, my spouse whom I have redeemed with my blood. "Save me from the lion's mouth," "me" meaning my body, all my chosen ones whose head I am.[77] I gleaned this insight from the fogs of pagan fable, where Homer pretends that Thetis prayed thus for Achilles, her son: "Avenge me and my body" – that is, my son.[78] Therefore, stand before God and sing your psalms in such a way that the mind accords with the voice, according to Father Benedict's testimony.[79] Chant through your psalms, directing your heart to God; but when you come to a particularly emotional place, for instance, "Your name, o Lord, is forever," and your memory, in which you gave

---

[77] Ps. 21:21–22. Cf. Book II, n. 52; Augustine, *Enarrationes in Psalmos* 39:5 and 39:12. The Psalms are for the most part personal prayers in the first person, addressed to God (e.g., in his example, "Deliver, o God, my soul from the sword"). Having said that the Psalms, like everything else in the Bible, are "God's Word," Goscelin now tries to explain what we are to make of that first person: it *is* God speaking, but on humanity's behalf; the reciter of the Psalms therefore not only speaks in her own voice but also impersonates Christ.

[78] Goscelin, like generations of educated Western Europeans in the Middle Ages, knew his "Homer" not in the original Greek but in the Latin verse paraphrase known as *Ilias Latina*, which was commonly studied in schools. (Ed. in Juan de Mena, *La Iliade de Homero*, eds. T. Gonzales Rolán, F. del Bario Vega and A. López Fonseca [Madrid: Ediciones Clasicos, 1996]; here, lines 83–91, p. 118.) Note the slightly dismissive "Homer pretends" ("fingit"); the fictive pagan parallel needs to be sharply distinguished from the divine language under discussion.

[79] Rule of St. Benedict, ch. 19.

yourself for us; or "Bless the Lord, o my soul, and let all that is within me bless his holy name," and similar verses which hold you in heavenly love, dwell on it, let it sting your heart, respond with long, holy sighs.[80] Saint Gregory teaches us to sigh with the frequent repetition of words in the offertories: "That he may see the good, see the good, good, the inestimable good."[81] Pour out your soul to God in your profound desires and sighs. And you may pray for anything with just one verse from the depth of your soul: "Let your tender mercies come to me and I shall live"; "My soul shall live and shall praise you." Or for someone you love: "Deal with your servant, Lord, according to your mercy."[82] Few words will suffice; your clamorous heart and vociferous desires will say more.

The Holy Day of Redemption

Sanctify all hours with Christ's suffering.[83] In the middle of the night adore him captured and incarcerated, in the morning as he is being flagellated, in the third hour as he is handed over to be crucified. Shouting, "Let him be crucified," they crucified him with their tongues. In the sixth hour venerate him as he is being nailed to the cross, in the ninth hour venerate him dead, in the evening as he is being buried. Then, at cock's crow, when the morning star rises, greet the Lord's resurrection with a morning prayer of praise. In the third hour recall the advent of the Holy Spirit. In the sixth hour think of the Lord visiting us in the Sixth Age of the world, sitting at the well, instituting Holy Baptism for us.[84] In the ninth hour recall his

---

[80] Ps. 134:13, 102:1.

[81] Goscelin is pointing out that in Gregorian chant settings of the Psalms or other Biblical texts, words are often repeated; he interprets such repetitions not merely as a convenient way to fit text to tune but as emphatic, emotional, and expressive. The example given is from the offertory of the 21st Sunday after Pentecost. Talbot refers to *Paléographie Musicale* I (Solesmes: Saint-Père, 1989; rpt. Berne: Herbert Laus, 1974), pl. 125, a facsimile of a tenth-century antiphonar from St. Gall, showing this particular passage with neums (an early form of musical notation). Even for readers without any knowledge of music or medieval notation, it is a striking visual example of what Goscelin has in mind.

[82] Ps. 118:77, 118:175, 118:124.

[83] Devotions of this sort, contemplating the cross and recapitulating the stages of Christ's passion, are attested from the ninth century and become widespread in the eleventh. See several examples in André Wilmart, "Prières médiévales pour l'adoration de la croix," *Ephemerides Liturgicae* 46 (1932): 22–65.

[84] The widely accepted notion of the Seven Ages of the World comes from Bede, *The Reckoning of Time*, trans. Faith Wallis (Liverpool: Liverpool University Press, 1999), 39–41, 157–59, editor's comments pp. 355–66. The two events

ascension to heaven, to fulfill God's plan: as he was brought low by
death, so he would be glorified by his ascension. And consider how
the order of God's plan had been set from before all time. Man was
created on a Friday, on a Friday he was redeemed. On a Friday the
Redeemer was conceived, and on a Friday he died and was buried.
On a Sunday he was born, on a Sunday he rose again: the first time
he emerged from a closed womb, the second time from a closed
tomb. Here is something I heard from a learned monk:[85] the Virgin,
unique among all others, who would give birth to God, once rose in
the middle of the night, as was her sacred custom, to sing divine
hymns. As she rose intoned the gradual psalm; and when she arrived
at the verse where it says, "May the Lord watch over your comings
in and goings out"[86] – at that very moment the Archangel Gabriel
entered with heavenly splendor, so that the Virgin appeared to be

specified, although connected by the idea of water and fountains, are separate
incidents from Christ's ministry on earth: his baptism in the Jordan, held to be
the origin of Christian baptism, and (presumably) the episode of his encounter
with the Samaritan woman.

[85] An intriguing passage, as are many of the ideas Goscelin claims to have thought
up himself or received orally from others. In the first place, Goscelin is interested
in meaningful temporal coincidences – as with the important events of salvation
history occurring on the same weekdays. He is also continuing his suggestions for
synchronizing a meditation on scriptural events with the day's prayer routine. But
another point of the anecdote would seem to be the power of psalmody. Mary, by
chanting the liturgically prescribed Psalm, in a sense brings on the Archangel's
visit; by implication, presumably, Eva can bring acts of divine mercy upon herself by uttering the Psalms. It is worth noting, too, how sexualized this annunciation scene is: the angel's powerful "entrance" and the virgin's "acceptance" of
him is continued in the next sentence with the conception (and then birth) of
Christ, his "coming in and going out" of Mary's womb. The notion that it was the
angel's greeting which impregnated Mary was commonplace; hence, Goscelin's
take on the Annunciation as a sexually efficacious speech act would seem neither
shocking nor unexpected, and it fits in well with his general theme here, of the
power of psalmody. What is interesting is that the focus here is solely on Mary's
speech act, not on Gabriel's, which is not even cited.

[86] Ps. 120:8. This is one of the "gradual psalms," so called because they were meant
to be recited on approaching the temple, on the steps (*gradus*). In medieval
monastic usage, the gradual psalms were recited silently before the office of
Matins, held in the very early morning hours, as the monks moved from the middle of the choir to their seats. (Thomas J. Heffernan, "The Liturgy and Literature
of Saints' Lives," in *The Liturgy of the Medieval Church*, eds. Heffernan and
E. Ann Matter [Kalamazoo: Medieval Institute, 2001], 89–90.) When he pictures
the Virgin rising and approaching the temple with these psalms on her lips, the
monk who is Goscelin's source is therefore imagining her performing his very
own daily routine.

receiving him with this greeting. More importantly, she received the one who the messenger said would be born of her, and the Lord would be watching over his "going in," in his conception, and over his "going out," in his birth. Thus, her spirit rejoicing from this angelic message in God her savior, she entered the Synagogue chanting the following psalm: "I was glad when they said to me, let us go into the house of the Lord."[87]

Note also that it was at mid-day, when the sun occupies the middle of the sky, that the True Sun, whose unjust suffering darkened the material sun, was poised on the balance of the cross: between the middle of the sky and the middle of the earth, sanctifying the sky with his head, the earth with his feet, and the world to his right and left with the embrace of his arms.[88] For the place of the Lord's passion is thought to be at the center of the earth, as David says: "The Lord our king from before all ages has wrought salvation in the midst of the earth."[89]

They also say that Judgment Day will be on the same weekday and the same month as the day of the Conception and the Passion; hence it is written, "the man is not at home, he is gone a very long journey," to heaven; "on the day of the full moon," which means the perfect assembly of all the elect, "he will return" to judge.[90] Therefore let us venerate with great reverence this day of redemption, which has known the Savior and presages the Judge. I admonish you, whatever you do on other days, sanctify that day with the highest devotion in prayer and tears; and offer up especially that time from the sixth to the ninth hour with a contrite heart, as if you were handing it to the Lord himself, hanging on the cross.

One who is most humble and who used to be most devoted to you has devised this devotion for himself: in that salvific hour when the Lord yielded up his ghost, he will chant these five psalms to the five

---

[87] Luke 1:47; Ps. 121:1.
[88] Gregory, *Moralia in Job* 7:2:2 (CCSL 143, Vol. 1, 334–5).
[89] Ps. 73:12.
[90] Prov. 7:19–20. Since all Biblical verses were held to be meaningful in several ways – in literal and various kinds of allegorical senses – quoting out of context was not considered a distortion; on the contrary, exegetes often seem to take pleasure in teasing unexpected or, to our thinking, even perverse meanings from a Biblical text. This is an almost comically egregious example of this practice. In their context, on the literal level at least, the verses have nothing to do with the Second Coming: they are part of a prostitute's seduction speech, as she assures her prospective client that her husband is far away and unlikely to barge in on the encounter.

wounds of the hands, feet, and side, with prostrations: from "God, my God, look upon me" to "The Lord is my light."[91] And then, after the Lord's Prayer, he adores Christ born, Christ tempted, Christ crucified, Christ dead and Christ buried, descending to the dead, rising again from the dead, ascending into heaven, sitting at the right hand of the father and hence coming again as judge.[92] I read in a book of miracles that the great St. Martin, the pride of Tours, prayed before the tomb of the newly buried blessed virgin Vitaliana. He greeted her with a holy salutation and inquired urgently, "How is it with you, blessed virgin? Have you already come before the face of the Lord, and have you seen the glorious bridegroom, Christ?" And a voice immediately responded from the tomb: "No, holy father, for just this one sin is in the way, that I washed my head on Fridays, and therefore did not celebrate the memory of the Lord's passion with due reverence." And St. Martin said to those who were with him," What shall we sinners do when such a holy soul is hindered from the glory of the face of the Lord for such a minor offense? Who can even know all the ways in which he has failed?" But after he had made on her behalf acceptable sacrifices to the Lord, he went back to her resting place and said exultingly, "Rejoice, holy virgin, for after three more days you will see God forever." And three days after he had said this, St. Vitaliana shone forth in miracles, thereby declaring that she had now gained God's presence and grace.[93] How true is that truth witnessed in the Gospel: "The God of Abraham, the God of Isaac, the God of Jacob is not the God of the dead but of the living."[94] For all things live for him.

How much faith and perseverance can achieve, learn from the life of St. John the Almoner. A woman wanted to confess her sins to that patriarch but was quite unable to do so because her shame completely closed her mouth. The bishop said: "Can you write it down and seal it, and entrust it to me to keep unopened and untouched?" She said, "That, father, I can do; and I know I can trust you not to

[91]   That is, Goscelin himself is in the habit of reciting Psalms 21–25 every Friday at noon, followed by the specified prayers.
[92]   Most of this list is the language of the Apostolic Creed.
[93]   Gregory of Tours, *Liber de gloria confessorum*, Ch. 5, PL 71:833. In Goscelin's rendition of the story, evidently from memory, the "sacrifices" seem to be masses said on her behalf ("hostias immolavit" can mean "offered sacrificial animals," but had also come to mean "offered the Host," i.e., celebrated Mass). In Gregory's narrative, Martin does not celebrate mass but cures several sick people and performs other miracles.
[94]   Mark 12:27.

read it." She went away, wrote it, sealed it, and placed it in the bishop's faithful hands. Not long after, the bishop passed on to the Lord; heaven had his spirit, and the tomb received his body. The woman came running, beside herself, and looked for but could not find what she had left with him. No one knew where it was, and she already feared that she would be exposed to all. O woman, why do you tremble? Your own agitation may betray you, but never John's sincerity. Take a deep breath and persist, for your great faith will find what it is looking for. For three whole days, without interruption, she lay prostrate before the saint's tomb, demanding her deposit with infinite cries and sobs. On the third day, in the evening, when she had collapsed, weakened by fasting and waking, behold, she saw clearly and with her bodily eyes, how John and the two bishops between whom he lay all exited from their tombs together, with their bishops' staffs and habits. He addressed her in this manner: "Why are you disquieting us, woman, with your wailing? Could you not at least spare my brothers here all this crying? We are drowning in your tears." And he handed her the sealed tablets: "Do you recognize these?" he said. "I have guarded them the way you entrusted them to me. Open the seal and read." She recognized them, eagerly took them, broke the seal, opened them: all her sins had been deleted, and she found only this written: "For the sake of John, my servant, your sin is forgiven." Thus tenderly consoled by them, she saw them all simultaneously re-entering their tombs.[95]

Thus perseverance won out; and the first one to see the resurrected Lord was the persevering Mary. A similar story is also told of St. Basil the Great, where another woman who had written down her sins received her tablets back after the death of the saint and found them deleted by a divine hand.[96]

The Riches of the All-Creator

Now, lest you fail in the poverty of Christ and in your solitude, admire the great deeds of God and the richness of things. How can I express how immense the entire world is, when we mortals of any nation inhabit and possess barely one fifth of it! The two outermost circles are uninhabitable with cold; the middle one drives us away with the heat of fire; it is only the two placed in between that are habitable, with a moderate balance of heat and cold. But we earthly

---

[95] "Vita S. Ioannis Eleemosinarii," Ch. 51 (PL 73:380–82).
[96] "Vita S. Basilii Caesareae Cappadociae Archiepiscopi," Ch. 10 (PL 73: 307–309).

souls inhabit only one of these, for who could cross the torrid zone to the other one? Therefore this zone that is inhabited by all humankind is just one fifth of the entire earth. Here are all the living souls, all the conflicts of nations, the immense oceans, the countless rivers, the vast solitudes of land, mountains, valleys, cliffs, rocks, heights and unreachable depths, the endless forests, fields, plantations, pastures, coasts and shores, the multitude of all buildings, cultivated lands, and all the arts; in this fifth, all houses are found, and yet this fifth spreads out in such vastness that none of its inhabitants or things need feel crowded by the copiousness. If then just one part of the earth's circle is so large, how large must we imagine it in its entirety? And compared to that whole size, what is the little portion of space taken up by your cell, such a tiny thing against such a vast space? But the entire immensity of the world, compared to the sphere of the heavens, seems as small by comparison with the home of the stars as your cell does compared to the whole realm of the earth. And the sun's globe, which flies around the sky and the earth at unimaginable speed, is far larger than the entire mass of the earth, even though to us earth-dwellers it seems to be measurable by a palm's width. What might be the dimensions of the entire ether if its eye, the sun, seems so small even though it is larger than the entire world? And every single star is believed to be bigger than, say, Europe, which we reckon to occupy one third of the earth.[97] Therefore,

[97] Goscelin's cosmography, while entirely made up of traditional elements, does not yield a very convincing total picture – which itself seems standard for his time: the meaning and interpretability of each "fact" taken by itself takes precedence over a scientifically consistent overall explanation. This meditation contains a few elements of the standard "T-O" map, known, at least in diagrammatic simplification, to any educated person at the time, since it was often depicted in standard school texts such as Isidore of Seville or Martianus Capella. (In this schema, Europe does occupy roughly one third of the earth.) Somewhat at cross-purposes with this, the main model here seems to be the "zone map," also frequently diagrammed in standard school texts, which in principle presupposes a spherical earth, and in which (as he says) Europe would take up rather less than one third. But this inconsistency does not bother Goscelin and his contemporaries. (Cf. the roughly contemporary "Adelae Comitissae" by Baudri of Bourgueil, which is based primarily on a T-O map but does describe the zones also. See my translation in *Journal of Medieval Latin* 11 [2001], lines 784–89 and note.) In most zonal maps, both temperate zones are thought to be inhabited, though some hybrid maps, like Goscelin, cluster all human life in just one of the temperate zones, leaving the other one empty. His cramming all geographical features, including the oceans, into the Northern temperate zone is of course quite illogical, but it suits his theme here: large and small, contained and immense, brimming with detail yet uncrowded. See David

to one who considers the heavens, can the empires of this earth be anything but mouse holes, and can those who would govern them appear anything but laughable? Are the high gables of cities, castles, and houses anything but hovels, root stocks, and little mole hills made of dirt? All the endeavors of human presumption seem as puny to the majestic angels as the efforts of bees, ants, and other tiny animals appear to us. Where, finally, can man, the worm, hide from his creator – man, who in his feeble arrogance looks as distasteful to the higher created spirits as those individuals graced with humility do to their arrogant fellow-humans? Hence Isaiah, who saw God face to face, and from that glorious vantage point despises earthly haughtiness: "All nations," he says, "are before him as if they had no being at all, and are counted to him as nothing, like a little dust and a drop in a bucket."[98] Jerome, interpreting Isaiah, explains this verse in this way: all the peoples of the entire human race, compared to the multitude of angels, are like a drop in a bucket.[99] But the creator of all things, who created everything and all matter out of nothing, fashioned man, made from matter contemptible to the higher spirits, in his own image. By becoming one of our kind he ennobled us so much that he valued us at the price of his blood. The seventy-two human languages are represented in the number of Christ's disciples.[100] But in these more than seventy thousand peoples and nations are contained. In India alone, we read that there are more than five thousand large cities and nine thousand tribes! We know that many peoples can be subsumed under one language, as for instance, the Greeks comprised Athenians, Miscenians, Thebans, Graii, Argi, Argolici, Achini, Danai, Myrmidons, Dolopes, Cycropides, Inachides, Corinthians, Galatians; or the Gauls comprise Franks, Allobroges, Auvergnates, Beturici, Normans, Cetomanni, Angevins, Poitevins, Basques, Catalans; the Teutons comprise Alemannians, Bavarians, East Franks, Danes, Saxons, Thuringians, Lotharingians, Brabandians, Flemings, and Angles, and other languages comprise many more peoples.[101] From this huge harvest, which still compares to a drop in

Woodward, "Medieval Mappaemundi," in J. B. Haley and David Woodward, eds., *The History of Cartography* I (Chicago: University of Chicago Press, 1987), particularly the overview of different types, with illustrations, 296–97. (Note, however, that the diagrams for figs. 18.5 and 18.6 are reversed.)

[98] Is. 40:15–17.

[99] Jerome, *Commentarium in Esaiam* 40:15. (CCSL 73, p. 461).

[100] Cf. Luke 10:1.

[101] The lists do not correspond to any of the standard encyclopedic reference works (Pliny, Isidore), but Goscelin may well have had reference lists of place names

a bucket or a little bit of dust compared to the heavenly multitudes, huge sheaves are collected from this world in the heavenly grange, for Christ, the grain of wheat that died falling on the ground, bore much fruit. Hence, the incomparable army of the nine orders of angels is being augmented; earth dwellers are ascending to the place from which the heavenly spirits fell, and the tenth order is being reconstituted from humans. From our first forefather until the end of time, from before as well as after the flood, under the patriarchs, under the Mosaic laws, under the prophets, under the grace of the Christian seed, the heavenly people is constantly growing and multi-plying, and we may hope that more will rise up there than the num-ber of spirits who fell, for the Redeemer knows how to repair the loss to his kingdom so as to make it even more sublime. John says in the Apocalypse: "I saw a great multitude which no man could number, from all nations and tribes and peoples and tongues, standing before the throne and in the sight of the Lamb, clothed with white robes" of eternal celebration and joy, "and with palms in their hands," that is palms of victory.[102] What mind is sufficient to grasp how huge is the sky, how great are the palaces of this world, and how diverse, how uncountable are the visible works of God? But if all these transitory, temporal things are so great, how great and how far above the high-est of what is visible, how far exceeding the grasp of any mind, are those things which eye has not seen and ear has not heard. Neither has it entered into the heart of man what things God has prepared for them that love him, and what you, God, have prepared for the poor in your sweetness, how many mansions there are in the house of Christ's father;[103] how distinct yet how united are the orders and the merits of the patriarchs, prophets, apostles, martyrs, confessors, vir-gins, widows, and all the elect; or how great is the distance from humans to angels, from angels to archangels, from archangels to thrones, from thrones to dominations, from dominations to princi-palities, from principalities to authorities, from authorities to powers, from powers to cherubim, from cherubim to seraphim, and from them to the King, Lord, Emperor Himself, the Great One of all the universe, infinitely exceeding his entire creation, reigning, disposing,

---

at his disposal. It is tricky to give modern equivalents for Classical and medieval names, since in many cases they do not correspond ethnically or politically. "Allobroges" are from around Geneva; "Beturici" are from around Bourges; "Cetomanni" from Maine/Le Mans.

[102] Apoc. 7:9.
[103] 1 Cor. 2:9; Ps. 67:11; John 14:2.

fulfilling all things justly, kindly, and mercifully, balancing within his circumference the highest and the lowest, offering himself to the small and the great as eminently sufficient, world without end.[104] Yet while every thing is set in its rank and place, the entire kingdom is nonetheless one, from the lowest to the highest, in perfect charity and concord, one city, one people, one house, one church, one bride, one body and soul, one single harmony of all things, the harmony of eternal love. For as many grains make up one loaf of bread, many threads one garment, many stones one temple, and many members one body, thus the building of God's court is one made of many.

Therefore, my beloved, do not languish in the poverty of your service to Christ, who fills the heavens and the earth with such generosity, who presides over such a rich *familia*.[105] Do not consider yourself lonely when you have the company of so many citizens of heaven. Let this great feast of joy shut out sleepiness, sluggishness, sadness, depression. Do not regret that you have despised that despicableness which idolaters and even the despisers of God himself have managed to despise. It would be shameful if their vanity were more patient in hardship than the faith of Christ's soldiers, to whom the kingdom is promised.

If you want to know how small are all those things that seem greatest to us in the eyes of the creator, consult our holy father Benedict. He saw that entire sky and the entire earth, and all that is in them, simultaneously gathered together – the sun, the stars, the seas, the peoples, the cities, the kingdoms, God's grace spread them all visibly before his eyes as if to say, "Look how small are those things for which you spurned me, compared to the greatness of the prize that I am holding for you, which you can now see only partially, darkly, but then will see face to face, when you come to that perfection."[106] And St. Gregory bears witness to this contemplation: "To a soul that sees God, all creation seems narrow." His dialogue itself will explain it better to you.[107] But how large and capacious a heart had he who saw such great things instead of small ones! To

---

[104] See Pseudo-Dionysius, "Celestial Hierarchy," 6–10 (Pseudo-Dionysius, *The Complete Works*, ed. and trans. Colm Luibhéid and Paul Rorem [Mahwah, NJ: Paulist Press, 1987], 160–174).

[105] The Latin word *familia* describes a unit larger, more hierarchical, and more public than our "family," yet more intimate and affective than our "household" or "court."

[106] Cf. 1 Cor. 13:12.

[107] Gregory, *Dialogues* 2:35 (PL 66:200; ed. Adalbert de Vogüé [Paris: Cerf, 1979], 240–41).

him, the path to life did not seem narrow, for he hastened along Christ's way to Christ's life. "I have run the way of your commandments, and you have enlarged my heart."[108] Regard your whole life as but one day compared to eternity, and say with the psalmist: "You are my God and my savior, and on you have I waited all the day long"[109] in my peregrination. Do not falter on this long way, for it is taking you to your eternal homeland. All finite things should seem short to one who is striving towards infinity. Let not the multitude of foes terrify you: "more are with us than are against us," as the apostle witnesses.[110] Elisea was prophesying and exposing the Syrians' hostile ambushes to the Israelites; and the King of Syria with a great army was hunting him to death. Elisea asked God to open the eyes of his trembling servant, and the boy saw the surrounding mountains fill with God's chariots and horsemen all around; thus he understood that Elisea could not possibly fear an enemy, however great, since he was defended by an even greater multitude.[111]

And do not think yourself straitened by your space. Those are more straitened who in the vast ocean of the world have no place where they may flee the ebb and flow of the masses; and Noah's dove, sent from the Ark, had nowhere to perch, and the Son of Man had nowhere to lay his head.[112] In every tribulation it is a great comfort to one's soul to have a secure place and dwelling. The daughter of Zion lived among the gentiles and found no rest; but the Lord our God will lead those who put their hope in him to a secure place. Aeneas, after long wanderings and uncertain dwellings on land and at sea, finally found a secure house when the time had come, and he founded a city; but in escaping from the perils of the sea he entered the dire perils of wars. Was this the "sure rest after all his toils"?[113] Yes: compared to instability, war in a fixed location seemed like rest, where at least he might hope to find a grave for his weary bones. But he who has no place to put his foot is buffeted by every current.

Therefore, my dearest, you owe tireless thanks to the ineffable mercy of the Lord, for he who is mighty has done great things to you; he heard your desires and gave you a house where you might

---

[108] Ps. 118:32.

[109] Ps. 24:5.

[110] These precise words are not found in "the Apostle" (which usually means St. Paul); perhaps Goscelin is thinking of Romans 8:31.

[111] 4 Kings [KJV: 2 Kings] 6:17.

[112] Genesis 8:8–9; Mt. 8:20.

[113] Aen. 3:393.

shelter with him, in a place where no one could have hoped for one, and hence introduced you into his chamber.[114] Trusting in the Lord you can remain strong and live securely, and die even more securely; dying every day to the world and living for God, you will learn not to fear death as something formidable, like the abyss of hell, but rather desire it as a rest and as the entrance to life. Once, in days past, when you were agitated and in tears, I succeeded in comforting you with this verse, and I pointed it out with notes[115] so that you might savor it more attentively: "Expect the Lord, do manfully, and let your heart take courage, and wait you for the Lord."[116] He has already looked upon you, he has already visited you, and has already come to you more graciously than you expected; only now act lest the grace he gave you be idle within you. You will await him with all the more trust, patience, and forbearance; and when he comes to reward your labors and still your long hunger, you will be all the more eagerly sated with the goods of Jerusalem, for having been brought to Zion from this prison house. "Who," said Job, "has sent out the onager free?"[117] An onager is a wild donkey, which signifies the anchorite.[118] The Lord sets the onager free when he releases the soul from outward worries, calling it to the freedom of contemplating him, and saying to those he has freed: "Free your mind and see that I am God."[119] So many people, both in monasteries and in the world, sigh for the lot of which Mary's defender said: "Martha, Martha, you trouble yourself with many things" – you with many, Mary with one – "but only one thing is needful," namely that you come from the many to the one in which all things are contained, for "Mary chose the best part."[120] If you suffer adversity, if depression is occupying your mind, always breathe with the hope of better things, for

---

[114] Luke 1:49; Song of Songs 1:3.

[115] "Notis intentabam." It is not clear what exactly Goscelin means: did he annotate the passage? Highlight it with signs in the margin? Possibly – given his musical credentials – even write it out with musical notation? On musical notation possibly by Goscelin, see Richard Sharpe, "Goscelin's St. Augustine and St. Mildreth: Hagiography and Liturgy in Context," *Journal of Theological Studies* n.s., 41 (1990): 515–16.

[116] Ps. 26:14.

[117] Job 39:5.

[118] This interpretation ("onager heremita") is found in Eucher of Lyon's *Formulae*, a kind of allegorical Bible dictionary (ed. C. Wotke, CSEL 31 [Prague: Tempsky, 1894] p. 26).

[119] Ps. 45:11.

[120] Luke 10:41–42.

in adversity virtue is trained to greater strength, for a victorious outcome. We have passed through the fire and the water, and you have brought us to refreshment.[121] A weary heart tends to be more weighed down in the evening and night, and with the morning light it is refreshed, as if renewed after the darkness. We must endure the darkness of the cavern. "After the darkness," said Job, "I hope for the light."[122] In the evening, weeping shall have place, and in the morning gladness.[123] Evening means this transitory life, and morning means the eternal light. Day succeeds night, summer follows winter, calm follows storm, Easter lent, joyfulness sadness. The earth, beaten with frost, snow, hail, rain, and every roughness of winter, newly breaks out in leaves, flowers, seeds, in every happy birth and fructification, in every joy of human happiness. Thus earthly anxiety gives birth to heavenly rejoicing, just as on the other hand fleeting joy brings forth eternal laments.

Therefore persevere in the Lord and take comfort. If it is feasible, take a daily viaticum of heavenly nourishment, to lighten the burdens of your earthly journey, so that your soul, resting in the Lord your Savior, may not weaken, for the bread of life himself says: "He that eats my flesh and drinks my blood abides in me and I in him."[124] This bread of life, this bread of angels, seek daily: "Give us this day our daily bread."[125] It is a great mystery: he who is joined to a harlot will become one flesh with her, but he who is joined to the Lord will become one spirit with him.[126] And he who partakes of the Lord's body and blood, what is he in-corporating but the Lord himself, so that he is tied to him not only in spirit but also in flesh? For as Eva was fashioned from the side of Adam, thus the redeemed Church grew from Christ's side. Taking his body into herself, she, too, by inseparable mixture becomes Christ's body. "And they will be," he says, "two in one flesh."[127] Thus they are no longer two but one flesh.

See, my dearest, how great an obligation of pure and chaste living is laid upon us for participating in such a great mystery. The precious teacher and martyr Cyprian praises daily communion, saying, "As

---

[121] Ps. 65:12.

[122] Job 17:12.

[123] Ps. 29:6.

[124] John 6: 57.

[125] Luke 11:3.

[126] 1 Cor. 6:16–17.

[127] 1 Cor. 6:16.

I sin daily, I hope for daily medicine."[128] Others step up to communion more rarely, according to their faith and their reverence. You, however, according to what God prepares for you, do your best to be refreshed by this life-giving food as frequently as possible. For it is so plentiful that, as we read of the manna, he who takes less will not have less, and he who takes more will not have more of it;[129] but it will profit most those who take it with the most devoted faith and sincerity. For if the corruptible body is revived by daily food, will not the soul be revived by angelic food, and will not the flesh of the eater also be revived in its strength and purity? "Behold," says the Lord, "I stand at the gate and knock: if anyone shall open the door to me I will come in to him and will sup with him, and he with me."[130] If you dine on this food with Christ and his angels, with your mind not roaming outside but concentrated inward, on the Lord, you will not be lonely, and you will not suffer deadly depression; but in the strength of the heavenly food you will pass rejoicing to the feast of eternal peace.

HERE ENDS THE THIRD BOOK OF EXHORTATIONS.

[128] "De Dominica oratione," 12, *Sancti Cypriani Episcopi Opera*, CSEL 3A (Turnhout: Brepols, 1976), 96. Daily communion, while not uncommon in Cyprian's day, would have been unusual in Goscelin's, in practice and even as an ideal; he all but acknowledges this in the following sentences. Most decrees and regulations in the early and central Middle Ages were concerned with establishing a bare minimum (usually once a year); the *consuetudines* of religious orders tended to prescribe a limited number of high feasts (e.g., seven a year) on which communion would be received. See *Catholic Encyclopedia*, s.v. "Communion, frequency of."

[129] Cf. Exodus 16:17–18.

[130] Apoc. 3:20.

Here Begins the Fourth Book

On Humility

Your streets, Jerusalem, are covered with pure gold and translucent glass.[1] Thus says John, the master of divine secrets, in his theology. Pure gold, tried in the furnace of poverty and patience, and the translucent glass of a pure mind illuminate the streets on which Humility, having traveled through Egypt and the desert and having vanquished her enemies, shall walk the way of the Lord's commandments. Her heart will open wide as she ascends to the city of heavenly peace with its golden walls and jeweled turrets, rising from humble foundations but standing taller than the stars. There, my soul, my special one, I would like you to travel by the roads[2] of humility. I know that you devoutly strive for ever greater humbleness; you say entreatingly: "My soul has cleaved to the pavement; quicken me, Lord, according to your word."[3] But I still want you to be cautious of human inconstancy, often our downfall. Because we are vessels made of dirt, we are impatient of God's gifts; the more we lack in virtue, the more insolent we are in disparaging the good he gives us. It is theft if we arrogate God's free gifts to ourselves. For as we do not exist of ourselves, thus we have nothing of ourselves besides sin. And yet it comes naturally to our ignoble flesh and our filthy, rotten indignity to rise up insolently at the prompting of the unclean spirit of pride, even as God visits us with his mercy. Against this arrogance, we read: "For if any man think himself to be something, whereas he is nothing, he deceives himself."[4] Therefore, presumption is the origin of every downfall. Hence David: "Let not the foot of pride come to me, and let not the hand of the sinner move me. There the workers of iniquity are fallen; they are cast out and could not stand."[5] And, "When they were lifted up you have cast them down."[6] Humility is the guard of virtues; if anyone loses it, he loses

---

[1] Apoc. 21:21.
[2] Reading "per strata" for Talbot's "perstrata."
[3] Ps. 118:25.
[4] Galat. 6:3.
[5] Ps. 35:12–13.
[6] Ps. 72:18.

his virtues, and he gives up his vineyard unguarded to the plunderers. But godless Pharaoh, the worldly king of Egypt, will persecute anyone who starts out on a pious life and begins to make his way from his country to the promised land. Pharaoh mounts his wagons and his horses – that is, he mobilizes vacuous, fickle souls against him; and he arms these with derision and reproaches, and hurriedly rides forth to trample the nascent seed. "Bah, look at him praying, fasting, and giving alms – just so he can leave us mere mortals behind and get to heaven as a servant and a saint of God." Thus, a certain scoffer saw St. Trudgaud, already a grown man, begin to learn the rudiments of the alphabet. "May a toothache strike me," he said, "if you ever master the psalter!" Well, within a year the saint had mastered the psalter, and the insulter was insulted by a toothache until the day he died.[7]

So when Christ's recruit persists in his resolution, then that coiled Leviathan, that Proteus[8] who can take any shape he wants, will approach those whom he had vainly tried to persuade and will begin to whisper fraudulent flatteries. Thus he hopes to prevail over the mind which persecution could not break, and the will that won the day in the battlefield may yet be slaughtered inside the safe walls of a good conscience: "What a blessed little thing, what a good little saint you are; you are so close to heaven, sweetheart." But on the other side is heard the voice of the Lord: "Daughter, they that call you blessed, even they are deceiving you."[9]

But that you, my sweetest, are well received by the people there; that the venerable mother and all the sisters shower you with love; that dignified fathers and bishops visits you; that the dear lady loves and cherishes you who prepared this place for you and, as a true follower of Christ, is now a most kind friend to you in a truer way than before (and may God repay her in all eternity for all her kindness):[10] all of that, I believe, is God's goodness breathing on you. Receiving

---

[7]   Identified by Talbot as abbot of St. Bertin, 996–1000.

[8]   The ms (and Talbot) has "Prometheus," but Proteus, the shape-shifter, is clearly intended.

[9]   Is. 3:12.

[10]   Latzke (p. 140) suggests reading "benedicta domina" as a proper name ("Lady Benedicta"), identifying her with the "Benedicta Reclusa" eulogized by Baudri of Bourgueil ("Carmen 77", ed. Karlheinz Hilbert [Heidelberg: Winter, 1979]). In any event, this passage suggests, and Hilarius's poem confirms (line 77) that Eva had a predecessor at Angers who recruited her and introduced her to the anchoritic life. One can infer from this remark that their friendship predated the older anchoress's conversion.

you in your exile, he brings you comfort through all these good people. In the same way, he has sometimes softened the hearts even of godless kings towards his elect; thus Abraham, Isaac, and Jacob rose high under foreign princes; thus Joseph under Pharaoh, thus Daniel under Nebuchadnezzar and Darius, thus the sons of Israel as captives under Cyrus, Ahasverus, Ptolemy, and other tyrants. For the heart of a king is in the hand of the Lord who made everything,[11] and the Lord will give grace and glory to those who are his. Even sweeter, then, is the divinely inspired affection of the Lord's faithful; may it warm you and refresh you. But when it became necessary, the Lord hardened Pharaoh's heart – or rather, it already was hard, but he did not free him from his hardness – and he turned the hearts of the Egyptians to hate his people, to deal deceitfully with his servants[12] – or rather, they hated already but he did not turn them to love, so that the elect might benefit by the persecutions and the persecutors might perish. Therefore be watchful. Let no one take anything away from your devotion. Firmly ground yourself in the peace of Christ through your humility, and arm yourself with both external and internal fortitude in temptations. Lest you abuse God's forgiveness, always beware of the snares of the foe.[13]

A Tall Structure Must Rest on a Firm Foundation

Humility, therefore, is both the foundation and the bulwark of good works. When Solomon, in his wisdom, was going to erect the highest peak of the temple, he dug the foundations into the lowest depths. And the Lord says in the Gospel: "He who hears my words and does them, I shall liken him to the wise man who, when building a house, dug deep, so that no storm could move it at all, for it was founded on solid rock."[14] A lofty tree grows up to great heights from a deep root. Grains are broken into bread, grapes are pressed into wine, a buried seed springs up and bears fruit. Rome, founded as the smallest of all cities, grew to be the largest of all. The Church started small, with twelve apostles, and it spread out to the ends of the earth. With military might Rome obtained the pinnacle of the world; with a martyr's patience, the Church subdued the world and even Rome herself. God, who ordains everything, prepared this earthly kingdom for his

---

[11] Prov. 21:1.
[12] Ps. 104:25.
[13] I.e., rather than relying exclusively on God's forgiveness, try not to sin in the first place.
[14] Luke 6:48.

apostles and for Christianity. Thus a little thing grew large, low overcame high, patience vanquished strength. Benedict, the teacher of
virtue, has set up twelve grades of humility for you.[15]

I will now explain to you several devices of God's dispensation,
which the healthy should fear and the wounded may embrace. The
just should not presume upon them and the guilty need not despair
of them; innocence cannot be certain of them and the lost need not
founder. He who created everything, governed everything justly and
kindly, and, searching the reins and hearts of everyone,[16] allots to
each his own. According to his true and inscrutable judgments,
always foreseeing all things from time immemorial, he weighs in his
balance all different qualities and all different minds. Unmoved, he
moves everything, unchanged, he changes everything, yet never
alters his sentence or his counsels. Calm and tranquil, he disturbs
and agitates everything; most stable, he turns and overturns everything, putting the highest low and the lowest high. He throws down
the upright, helps up the fallen, subjects the strong to trials, heals the
contrite, weakens the robust and strengthens the infirm, incriminates
the just and justifies the unjust, humbles the high and exalts the humble. The virgin falls, the whore rises, the chaste is violated, the prostitute made chaste.

Why? That no flesh should glory in his sight,[17] and that those who
are nothing without their creator's gift should not attribute anything
to their own powers. He himself wastes and destroys, roots up and
pulls down, that he may build and plant.[18] By the strange dispensation of the great creator, many fall, either because they have been
arrogant or lest they become arrogant, and tumble diminished from
their high places, ignominiously or, again, so that they may rise up
more gloriously. For after the fall of our first parents, the Redeemer
raised up humankind so much more splendid than they were before
the fall, that we rightly call that guilt "fortunate" which merited us
such a great redeemer;[19] through him we have triumphed in a nobler
victory. They do well to destroy who will build something better.
I, a useless little man, who only encumber the ground,[20] am often
annoyed when I see flimsy buildings, and, completely lacking in

[15] Benedictine Rule, Chapter 7.
[16] Apoc. 2:23.
[17] 1 Cor. 1:29.
[18] Jer. 1:10.
[19] From the "Exultet," part of the liturgy for the Easter Vigil.
[20] Luke 13:7.

material means, I plan great things. There are perfectly well-regarded churches which I, given the power to do so, would not suffer to stand unless they were as grand, magnificent, soaring, vast, light-flooded and exquisitely beautiful as I would wish them to be. What, then, will the noble architect of the eternal palace do, who will build his houses of nothing less than pure gold and silver tried in his furnace, and has fashioned the walls and towers of his Jerusalem of gems and precious stones? Will he not tear down what is useless and ruinous and not worthy of him, and renovate that which is becoming of his glory as the place where he will reside? For only holiness lasting unto the length of days becomes his house.[21] The Lord ordered that the fruitless tree be cut down; a respite was asked for, manure was applied, and out of that slimy, thick substance sterility was made fertile.[22] Thus out of the slime of sin, the good creator coaxes the negligent soul to grow fat and bear fruit. He converts our crimes into weapons of virtue, and out of our badness he fashions health and medicine for us.

Commenting on David's adultery and murder, St. Gregory asks why the omnipotent God subjects to such baseness those whom he means to glorify for all time.[23] The answer is that he does it to humble deeply those who will be exalted highly, to turn baseness and abjectness into sublimity. "Lord," said Peter, "why cannot I follow you now? I will lay down my life for you."[24] What presumption! Are you going to forestall him who came to redeem the world? Is he the one who is lost, and you will save him? If the redemptor had followed your advice and had not died, neither you nor the world would have been saved. Not so fast, Peter! You cannot lay down your life for the Lord unless he first lay down his for you. First you must realize who you are, and what you can do without him who said, "without me you can do nothing." First you must deny him three times; you must be a denier before you can become a martyr. There are sick people who fancy themselves well, but the doctors are mindful of their mortal danger. Hence St. Augustine's little verse:

> The sick man trusted he was well,
> But the doctor his pulse could tell.[25]

---

[21] Ps. 92:5.
[22] Luke 13:8.
[23] Moralia in Job 33:25, CCSL 143b, 1649–95.
[24] John 13:37.
[25] Sermon 80:4, PL 38:95.

The doctor knows what is ailing each patient, what will harm him, what medicine he needs. Not surprisingly, Truth spoke the truth, and Peter, the liar, fell when left to his own devices. Night came, and the braggart, to avoid death, denied him for whom he had promised to die. The rooster crowed and exposed the denier. But from this fall, the prince of faith, the foundation of the Church learned to stand so firmly that he was able to stabilize others as well. Paul, too, experienced temptation after being taken up into the third heaven, though he did not fall: he was given a thorn in his flesh, an angel of Satan. Why? "Lest the greatness of these revelations should exalt me."[26] The Lord said to those who will hear him, "Even before you call on me, I tell you, 'I am here.' "[27] Yet when his most faithful martyr Paul, who carried his passion in his body, prayed to him for the third time in the anguish of his soul, the Lord did not give in to him but said, "My grace is sufficient for you, Paul." I know what you ask, I know what you want, and I also know what will be better for you. A greater illness will be driven out by this illness, this infirmity will work healing in you, for "power is made perfect in infirmity."[28] The antidote called "Tyriacum" is made from snakes. The potion will cure snake bites, even deadly ones; miraculously, poison drives out poison. Thus, in Paul, the poison of the thorn in his side drove out the poison of arrogance.

He who distributes all graces has thus apportioned his gifts that each may see in the other what is admirable and in himself that which humbles him. John admired Peter as the leader of the apostles and of the Church; Peter admired John as a virgin and as Christ's special beloved. John blessed Peter as one who loved the Lord more than all others; Peter blessed John as the one who with confident familiarity leaned on Christ's bosom. John cherished the keeper of the keys of heaven, Peter cherished the one who drank the Gospel directly from Christ's heart. John thought Peter the greater for following Christ on the cross; Peter thought John the greater for being spared by the prerogative of grace because the Lord loved him: "Him I want to remain; you follow me."[29] Paul admired Peter for presiding over all the others; Peter admired Paul for working harder than all the others. Paul cherished Peter as the more eminent, Peter

---

[26]   2 Cor. 12:7.
[27]   Bened. Rule, Prologue; cf. Isaiah 58:9.
[28]   2 Cor. 12:9.
[29]   John 21:22.

cherished Paul as the more learned. I also read once of a pious contest between John and Andrew, when John said he would rather be the one first chosen by the Lord, and Andrew said he would rather be the one whom the Lord loved most.[30] And, in short, the Lord made the denier a prince, the persecutor a teacher, the publican an evangelist, and the whore his friend. And many who were innocent, blameless of life, and gifted with great virtues, he has ennobled further by giving them humility. The arrogant see in others what they despise and in themselves what they think exalts them; the pure and the humble, even if they excel before all others in many virtues, in their own minds occupy the last place. David had crushed the lion and the bear, and brought down Goliath; then he became a refugee from Saul and compared himself to a flea. He never forgot that he had been raised from his flock of sheep to the throne, and amid his many claims to great virtue, he humbled himself so much before God that his own wife despised him for a fool.[31] When Peter was so great that his mere shadow sufficed to cure the sick, he did not forget where he had come from: that he had ascended to the apostolate from the fishing nets.[32] When a Roman general returned victorious, the crowd that met him filled the earth with its singing and the skies with its cheers. But next to the victor in his golden chariot, reveling in the heady triumph, sat an admonisher, who for every cheer from the crowd hit him with a golden rod and said, "remember that you are human, a beast."[33] This was done to remind him, even in his victory, that he was not invincible – lest human folly, forgetting its condition, deteriorate into tyranny and vainglory. To us Christians, it is said even more clearly: "Remember that you are dust and will return to dust."[34] Man, created free, will be tempted by his very freedom into the vice of arrogance; he will fall of his own accord, so that, raised up from the dust by his maker, he may learn to stand.

The Rewards of Pride and Humility

How vile earthly arrogance is before the Most High always becomes clear in its fall. Through the Prophet, God threatens those souls who abuse their liberty: "Because the daughters of Zion are haughty," he

---

[30] I.e., each declared the other's distinction superior.
[31] 2 Kings (KJV: 2 Sam) 6:20.
[32] Acts 5:15.
[33] Tertullian, *Apologeticus* 33.4. (*Apologetical Works*, trans. Rudolph Arbesmann et al. [New York: Fathers of the Church, 1950], 89.)
[34] Gen. 3:19; also the formula used during the imposition of ashes on Ash Wednesday.

says, "and have walked around with their heads held high, and wanton glances in their eyes, and clapped their hands and walked with assured steps: the Lord will make bald the crown of the daughters of Zion, and the Lord will uncover their hair. On that day the Lord will take away the ornaments of their shoes and little moons and chains and necklaces and bracelets and bonnets, and bodkins, and ornaments of the legs, and sweet balls, and earrings, and rings and jewels hanging on the forehead, and changes of apparel, and short cloaks, and fine linen, and crisping pins, and looking glasses, and lawns, and headbands, and fine veils, and instead of a sweet smell there shall be stench, and instead of a girdle a cord, and instead of curled heir, baldness, and instead of a stomacher, hair cloth. And her gates shall lament and mourn, and she shall sit desolate on the ground."[35] All this was fulfilled in the capture of Jerusalem by Nebuchadnezzar and the Babylonian captivity of the Jewish people. And it still often happens today. The daughters of Zion are the virginal souls who through their innocence and natural integrity are comely and self-assured daughters in the beauty of purity. If they do not bear their happiness well and do not respect the Creator's majesty, and instead go around joking, playing, with their heads held high like the image of pride, they fall headlong into the trap. They are "made bald" as their chastity is torn away and the ornaments of virtues are stripped. For the feminine ornaments the prophet lists stand for the virtues. Then it happens that instead of the sweet perfume of good reputation and esteem, there is the stench of ignominy and infamy. Every reason for pride is stripped away, and she sits on the ground, shorn, confused, and desolate, remembering that she is dust and mourning and sorrowing for her inane gaiety. And yet she is better off now. In his wrath, the Lord was bent on punishing the arrogant, but now that she is prostrate, his pity, better than lives,[36] is already gathering her up to console her in her misery and turn her mourning to happiness. For he looks upon the humble and does not despise a humble and contrite heart, and he finds his rest with the humble and quiet who tremble at his word, and raises up the needy from the earth, and the poor he lifts out of the dirt.[37] Jeremiah laments Jerusalem's captivity: "The Lord has cast down Jerusalem; he has overthrown all the walls thereof. She is violently cast down, and she does not have a comforter. From the daughter of

---

[35] Is. 3:16–26.
[36] Ps. 62:4.
[37] Ps. 50:19; Is. 66:2; Ps. 112:7.

Zion all her beauty is departed," etc.[38] But the Lord will console Jerusalem, and will amend her every ruin, and all that is ruinous will be restored. As the Lord threatens the arrogant through Isaiah, through the same[39] he also consoles the humble. "Fear not," says the Lord, "you will not be confounded, nor blush; for you shall not be put to shame, because you shall forget the confusion of your youth and shall no longer remember the reproach of your widowhood. For he that made you shall rule over you, the Lord of Hosts is his name, and your redeemer, the Holy One of Israel, shall be called the God of all the world. For the Lord has called you as a woman forsaken and mourning in spirit, as a wife cast off from her youth, said the Lord your God. In a moment of indignation I have hid my face from you for a little while, but with everlasting kindness have I had mercy on you. For the mountains shall be moved and the hills tremble, but my mercy shall not depart from you, and the covenant of my peace shall not be moved, says the Lord that has mercy upon you. Poor little one, tossed with the tempest, without all comfort, behold, I will lay your stones in order, and will lay your foundations in sapphire. And I will make your bulwarks of jasper and your gates of graven stones, and all your borders of desirable stones."[40]

Thus the grace of the merciful Lord raises up those whom he has crushed to shatter their arrogance, higher even than before. Solomon's temple was burnt by Nebuchadnezzar after four hundred and thirty years, which signifies shame burned by the devil; but seventy years later it was rebuilt far more magnificently. O pride, how much you destroy! O humility, how much you preserve, how much you rebuild! Therefore, David willingly humbled himself from his regal height to the level of a small child: "The Lord," he said, "is the keeper of the little ones; I was humbled and he delivered me." "Before I was humbled, I offended": running my vain course, I had fallen into the abyss of pride; "therefore I will keep your word," having been taught by my humiliation to proceed more cautiously. Therefore: "It is good for me, Lord, that you have humbled me, that I may learn your commandments," which are: "Unless you be converted, and become as little children, you shall not enter into the kingdom of heaven," and "Who so humbles himself as this little child, he is the greater in the kingdom of heaven."[41]

---

[38] Lamentations 2:5, 1:9, 1:6.
[39] Reading "per eundem" for Talbot's "pereuntem."
[40] Is. 54:4–6, 8:10–12.
[41] Ps. 114:6, 118:67, 71; Matthew 18:3–4.

He who wants to glory, therefore, may glory in the Lord, and be humble in himself; for no one can achieve anything unless it is given to him from heaven. "And no one can come to me," says the Lord, "unless it is given to him by my father." If you have received, why should you glory as if you had received it, as if you had the divine gift by yourself? No one can have what the Lord did not give him, no one can keep what the Lord will not keep. Unless the Lord build the house and guard the house, they labor in vain that build it, and they watch in vain that keep it.[42] The good Lord made all good things, and made everything well, but unless the giver preserves the gift, it perishes. He gave everyone the grace of being born a virgin; but he gave perseverance in virginity only to those who merited it through their humility. He himself foresaw everything from all eternity. Many women wished to persevere but could not obtain the gift even through prayers; others who did not wish to persevere were preserved in virginity by afflictions and chastisement. Others incurred the Serpent's bite either through the ignorance of youth or Dina's curiosity,[43] but the Lord cured them, quickly expelling the venom; for the sooner they come to their senses, the more curable they are. Similarly, some sought martyrdom but did not find it; others tried to avoid it but suffered it. Man cannot become an angel, but through his creator, made man, he can be associated with the angels. We do not call someone a martyr unless he has suffered persecution; but one who lives in a martyr-like way partakes in martyrdom. Likewise, a widow can join the virgins if she seeks virginal chastity, albeit after suffering the wounds. John Chrysostom, which means "golden mouth," said, "The Lord found a shepherd and made him a prophet. He found a minstrel and made him king. He found a fisherman and made him an apostle. He found a publican and made him an evangelist. He found a whore and made her equal to virgins."[44]

Again, others have preserved their virginity amid all those who pursued their chastity, and miraculously escaped from the very mouth of perdition. Thus, resplendent Agnes, glorious Lucy, heroic Potaminia

---

[42] 1 Cor. 1:31; John 6:44; Ps. 126:1–2.

[43] The rape of Dina as she "went out to see the women of that country" (Gen. 34:12) was commonly interpreted as a warning against women's "curiosity." See Joy A. Schroeder, "The rape of Dinah: Luther's interpretation of a biblical narrative," *Sixteenth Century Journal* 28: (1997): 776–80; John R. Clark, "The Traditional Figure of Dina and Abelard's First Planctus," *Proceedings of the PMR Conference* 7, (1982): 117–128.

[44] Sermon on Pentecost, PG 52: 803.

carried away the palm from the infernal swamp of lions and pimps.[45] Potaminia, according to Eusebius's History, first suffered all kinds of torture, and then was put into a brothel. All the young bird-catchers ran to the devil's prey. But God brought help to his beloved through her very enemies: Basilides, the leader of the torturers, fervently defending the virgin's dignity, beat them back. The virgin, groped and threatened from all sides, said to him, "Believe me, Basilides, you shall not lack recompense for this good deed." Then, killed slowly with boiling pitch, Potamiana triumphed with the double palms of virginity and martyrdom. Later she appeared to Basilides and put a crown on his head, with these words: "Christ said that he who receives a prophet in the name of a prophet shall receive the reward of a prophet.[46] You defended my chastity, therefore you shall participate in my crown." This awoke him from his sleep and from his error; he confessed Christ and soon won the crown by beheading.[47]

At this point it also seems pious to remind you what St. Ambrose testifies in "The Praise of Virginity." Not having access to his book or to his dignified eloquence, I shall have to stammer through this magnificent story in my own inarticulate words.[48]

---

[45] Goscelin is punning on *leo*, "lion," and *leno*, "pimp."

[46] Matthew 10:41.

[47] Eusebius, *Ecclesiastical History* 6:5 (and Palladius's *Lausiac History* 3), enriched with reminiscences from other virgin martyr legends, e.g. Agnes. The early Christian stories of virgin martyrs, which feature young women tortured and threatened with rape, were popular throughout the Middle Ages and were often recommended as edifying reading to women. (The *Ancrene Wisse* appears in manuscripts together with Middle English renditions of several such legends, the so-called "Katherine Group.") The significance and sexual politics of these stories, and especially their emphasis on violence and sexual violation, have been studied and debated extensively in recent years; see for instance Jocelyn Wogan-Browne, *Saints' Lives and Women's Literary Culture c. 1150–1300: Virginity and its Authorizations* (Oxford: Oxford University Press, 2001), 106–17; Karen A. Winstead, *Virgin Martyrs: Legends of Sainthood in Late Medieval England* (Ithaca: Cornell University Press, 1997), 1–63; Elizabeth Robertson, "The Corporeality of Female Sanctity in the Life of Saint Margaret," in *Images of Sainthood in Medieval Europe*, eds. Renate Blumenfeld-Kosinski and Timea Szell (Ithaca: Cornell University Press, 1991), 268–87; and Sarah Salih, "Performing Virginity: Sex and Violence in the *Katherine Group*," in *Constructions of Widowhood and Virginity in the Middle Ages*, eds. Cindy L. Carlson and Angela Jane Weisl (New York: St. Martin's 1999), 95–112.

[48] Ambrose, *De Virginibus* 2.4 (PL 15:212–16). The wording would seem to imply that even though Goscelin is quoting from memory here, he does for the most part have the books he cites within reach. For that matter, he might also have Ambrose handy, and the disclaimer could be merely a "modest" acknowledgement that he

A virgin was destined for the brothel for her faith in Christ, and no torturer, swordsman, or executioner had even so much pity in him as to burn, tear, or mutilate her. The butcher would not suffer her to be mercifully strangled rather than violated; the killer had not compassion enough to save her from the corrupter. Amid bitter sighs, she exclaimed: "Lord Jesus, I was owed two crowns, the crown of virginity and the crown of martyrdom. Now if I must pawn my virginity for the martyrdom, and one crown must be purchased by damage to the other, you, Lord, for whose sake I bear these injuries, will see everything in your liberating mercy. Whatever I must bear for your holy name, it is certain, Lord God, that I can never deny you. In such a dire choice between two evils, it is better to die in body than in spirit. But the enemy is denying me martyrdom; he would rather see me destroyed by rape than by the sword; he would rather have me live a whore than die a martyr. Both things are up to you, Lord, to preserve virginity and to confer martyrdom. So if I am unworthy to be either your spouse or your martyr, I shall endure as your whore while steadfastly confessing you." As she is sobbing these words, they throw her into the brothel. The grunting, swinish band of rapists is all around her. In the middle stands the victim of God, like a dove among crows, like a lamb beset by wolves. O, the fear of rape is so much graver than the fear of torture! The danger to her chastity so much worse than threats to her life! O Lord, timely helper in all tribulation![49] A young boy, still beardless, outstanding among the others in his maidenlike chastity and decency, yet acting more thoughtless and reckless than all the others, enters first as if to violate her. But the Lord has recognized him as a lamb in wolf's clothing, and has found a way to protect his own lamb. The boy says to her: "Fear not, my lady; I have come to save you, not to destroy you. Just do as I tell you. We are alike in age, stature, and looks. Let us simply trade clothes, so that you put on men's clothes and I girls' clothes. Then go out in my stead and escape; I shall remain in your stead and fool the rapists. And they will not easily catch you: coming out of a place like this, it is only natural that you would cover your face for shame."

By this ruse the virgin escaped, walking right through her foes. With the next rapist, the holy ruse was discovered; a clamor ensued; the boy, dressed like a girl, was hauled away to be killed. The girl, dressed like a man and with a man's courage, put herself in the path of

---

means to rewrite this particular story quite extensively and show off his own "dignified eloquence."

[49] Ps. 9:10.

the furious crowd, shouting, "Hit me, me! I am guilty of this thing; an innocent should not be punished instead of the guilty one." On the other side, the boy fought to be killed for the virgin, protesting that it was he who masterminded the deception. In this holy contest, the two of them, about to grace the starry chorus of virgins with their roses and lilies, were beheaded together, together slaughtered for Christ. O their inseparable love, their happy embraces as they dwell everlastingly in heaven! Who, sweet Jesus, glorious in your saints, can justly sing your praises? She feared to be shipwrecked by shame, and you not only allowed her to triumph unsullied, but you even gave her a companion of equal age and equal dignity to be with eternally! They are joined tightly in your love. You, having brought them together, embrace them both with your right and left arms.[50] Praised be your mercy forever.

Progress in Humility

Why then to do you keep sighing, o man? Is it not enough for you to be accepted by God's grace and become a citizen of the heavenly homeland, unless you can also be first in rank? Are the riches of God's goodness insufficient for your estate? Are you angry that you are only a man and cannot become of angelic nature, even though Christ did not disdain to call himself the Son of Man and dined even with sinners? First go and become as holy as the publicans of the gospel.[51] Weeping about your sins would become you more than insisting on your rights. Will you ascend through the clouds and become like the most high? But ascend by going down, lest you fall as you climb. Be the image and likeness of him who said, "Learn of me, because I am meek and humble of heart."[52] Do you have your eyes on the seat on the right or left of Christ? But that seat is not up for ambition, certainly not ambition that is not inspired by love. It will be given to those for whom Christ's father has reserved it; he will deny it to those who have raised themselves up above all others. It is not up to me, he said, to give to the exalted what has been set aside for the most humble.[53] Hence, he who would be first should be

---

[50] Note the echo of the "stabat mater" tableau in Book I (p. 29), where Christ embraces "a virgin of each sex" with each arm – John and Mary, but by implication also Goscelin and Eva.

[51] E.g., Mt. 9:10–12. The "publicans" of the Bible were tax collectors on behalf of the Roman authorities, hence seen as collaborators and highly unpopular. In the Gospels they are consistently named in one breath with sinners: "Why does your master eat with publicans and sinners?"

[52] Isaiah 14:14; Mt. 11:29.

[53] Mk 10:40.

last of all through his own self-abasement, and should believe with all his heart that is inferior to all.[54] Thus the last shall be first, because no one can be worthy of the heavenly community unless he believes himself to be unworthy, as St. Augustine wrote.[55]

Winnoc, the excellent soldier of God, served under our holy father Bertin, and since he was making such excellent progress, the father had already placed him in command over his brothers in some cell.[56] And even though he was of distinguished royal parentage, outstanding in chastity and integrity, obedience and thrift, and praiseworthy in every aspect of saintliness, we read that the Lord had gifted him with such humility that he believed himself lower than all others. He turned the millstone with his own hands and served everyone with this rustic labor, following the Lord who came to serve, not to be served. But by God's gracious gift the millstone began to turn on its own, constantly, doing the labor of many; and he, as we sing, "sang and prayed, intent on heaven, and lifted hands and eyes towards the sky."[57] A skeptic once came to watch this with jealous eyes: the turning mill stopped, and he was stricken with blindness and a tremor of his whole body. But with the saint's indulgent help, he was cured, and the millstone turned again. It is the purity of humility that earned him this grace, for God resists the proud but gives grace to the humble.[58] Even if it is his own bride who waxes presumptuous, she will not get away with it. The groom who accepted her will become angry, and will push her away from him with these words: "Go out, follow the steps of the flocks," that is worldly luxury, "and feed your goats," that is the lascivious delectations of desire.[59] The queen is thrown out of the king's bedchamber, and the handmaid is taken in.

The Righteous Must Fear, the Fallen May Hope

If both the judgments and the mercies of our highest ruler are so great, then the innocent must fear, the fallen may take heart; the

---

[54] Rule of St. Benedict, ch. 7. The whole section is loosely based on this chapter.

[55] Mt. 20:16; *Enarrationes in Psalmos* 18:3.

[56] "Vita Audomari Bertini Winnoci," ed. Levison, MGH Scriptorum rerum merovingiacarum, 5.771–73. A "cell" is a small monastic outpost, a priory dependent on an abbey. Winnoc was in charge of a cell at Wormhoudt near Dunkirk.

[57] Goscelin is citing from the monastic office for the feast of St. Winnoc that would have been performed at St. Bertin.

[58] James 4:6.

[59] Song of Songs 1:7. Again, the quotation and its exegesis are almost perversely out of context. In context, the bridegroom is giving the bride directions on how to find him – by grazing her flock close to his.

virgin must be afraid and the married woman may be confident. The
bride must beg and pray, "Cast me not away from your face, Lord,
and take not your holy spirit," that is, your love, "from me"; for
searching our hearts and reins – that is our intentions and our
thoughts – he humbles one and exalts another, for in the hand of the
Lord there is a cup of strong wine full of mixture.[60] Only humbleness, the timid one, is safe under such an examiner. No one should
puff himself up, no one give himself up for lost. The righteous and
the guilty, the celibate and the married – we believe that before the
redeemer of all, all can be saved. Mary conceived him, Anne held
him: a virgin gave birth to him, a widow carried him. The spouses
Zachary and Elizabeth prophesied him and greeted him with a bene-
diction. Even more astonishingly, when he was already a grown
man, and his miracles had already proclaimed him God, a whore presumed to wash his feet with her tears, dry them with her hair, and
warm them with her kisses;[61] and weeping, drying, and kissing,
placed all her crimes at his feet, washed them off and wiped them
out. A Pharisee, who vainly believed himself to be righteous, said
angrily: "If he were a prophet, he would surely know what manner
of woman she is that touches him, that she is a sinner." But she, by
eagerly trying to please him, was accepted by the merciful Lord and
earned his praise, surpassing the righteous Pharisee. "Many sins are
forgiven her," said the Lord, "because she has loved much," because
love covers a multitude of sins. She gave herself over to the physi-
cian, and by the word of the Lord she was cured of every wound of
sin, like another publican in the gospel, the ailing one who dared to
demand the cure of justice for his spiritual sickness.[62] In the same
way she attained such friendship and intimacy with the Lord that she
could salve even his head with sweet ointments. Who can understand
the mercy of the Lord? It is a miracle, a worthy spectacle not for men
alone but for all the celestial powers! The Baptist trembled and did
not dare to touch Christ's sacred head – the Baptist, than whom none
greater would arise among those born of woman.[63] And that sinner,
whose touch even the unclean Pharisees abhorred as an uncleanness,
not only touches the Lord's footsteps but, from the great burning of
her heart, salves even his head with ointment and massages it with

[60] Ps. 50:13, 7:10, 74:9.
[61] Reading "osculis" for the ms.'s (and Talbot's) "oculis." (See the corresponding
list of verbs, "flendo, tergendo, osculando," and the Biblical source.)
[62] Luke 7:39, 7:47; 1 Peter 4:8; Luke 18:10–14.
[63] Mt. 11:11.

both hands. She envelops his hair in the sweetest scents, she infuses, smoothes, soothes, caresses, grooms; and the sweet oil that dripped from the Savior's head filled the entire house with its perfume.

How great are you, Lord, and yet how small, how mighty and meek, how exalted and humble! Your own Baptist, the most holy among men, even greater than a prophet, does not dare touch you, and the wicked woman confidently dares! The dominations adore, the powers and all the hierarchies of heaven tremble, and a little prostitute boldly embraces that head! O Lord, so magnificent over all things, so gentle to the lowest! Incomprehensible to the highest, you are easily grasped by the lowest; you rise above the highest and lower yourself to the most humble, commune with them, obey them. And even though these hands had toiled in obscenities, they did not sully the Lord in his purity. Rather, touching him who sanctifies all, she herself was sanctified. She ministered to her beloved in a saintly way, no longer unclean but holy. His devoted handmaiden anointed his head with pleasing ointments – the same head which the godless would beat with bloodied hands, and would crown with wounding thorns. Where do we find holiness, justice, innocence, virginity, the beauty of immaculate life? Behold, she who was a pit that housed seven demons, the receptacle for the seven mortal sins with all their forces, has had her demons cast out and has become the sacred vessel for the sevenfold grace, full of the spirits of wisdom, of insight, of counsel, of fortitude, of knowledge, of devotion and of the fear of the lord. In the dens where dragons used to live, now rises the verdure of the reed and bulrush:[64] the devil has been cast out that the divine reed pen may write the law of the Lord in the purified heart, to meditate upon it steadfastly day and night. In time the heart will bear fruit; like bulrushes, righteousness and purified discipline and the holiness of the Lord will green in the chastened body, and with the power of chastity the flesh will flourish again. And when the filth of the enemy has been purged, God's mansion is ready to be decorated.

When I first came to join the bishop at Potterne or Canning[65] as a very young man – you were only a baby – I was assigned lodgings so desolate, filthy, dank, and fetid that they seemed more like a pigsty than a human habitation. I remained silent, but I was angry, and I thought I would not be able to bear it. But soon all the dirt was

[64] Is. 35:7.
[65] Goscelin is recalling his arrival in England with Bishop Herman, in about 1058. He was in his twenties at the time.

removed, the walls and floors were cleansed of their filth, the place was sweetened with green leaves and sedges and burning herbs, the walls and ceilings were covered with curtains and drapes, the seats with blankets, and when everything was carefully prepared, I was led in as the new tenant. I could not believe this was the same house I had seen before. It was so different from its previous state as honor is from shame, beauty from fetidness, splendor from horror, ornament from squalor, incense from stench. What I had first abhorred I now loved, what I had run away from I was now eager to inhabit.

Thus, a mortal man hates what is ugly, but loves it when it has been transformed to beauty. Will not the Omnipotent like to inhabit what he has made in his own image, even if it was ruined but then restored more beautifully than before? A likeness of human beauty can be fashioned from a log: such is human ingenuity. From a sinner sanctified can be fashioned the likeness of God: such is the change wrought by the right hand of the most high.[66] If anyone does not believe that what has been founded well can be restored even better, let him be careful not to slight his maker's goodness.

God is no respecter of persons.[67] Jew or Greek, Barbarian or Scythian, slave or free, virgin or whore, they are distinguished not by their status or their role in life but by their merits, their faith, their love, their humility, and Christ is all things to all people. If you are called a slave, do not let it weigh on you; but if you can, try to become free. "Slave" means those who serve in the bonds of marriage; "free" means those who have been freed from marriage. In that happy reign of Christ and his saints, there will be no pain, no punishment, no damage, no detriment, no reproach from past sins: "that my glory may sing to you," says David, "and I may not be stung" by the prick of conscience; may I receive perfect joy.[68] And no one will look for more than he will have in that plenitude of all goods, in that satiety of all desires. Even the lowliest of all will lack for nothing. Even though the rewards vary according to merit, nonetheless all that one has will belong to all; for as one body joins together all the limbs, so one love will let all share in everyone's joy. O that I were the humblest guest at that feast! I will not demand more, for I will already possess all with all, for God will be all in all.[69]

---

[66] Ps. 76:11.
[67] Acts 10:34.
[68] Ps. 29:13.
[69] Eph. 4:6.

Give me, Lord, for my paucity of virtues the virtue of humility, that I may presume on your gifts when I cannot presume on my merits, that you would count me among the least of your people. Truly, I do not deserve it, but your great redemption of the world, more precious than all the majesty of all things, deserves much more than just the redemption of a sinner. Against that sacrifice of redemption, worthier than any price, let my sins be hung in the balance of the Cross: the enormous grace that exceeds all crimes will outweigh them; that goodness will be greater than all iniquity. Satan with his accusations will be confounded and thrown out. When he presumes to accuse the sinner he will condemn himself, in him who never sinned but was beaten for our sins.[70] His merciful intervention can forgive more than the world can sin. Let me worship, Lord, your cross, which redeems me; let me worship your mercy, which accepts me; let me fall at the feet of all your saints, for if I cannot imitate them in virtue, I can make them my patrons by my veneration.

With these meditations, unpolished in style but shining in faith, I have endeavored to give you, o sweetest child of my soul, a bulwark of all virtue.[71] Humility herself is accompanied by hope, so that confident in fear and somewhat fearful in hope, she may always be unshaken; no caressing breeze will lift her up and make her light-headed, and no storm will break her and destroy her. All should venerate and love the Lord's mercy of infinite goodness, those whom he has miraculously preserved in virtue as well as those whom he mightily raised up from a fall and restored to youth like an eagle.[72] She loves much who has been forgiven much; should not she love even more who has been spared much sin? If you are tempted by the winds of human favor, for the life of man upon earth is a temptation whether in good times or bad,[73] openly expose your sins, for no one is so innocent that she has no sins. "Who can understand sin? From my secret ones cleanse me, o Lord, and from those of others spare your servant," that is those that seek to trap me through flattery, "and I shall be cleansed of the greatest sin," pride. God, you know my

---

[70] See Book II n. 27.

[71] Goscelin here says explicitly that he means the preceding text as a model of meditation for Eva – in the style of Augustine, John of Fécamp, or Anselm. Moreover, the passage shows that he also seems to have in mind a more general audience, for instance when he counsels those who are married to free themselves from their marital obligations if possible – obviously not applicable to Eva.

[72] Ps. 102:5.

[73] Job 7:1.

foolishness, and my offenses are not hidden from you. Let not them
be ashamed for me who look for you, o Lord.[74] Since I cannot see
anyone's heart but my own, I shall believe all others to be better. In
a regatta or in a foot race, the one who was last may overtake the
first, and the one who ran ahead may tire and fall behind. Thus in the
campaign of this life, the determined winner is often beaten by him
whom he has been so eager to surpass; the worker who came towards
evening may take the prize away from the one who has been toiling
since morning.[75] The prudent look not at the merits of those they
might surpass, but the merits of those who might surpass them.
When Solomon's temple was built, you heard no hammer, no axe, or
any tool, for the stones had been previously hewn and tooled.
Believe that those stones will fit into the celestial edifice without the
hammering of a second purification, who are now being prepared by
monastic discipline under someone else's command; think of yourself as a useless animal that feeds on the alms of the world, and that
you owe everyone prayers.[76] Yet do not relinquish the part Mary
chose. Once you resented being called a nun; now do not disdain to
be called a recluse, Christ's poor one, Christ's beggar.

But lest you presume on your own constancy, rather than give
credit to divine goodness, just as I told you above of innocence
miraculously preserved, hear now a story of sanctity undermined by
temptation and built up again from ruin. What I am about to tell I
have heard sung and recited; I did not learn it from books.[77]

St. Alexander was an anchorite living a solitary life in a forest
wilderness. He was already a great man; already his virtues enabled
him to touch heaven. But the old serpent was envious: see what an

[74] Ps. 18:13, 68:6–7.
[75] Mt. 20:1–16.
[76] I.e., even though the anchoritic life is generally considered harder than coeno-
bitism, and hence more meritorious, do not consider yourself better than nuns in
a convent; on the contrary, assume that they have a better chance of being saved.
[77] Related stories can be found in later collections of preachers' *exempla*; see
Frederic C. Tubach, *Index Exemplorum: A Handbook of Medieval Religious
Tales*, FF Communications 204 (Helsinki: Akademia Scientiarum Fennica,
1969), no. 2576 and Joseph Greven, ed. *Die Exempla aus den Sermones feriales
et communes des Jakob von Vitry* (Heidelberg: Winter, 1914), 21–22. I have not
been able to find an early example that might have been Goscelin's source; but
there may not be a written source, as he tells us he has heard rather than read this
story. The story, like many *exempla*, is loosely based on the literature of the
Desert Fathers, combining several motifs found there; in many respects it seems
close to the story of Mary the Harlot and the hermit Abraham. (See the
Interpretive Essay for further discussion of this story.)

elaborate, long-planned snare he set for the man. By divine permission, the devil secretly snatched a baby girl – the king's daughter, as the end of the story will show – screaming from her cradle.[78] Dressed as a monk, he entrusted her to the hermit with this explanation: "This baby was born to my sister; both her parents are dead. I took her with me out of pity, for otherwise she would have died. Now I am in great distress, for in my monastery, under my abbot, keeping her would be out of the question; and abandoning her would be a terrible crime. You, brother, in your holiness and your famous solitude, are the only refuge I can think of. Please take pity on this infant and be her foster father. Feed her and protect her for as long as she needs to be provided for." To cut a long story short, Alexander took her in, brought her up, and when she was grown he seduced her and made her pregnant. As the girl was carrying the proof of his crime in her swelling womb, the devil, the author and instigator of all iniquity, returned in the same disguise as before and demanded back what he had left there. The hermit, sighing sorely with pain and contrition, confessed his terrible crime to the malevolent traitor. I need not prolong the story unduly: the Enemy pretended to grieve with him over this great misfortune. He convinced the wretch that his crime was the more monstrous for his saintly reputation and advanced years. Nothing, he said, is more disgusting than an old man who lapses into sin. And if this filthy disgrace were to break open in public, especially given his former high esteem, everything would go down in a welter of confusion and scandal. The whole world would be up in arms not only against him but against all holy men, with hatred, disparagement, curses, jeers and derision; and all things sacred would be trampled and sullied. He would be responsible for the spiritual ruin of countless people, and that would be a graver guilt than the crime itself. There was only one remedy left to him, one way to stamp out so many ills with one evil deed: he had to strangle the hapless woman. If only he could bury his crime along with her, hide it from the sight of heaven as well as from all human attention, he could repent and do penance. He would stand a better chance of obtaining forgiveness from a merciful God than from the frenzied crowds.

The hermit, relying on this excellent teacher of perdition, did all that he said. No sooner had he buried his murdered spouse that the seductor suddenly broke out in shaggy hair and manifested himself

---

[78] "By divine permission" because the devil has no independent power; he cannot harm humans except insofar as God allows him.

in his true shape, seeking to destroy him with the shock of this sudden transformation. He seized Alexander and said, "There now, you depraved and sinful wretch – now you have become all mine. No one has ever followed my instructions more willingly and cruelly. What, you lost soul, was it not enough to rape her – you also had to stain your whorehouse with blood?" The terrified hermit cried out to Christ, and the fiend, who cannot bear to hear that great name, vanished and left his prey behind. The devil had been on the verge of destroying him with his terror; but now Alexander escaped from the terror to his Savior. For three days he lay prostrate and watered the ground with so much weeping that blood mixed in with his tears. Finally he was able to get up, and before his eyes there stood an oak, split open. Inside something glittered, like the shine of metal. He approached, curious to explore this; and when he put both his hands in the opening, the tree closed and held the traitor against God captive. There, to be brief, he is said to have stood for fifteen years, making do with no food but the occasional falling acorn or leaf, no drink but the dew and the rain. Finally, the time of his tribulations was up, and the day of divine mercy arrived. It happened that King Gundoforus – he was the father of the murdered girl – went hunting in that forest; and straying from his company, he wound up precisely where God's captive stood, suffering the long hot summer days and the stormy, frosty nights.

The king stood dumbfounded, as before a monster. The pious old man reassured him with a humble voice. He told him his entire life and his deception by the devil; with a nod of his head he pointed to the murdered woman's grave. The king counted up the years: there was no doubt in his mind, from the timing and the details of the narration, that this had to be his daughter, lost to him in her infancy. With his sword or a stick he exhumed her, and found a great miracle of God's mercy: after all these years she was undecayed, as whole and radiant as she had been in life. When her murderer saw this, he tearfully begged the king to obtain his daughter's forgiveness for him. The father, deep in prayer, took his child's undecayed finger, like the rod of manumission,[79] and in a forgiving gesture laid it on the hermit. At that same instant, the oak groaned and released its captive. Alexander, released from his sin and his long bondage, suddenly found himself free. Just so, the Lord absolved the paralyzed man in the Gospel, first from his sins, which were the cause of his illness, then from the bonds of his physical infirmity. Therefore, whatever

---

[79] The phrase recalls the Roman ritual of emancipating a slave.

adversities we suffer, we should first ask of God that the debt that occasioned the punishment be dismissed, and then that the punishment be mitigated. Ask for inner health first, and outward health will follow. When we have already despaired of a cure, health is doubly welcome when it does come; and God's mercy will flow more bountifully for having hesitated so long. Alexander rejoiced that out of the crimes of violation and murder he had created the fruit of martyrdom, and that she would enter heaven in triumph on his behalf, bound to him with the inseparable bond of love.[80] And the king built a huge monastery in that spot, endowed it with regal gifts of land, and settled a community of three hundred monks there. Moreover, he himself resigned his throne, and in that same convent fought in God's army in monastic holiness. Hence, the hermit, the girl, and the king are all venerated as saints. The seed of holy conversion germinated and bore rich fruit. Where once the devil tried so vigorously to destroy one soul, Christ gave in abundance to that same man and many others.

Thus does the Lord work the miracles of his mercy, and out of our evils shapes his goods. You, too, speak with the Psalmist: "I will be glad and rejoice, Lord, in your mercy,"[81] not in my own strength. One who has conquered all vice, or one who wears the crown of unvanquished virtue, may yet suffer greater wars in fighting vainglory than does the sinner, who is weighed down by very real causes for humility. A good conscience can be an enemy within the walls and a dagger hidden inside; one who is free of guilt may be in great danger if he does not know that God has other saints, and better ones, besides him. The prophet Elijah was worthy, in the end, to be taken up to heaven in a fiery chariot; but when he believed himself to be the only worshipper of God, immediately heard from God: "I will leave me seven thousand men in Israel whose knees have not been bowed before Baal."[82] When St. Anthony, confirmed in his sanctity by extraordinary fame and miraculous signs, believed himself to be the only or the first hermit in the world, he was ordered by a divine voice to seek out Paul, whom he would find to be better and more excellent than himself.[83] Zozimas had excelled in Christ's army from early

---

[80] This echoes Goscelin's language at the beginning of the letter, where he wishes for a similar "eternal bond of love" with Eva.

[81] Ps. 30:8.

[82] 3 Kings (KJV: 1 Kings) 19:18.

[83] Jerome, "The Life of St. Paul the First Hermit," in *The Desert Fathers*, trans. Helen Waddell, Vintage Spiritual Classics (New York: Random House, 1998), 36–37; PL 23:22.

childhood until his one-hundredth year, and it finally occurred to him that no one had lived in a more saintly manner, that no one had more perfectly fulfilled every rule of life. This is the response he received from heaven: "Zozimas, you have indeed fought well, within your human capacity. But you have never encountered a greater battle than right now: you must beat back your self-satisfied conscience, your most intimate enemy." Thus, at the command from on high, he left his family and found the sinful woman with whom, clean though he was, he did not dare to compare himself.[84]

Now, sweetest soul, it is up to you. Let these examples inflame you, and indeed as many others, even more instructive ones, as you can find. Kick away the vanity of the world, and let eternal love enrapture you to Christ's eternal joys. Arriving there thirsty, like the hart panting for the water brooks, pour yourself out before the Lord's face like water.[85] You must be like the Lord's garden, well irrigated, which will not lack water for the true gardener to make his seeds germinate. Dig yourself the wells of the patriarchs Abraham, Isaac, and Jacob, throwing out a heap of earthly desires together with all earthly hope. Always reflect on the past and the future, the first things and the last things, carefully cleansing your innermost being until you find the vein of the Lord's living water.[86] With all sorts of devotions to stir you,[87] from the depth of your heart and your profound desire for heaven, make an aqueduct of tears which will wash and whiten your dress, and you will praise the Lord from the fountains of Israel, which sees God. For Israel translates as "seeing God."[88] Sigh with Caleb's daughter, asking your heavenly father for irrigated land.[89] Ask him to give you the tears of compunction from the well of his mercy, who produced from the rock which prefigured Christ a spring of living water. Say, "You will feed us with the bread of tears, and give us for our drink tears in measure. And let my eyes shed down tears night and day, and let them not cease."[90]

---

[84] I.e., Mary of Egypt, see p. 89 ("Vita S. Mariae Aegyptiacae," PL 73:674).
[85] Ps. 41:2, 21:5.
[86] Genesis 26:15–33.
[87] The word "compunctio," (cf. our "compunction") here seems to refer to any meditative exercise that can stimulate emotion.
[88] The reference is to Genesis 32:28–30, where Jacob is given the name "Israel" after his fight with God's angel, although in fact it is not the name Israel that is glossed as "Seeing God" but rather the name Jacob gives to the place of this encounter, "Phanuel."
[89] Joshua 15:18–19.
[90] Ps. 79:6; Jer. 14:17.

You have enough material for tears. All worldly joy has been shut out; the crowd of family and friends is far away. You have been left alone as Christ's ward, that in him you may rejoice with your fellow citizens and fellow soldiers, the angels. Therefore in the spirit of humility and in contrite mind give yourself to God as a sacrifice, for an afflicted spirit is a sacrifice to God.[91] Yes, in the spirit of humility and contrition serve the Lord in fear, and praise him in trembling; pour out your heart with the sighs of all your desires to God your redeemer. Desire him, conceive him, embrace him with all your insides. Think how sweet, how gentle, how kind, how mild, how gentle, how indulgent, how lovable he is; how beautiful, how rich, how delightful, how glorious, how festive, how playful, how cheerful, how gracious, brightening everything with his face; how full he is of the infinite treasure of all that is good.

Love him alone, this loving Lord. Conceive him, give birth to him, engender, nourish him. He will not scorn to be born from your womb and to grow to the fullness of charity.[92] If in the presence of his stunning beauty you humbly blush of your own ugliness, by loving him you will yourself become beautiful. No African woman could be so black, no woman so discolored or so ugly, that if she loves him purely, she would not draw beauty and splendor from his beauty.[93] When the Lord looked at Moses, his face became "horned" from the splendor, that is, rays of light shone out from it as from the sun.[94]

---

[91] Ps. 50:19.

[92] Talbot reads "a paruo" for the ms.'s "ab aruo," which makes little sense. Talbot's emendation could be rationalized, with some shifting of words, "he will be born for you and grow from a little one to the fullness of charity," but it is a stretch. I have conjectured – perhaps too boldly – that the reading should be "ab aluo," "from your womb" (which makes sense in connection with "being born," and the previous sentence), and have translated accordingly. (See also Book II n. 44.)

[93] The famous line from the Song of Songs, "I am black but comely" (1:4), is behind this reflection. If the Song of Songs somewhat defensively acknowledges that the dark woman may be "comely," here (and in Jerome, see n. 95 below), blackness is taken – jarringly, for us – solely as a defect and an outward sign of inner "darkness." As Malcolm X noted in his autobiography, the light/dark, black/white metaphors, which cast white as "good" and black as "bad," run deep in our culture. On the intricacies of medieval exegesis of this passage, see Bruce Holsinger, "The Color of Salvation," *The Tongue of the Fathers: Gender and Ideology in Twelfth-Century Latin*, eds. David Townsend and Andrew Taylor (Philadelphia: U. of Pennsylvania Press, 1998), 156–86.

[94] Exodus 34:29–35. The Vulgate famously (and erroneously) translated the Hebrew as "horned" (KJV has "shining"); but, as this reference shows, even Vulgate users were aware that the "horns" referred to rays of light.

Moreover, he who was more beautiful than any human, prefiguring Christ and the Church, had an African wife, an African queen.[95] Such is the voice of the black woman, but beautiful because made white by Christ: "Lord, turn away your face from my sins"; and "make your face to shine upon me"; and, "May the Lord cause the light of his countenance to shine upon us"; and "Look upon me"; and, "The light of your countenance, o Lord, is signed upon us"; and "Give gladness in my heart."[96] Look how he extends his affectionate arms on the cross, inviting us to come to him with his redeeming kindness, prepared to receive, gather, embrace, warm us in his arms if we come. "Come to me," he says, "all you that labor and are burdened, and I will refresh you."[97] He will give himself to you either large or small, depending on your love and faith. "As you have believed," he says, "so be it done unto you." For one who trusts in the Lord, nothing is difficult. Recall what I used to whisper in your ear: "The things that are impossible with men are possible with God"; "All things are possible to those who believe."[98] Hear, and be bold.[99] He himself said it, and saying it did it. He who sits above the cherubim, can also be held as a baby in the arms and in the lap of those who desire him.

Speyer is a famous, wealthy episcopal city.[100] An image of the Holy Mother of Christ with the Child is worshipped there, placed so low that children can reach it. Once a small boy, his mother praying some distance away, went up to the image with a chunk of bread in his hand; he broke off a bite and held it out to the image of the weeping Christ Child and implored it with such words as German children might babble: "Baby eat, baby eat." When the sacred image did not move at all, the little visitor began to urge it with embraces and anxious sobs as if it were alive, crying again and again, "Baby eat!" Finally the image of the almighty baby seemed to hug the insistent child back, and address him with these words: "Baby, don't cry, after three days you will eat with me." The mother heard it and shuddered, and told the miracle to an elderly canon who happened to come by. "You will see," said the wise canon, "on that day you will no longer

---

[95] Num. 12:1; see also Jerome's letter to Eustochium (Epist. 22), 5.
[96] Ps. 50:1, 118:135, 66:2, 85:16, 4:7.
[97] Mt. 11:28.
[98] Mt. 8:13; Mk 9:22.
[99] The punning phrase is "audi et aude."
[100] See Albert Poncelet, "Index miraculorum B.V. Mariae quae saec. VI–XV latine conscripta sunt," *Analecta Bollandiana* 22 (1902), nos. 1671, 72. All analogues listed there are, however, considerably later than Goscelin.

have your baby." Soon, the little boy was taken by a fever and on the third day he died; there is no doubt that he is dining among all the innocent children of Bethlehem with the child who promised him a feast. I learned this story from the learned men who are set before the church as teachers, who exhort us to believe in countless miracles of this kind as examples of God's commiseration.[101] O happy purchase! How generous the vendor of the heavenly kingdom! The kingdom can be bought for a penny; it can be bought for a cup of cool water; it can be bought with a mite of bread; it can be bought with the wish of a good will. Simple, he offers himself to the simple ones who love him. Embrace him with the whole affectionate purity of your mind.

How blissful it is to get to him, you may learn from this exemplum.[102] A baptized Jew lay dying. He told his two brothers, whom he had often invited to the faith, that on the third day after his passing he would appear to them, so that they would believe. Three years and three days later, when they had already given up hope, the deceased appeared to each of them in a vision. With a cheerful face full of heavenly joy, he said: "I promised you that I would appear to you within three days of my death, and here I am finally come after three years and three days. I could not disappoint you by tarrying any longer. Note that this *is* the third day after my third anniversary. I am in such rapturous joy with my Christ, that I could not tear away my gaze from him to turn to you any sooner; and because of my happiness these three years seemed to me as three days would on earth. But now I have come to you with some urgency. If you would

---

[101] The vague reference presumably indicates that Goscelin does not recall the exact source and is quoting from memory (and the slightly defensive tone of the reference suggests that he, too, found the story spooky and of doubtful piety).

[102] Tubach, *Index Exemplorum* (see n. 77 above) lists several related exempla of an agreement to appear to friends after death (nos. 2214, 3976), but all citations are considerably later than Goscelin, and none features a baptized Jew. One wonders if the uprising ("seditio") in which the brothers die is a pogrom such as the one described by Guibert of Nogent, which would give the story a possible contemporary reference, and a darker cast than may at first appear. Goscelin is writing well before the 1096 Rhineland massacres, but incidents of anti-Jewish violence occurred in France and Germany in the run-up to the First Crusade (proclaimed in 1065). (*A Monk's Confession: The Memoirs of Guibert of Nogent*, trans. Paul Archambault [University Park: Pennsylvania State University Press, 1996], 111 and see R. I. Moore, *The Formation of a Persecuting Society* [Oxford: Blackwell, 1987], 29–30.) The story fits in well thematically with the eschatological vision beginning in the next paragraph: the conversion of the Jews was believed to be one of the signs of the imminent Second Coming.

like to be beatified with me[103] in all eternity, you must hurry to believe in Christ and be baptized, for know that you will surely die in two weeks' time." The next morning they told each other their identical visions, and convinced by this certain sign, they were both baptized, and on the predicted day they both were happily taken from this earth in an uprising. Happy are those whom you have chosen, Lord.[104] Therefore, my sweetest, hurry, run, fly to your good Lord with your whole mind; rage, rave, go wild, die for him in the holy impatience of love, though with fear and measured reverence, humble in your growing familiarity and devotion.

Already the world is passing and its concupiscence; already it is slipping away and fading. Lift up your eyes and see: the Lord is coming in His majesty, and for fear of Him the burning skies will dissolve in a mighty eruption. All elements will vanish and the stars will fall. The earth will split open; the nether regions will let out a despairing roar and give up the dead to their awesome judgment. From Zion will come a display of the Lord's magnificence, and our God will come openly to judge, as He once came unrecognized to be judged. The display of His magnificence – apart from the Godhead's own majesty – will consist of all the powers and all the entourage of the heavens, angels, archangels, thrones, dominations, principalities, powers and authorities, cherubim and seraphim, patriarchs, prophets, apostles, martyrs, confessors, virgins, hermits, the infinite multitude of all the elect. The angelic host, led by Michael their mighty general, will carry forth the cross of the Lord, the ensign of their triumphant emperor, and it will shine throughout the world. The sun will be seven times larger and seven times brighter; yet with the banner of the Lord's cross sparkling in the sky, the immense power and splendor of the sun will be altogether dimmed before the majesty of the greater light, and it will be invisible as now the stars fade in the midday sun. If our king's standard will be so magnificent, who can bear to see the King of Glory Himself?

And the whole sky will shine with the radiance of the sun, and David, in the voice of a father speaking of his son,[105] will say, "His throne as the sun in my sight, and as the moon that is perfect forever and will not wane."[106] And in that great convulsion of the advent of

---

[103] Correcting Talbot's "meum" to "mecum."

[104] Ps. 64:5.

[105] See Cassiodorus, *Expositio Psalmorum*, vol. 2, CC SL 98 (Turnhout: Brépols, 1958), 802, 809–15.

[106] Ps. 88:38.

the Supernal, the entire human race, from Adam to the last human being – we will all rise together in the blinking of an eye. Whatever the fire ate away, whatever the floods carried off, whatever the winds dispersed, whatever wild beasts devoured, whatever was incorporated in or digested by another body, whatever parts of the human body dissolved into nothingness, will all come back in incomprehensible suddenness; and whatever was distant from one end of the earth to the other will instantly coalesce in one point; and not a hair or clipped fingernail will perish. If anyone had more than a fair human share, it will not be taken away from him, but from the total mass a beautiful human being will be shaped; and if anyone was lacking anything, it will be made up from the bounty of creation.[107] We read that someone was born with double members, and grew into adulthood: he had two torsos joined back to back, four hands and four feet. This double man had but one soul. By contrast, it is said that within recent memory there was one woman with two souls. She was one up to the navel, and double above it. From a joined lower back she rose up into two. They spoke back and forth to each other, and ate together, span together, sang together. With great affection did these two souls join into one; and when one of them died, the survivor carried around the cadaver that was born part of her. The double body with the single soul, then, will be fashioned into one body from the total mass; and for the two souls, two entire bodies will be made from one.[108] We will all be renewed in our proper stature and beauty, as thirty-year-olds in our prime, according to Christ's age of plenitude.

Those who died as children will rise in that stature they would have attained had they reached perfect age. No shortness, no tallness, no grossness, no fatness, no blemish whatsoever will mar them, but everything will be perfect and full of vigor in the hand of our creator, all will be so consonant and fitting together that nothing will ever lack in glory and honor, and nothing better could be wished for.

---

[107] See Caroline Walker Bynum, "Material Continuity, Personal Survival, and the Resurrection of the Body: A Scholastic Discussion in its Medieval and Modern Contexts," *History of Religions* 30 (1990): 51–85.

[108] Note the echo of the Prologue, where Goscelin hopes that his soul and Eva's ("one soul in two people") will be refashioned as a single soul. Note also the sexual suggestiveness of "being joined from the waist down" – and the fact that Goscelin pictures both halves of this Siamese union as female. Cf. William of Malmesbury, *Gesta Regum Anglorum: The History of the English Kings*, ed. and trans. R. A. B. Mynors, R. M. Thomson and M. Winterbottom (Oxford: Clarendon, 1998) 1:384–85.

If someone was infirm, or blind, or lame, he will be so no more; the eyes of the blind will be opened, the lame will leap like deer, the tongues of the mute will be loosed. "And I shall save the lame," says the Lord, "and I shall heal whatever was infirm, and what was broken I shall mend, and what was weak I shall tie together.[109] Bring the blind and the halt to me, and bring the needy and the harborless into my house."[110] The Lord also said that heaven and earth will pass, but his word will remain in eternity. Who can imagine the glory of the bodies of the blessed, where every single face will shine like the sun? That is what the author of the resurrection himself testifies: "Then the just shall shine like the sun in the kingdom of their father."[111] All the harmonious bodies will be full of splendor and celestial rays, and their interiors, now cleansed to the utmost, will be filled with eternal brightness, and all will be more pellucid than any crystal and any glass, so that we may cry out in perpetual exultation: "Bless the Lord, o my soul, and let all that is within me bless his holy name."[112]

And through all the windows of the glorified body, through all its members, the sun's rays will shine, so that even our very bones will say: "Lord, who is like you?" "The bones that have been humbled shall rejoice, Lord, and my flesh will flourish again, and my heart and my flesh will rejoice in the living God" and the God of the living.[113] And the red blood will most pleasingly bathe our translucent veins and shining joints, as we now see the pink colors of the sun reflected in luminous clouds. What fragrance, what sweet breath will come from our mouths, sweeter than anything our senses can imagine! For if even now the bodies of saints, although still subject to decay, often emanate such miraculously sweet odors from their graves, what will they do when they rise again completely incorruptible?[114] The saints and martyrs will forever gloriously display the scars of all the wounds they suffered for Christ; what a sweet, lovely sight this will be, with no deformity at all! We will also see the wounds of the Lord's own hands, feet, and side, the five wounds that redeemed our five senses, that we may live with him in love and thankfulness.

[109] Zephaniah 3:19; Ezek. 34:16.
[110] Is. 58:7.
[111] Mt. 13:43.
[112] Ps. 102:1.
[113] Ps. 88:9, 27:7, 83:3.
[114] The "odor of sanctity," a sweet fragrance emanating from the dead body of a saint, is a commonplace of medieval hagiography.

In this transfigured state, then, will they take up their ornamental lamps towards the arrival of the Lord, and we shall be taken up into the clouds to meet Christ, into the air.[115] In a commentary on the gospel of the ten virgins we read that the many saints who, according to the gospel of Christ's passion, rose from their graves when the Lord rose and opened for us the way of resurrection, will also ascend together with him into heaven.[116] For it is fitting, according to this commentary, that the triumph of such a great victor should involve many; and they would not be true witnesses of the eternal resurrection unless they had been resuscitated forever. Thus they will come to the Judgment, already re-embodied, together with the Lord. We, on the other hand, who will be rising only then, will go out to meet them; and that is what is referred to when we read, "They went out to meet the bridegroom and the bride":[117] the groom being Christ, the bride the church of those saints who were resurrected with Christ, or also the host of angels. And then finally, when everyone has been resurrected, the Bride will be one and perfect, made up of all. The nations of the world who will then be in the flesh, will not die so much as be suddenly changed with the dead in resurrection.[118] This includes us, the living, who are left over, or rather, that part of us who will at that point be living a mortal life.

In the Judgment there will be four orders, two of the elect and two of the reprobates. The first order of saints will have the dignity of judges and will sit with the Lord and judge the world – those who abandoned everything for Christ, and followed the Lord through many tribulations in perfect justice and love. The second order will be the less perfect elect, of whom the psalmist says: "Your eyes did see my imperfect being, and in your book all shall be written."[119] These are the good and faithful married people, those who abstained from what is illicit, who shared their earthly possessions by giving alms and being hospitable; they will be saved through the fire of suffering here or the fire of purgatory there. This group also includes the greater part of our order,[120] who, spurned for their mediocre lives, are not strong enough to climb up the mountain with the Lord and cannot soar up to the heights of virtue. All those will be accepted

---

[115] 1 Thess. 4:16.
[116] Mt. 27:52–53.
[117] Mt. 25:1.
[118] 1 Cor. 15:51–52.
[119] Ps. 138:16.
[120] Those in religious life.

by the judge's mercy, and like the blessed of his Father will be invited into the kingdom.[121]

On the left, however, there is the order of evil Christians, who will be condemned by judgment. The second order on the left, the impious pagans, is not even worthy of judgment. This is much as it is in earthly realms: when someone has been judged an enemy or outlaw[122] he is not subject to trial but may be killed on sight. Thus for the pagans, the enemies of Christ, there will be no judgment but outright damnation, for he who does not believe is already judged. Then the just shall stand in great constancy against those who had oppressed them. All those who see it shall be troubled with a terrible fear, etc.[123] Then the martyrs will rise up against their persecutors, and the catholics against the heretics who fought civil wars, and whoever has suffered injustice will demand justice from the offenders. Then the horns of all the just shall be exalted, and the horns of the sinners shall be broken. The "horns" mean the kingdoms, powers, glories, and vanities, as Daniel's visions show.[124]

The Maccabees will surge against Antiochus, the Innocents against Herod, Stephen against those who stoned him, Peter against Nero, John against Domitian, Lawrence against Decius, and all will simultaneously punish their foes. All the kings will stand together before the Lord, and all will see the highest one, before whom kings will hold their mouths and their grandiloquent tongues. Then the Lord will judge between nation and nation, between kingdom and kingdom, between the Assyrians and the Hebrews, between the Romans and the nations they subjugated, between the French and the English,[125] between towns and households, fathers and children, brothers and sisters, husbands and wives, friends and companions, prelates and subjects, between all human trades and offices. There all will be shown plainly to all, whatever has been done, said, or thought. Blessed are those whose sins are covered![126] There, all hearts will lie open. The cross on which our Lord suffered will be there, the lance which pierced him, the nails which fixed him to the

---

[121] Gregory, *Moralia in Job* 26.50–51, CCSL 143b, 1304–05.

[122] Goscelin uses "utlagus," the Latinized version of the Anglo-Saxon legal term "outlaw."

[123] Wisdom 5:1–2.

[124] Ps. 74:11; Dan. 7–8.

[125] Goscelin uses the Classicizing terms "Gauls and Britons," but he surely means Norman French and English.

[126] Ps. 31.1.

cross, the crown of thorns, the whips, and all the instruments of his injuries. They will see the side, hands, and feet which they pierced, and "they shall look on him whom they pierced";[127] that is, they will realize that they have wounded the Lord of Majesty. The martyrs' tortures will also appear: Peter's chains and his reversed cross, Paul's sword, Stephen's rocks, Lawrence's grill; the whips, the racks, the red-hot blades, lead balls, wheels, and all torturers' instruments will be presented, all the saints' accusations will be recited, to the glory of the saints and the eternal damnation of the godless. And then, with the populations divided on this side and that, the Judge of the saints will seal his division with one eternal conclusion of infinite finality. He will welcome those on his right with these words: "Come, you blessed of my father, possess you the kingdom." Those on the left, he will eject with these words: "Depart from me, you cursed, into the everlasting fire."[128]

Then have mercy on me, Jesus savior of the world, together with your own Eva. Place us on your right, in the truth of your salvation; do not throw us away from your face, for you have signed us with the faith in your cross. And then the seducer, accuser, and confounder of the whole earth, Satan, will go into the pool of eternal fire with all his angels and with his whole body.[129] And Christ will triumph with his whole body; he will exalt those who will rule in heaven. He will lead his people forth in exultation and his elect in joy, and they will sing a new song to the Lord for ever and ever.

There will be new heavens and a new earth – not of other elements but the same ones transformed into another glory, just as our human bodies will be wholly other in a new blessedness but still the same bodies.[130] How happy, how true, how full, how perfect will be the joy, the celebration, the light, the peace, the security, where there will be no more death, no mourning and no crying, no pain, no worry, no fear, no enemy, no snares of demons, no night, no darkness, neither heat nor frost but happy and unimaginable temperateness; no

---

[127] Zach. 12:10; John 19:37.

[128] Mt. 25:34, 41.

[129] I.e., all his followers who make up his "body," as the Church makes up the body of Christ.

[130] For similar meditations on heaven in John of Fécamp, see Hugh Feiss, OSB, "John of Fécamp's Longing for Heaven," in *Imagining Heaven in the Middle Ages*, eds. Jan Swango Emerson and Hugh Feiss, OSB (New York: Garland, 2000), 65–81 and, on the inevitable failure of the imagination in such eschatological descriptions, see Daniel P. Terkla, "Impassioned Failure: Memory, Metaphor, and the Drive toward Intellection," in the same collection, pp. 245–316.

adversity, no sadness at the end of the day. For this happiness is so true that even though it will always be had to full satiety, it will always be sought with infinite desire. Now earthly time goes in a seven-day cycle; then, there will be one endless eighth day. For all members of Christ who rose again in glory, there will be a perfect and never-ending paschal day of the Lord, forever designated by the psalm title, "Unto the end, for the octave";[131] and the verse that says, "In the evening weeping will take place, and in the morning gladness": the evening means the prison of mortality, and the morning the paschal joy of the resurrection.[132]

How will we exult when we taunt death that has been trampled underfoot: "Death, where is your sting? Where, death, is your victory?"[133] The face of the sun and its rays will be everywhere, everywhere unthinkable splendor, not of this sun but one a thousand time brighter than even seven times its rays, as different from our sun as day from night. But even that sun will not be necessary in the new homeland of the blessed: what is a little spark of light compared to the True Sun? The maker of sun and light himself, the unfailing sun and day, will shine there, and spread his light in all things, everywhere.[134] Wherever you turn, wherever you might want to go, everywhere and in everyone you will see Christ. Then the Lord, remembering his mercy, will gird his loins and will proceed to the eternal remuneration. He will make his people lie down and rest. He will eternally satisfy the desires of those who hunger and thirst for justice. No longer judge but king, he will minister generously to his servants, all the countless multitudes. Like a shepherd he will order his flock and have them sit down, all groups, peoples, and kingdoms, cities and countries, households and families, in their proper order.[135] He will join Adam, Eve, the patriarchs with their offspring, Moses, Joshua, Samuel, the prophets with their tribes. He will join apostles with the nations and languages which they have made bear fruit for God: St. Denis with the Gauls and the Parisians, St. Martin

---

[131] Ps. 6:1, 11; Augustine, *Enarrationes in Psalmos*, CCSL 38.27–28. "Octavus" means "eighth," and Augustine interpreted it to mean an eighth day over and above, and outside of, the normal seven-day week of earthly life. What the title really means seems unclear; modern Bible commentaries surmise that it may have something to do with the psalms' musical setting.

[132] Ps. 29:6.

[133] 1 Cor. 15:55.

[134] Apoc. 21:23.

[135] Cf. the feeding of the 4000, Mt. 15:32–38.

with the people of Tour, St. Hilaire with the Poitevins, St. Augustine with the English, St. Bertin with the people of Sithiu, St. Edith with the nuns of Wilton, and all the other doctors and missionaries of the churches with their sheepstalls and their happy flocks; he will enrich them all with the most generous possessions and dwellings. The kings and princes, too, magistrates and governors, who capably administered God's business and guided his army well, such as David, Hezekiah, Josiah, Constantine, too, the great emperor and promoter of Christianity, chosen by God from his British origins to rule the Eastern Empire; the other caesars and consuls of the Roman Empire; also the holy kings of Britain, Oswald, Edmund, Kenelm, Ethelbert, Edgar, Edward, and with them a thousand other earthly kings will be magnificently crowned, and, like sons among fathers, will stand before God richer and more regal than they were when they reigned.

Once, on the vigil of the feast of St. Matthias the apostle, the canons offended by neglecting the duly owed office. That night, it is told, the prior saw the holy apostle himself being led into the church with the honor due to an apostle, by two archbishops; many crowned kings followed him, with a huge crowd of people and clerics. One of the kings, who was under an interdict, remained outside; through one of the bishops he begged forgiveness of the apostle on his holy feast day. Soon, the apostle called the king before him and absolved him, crowned the absolved one with his royal crown, and solemnly joined him with the others. When the divine praises of the glorious apostle had been sung, everyone recessed in the order in which they had entered. Only those responsible for the negligence were denied their place in the procession and were punished. So many kings and potentates followed just one apostle: how many do you think will be in that plenitude of the kingdom of God? Joshua, prefiguring our true Christ, led the children of Israel into the promised land and then divided it among them.[136] Just so our Lord will distribute the kingdom to everyone according to their different merits and according to the capacities and the desires of each heart. But, in the peace and unity of heaven, these distinctions will not lead to division or dissonance, but to a beautiful harmony of different honors, as a meadow is decorated with various flowers, a painting with various colors, or a necklace with various precious stones. Similarly, the sun has one sort of brightness, the moon another, the stars another, and each star

[136] Joshua 13–22.

differs from the next in brightness; so also, says the apostle, is the resurrection of the dead.[137] The purer someone was in life, the brighter he will be there; the chaster he was, the more translucent; the more he loved God and his neighbor, the more beautiful; the more knowledgeable he was about God, the more intimate he will be with him. As the bride who says, "The King has brought me into his chamber,"[138] the more downtrodden one was, the more sublime one will be; the more despised, the more honored; the more restricted, the freer; the more distressed, the more at peace; the poorer, the richer; the sadder, the more joyful; the more tormented, the more secure; the more disconsolate here on this earth, the more comforted among the angels; the more patient and indulgent, the more closely associated with the martyrs; in short, the more ills depressed us in life, the more we will be filled with good things.

No one, among all the distinct honors, will covet preferment; and as there will be no transgression, there will be no correction, no yoke, no reins, no bitterness among servants as no masters will sit in judgment. No one will be a slave, but all good servants will rule over their unjust masters.[139] Wrath, anger, terror, indignation will be far away; all lust for power will be extinguished. Tyranny, pride, brutality will go to the depths of hell. The greater will not oppress the lesser, but as fathers cherish their children, they will nurture them at their loving bosoms with a mother's tenderness. The least will harmonize with the greatest as the smaller bones harmonize with the larger members, as one soul animates the whole body. Charity will make everything equal. Since there will be no desire for iniquity, the law will give free rein to every inclination, complete freedom to everyone's personal wishes, all power to free will. We will be like gods and the sons of God, according to the prophetic voice of the psalm: "I have said, you are gods, and all of you the sons of the most High"[140] – so much more truly now the children of God as you will die no more but will be like God's angels.

All wishes will instantly be followed by their fulfillment, since no movement of the mind will be immoderate or culpable, but rather all holy and divine. For these glorified bodies will be as mobile as wishes – I do not mean fluid and changeable, but on the contrary most potently efficacious. Or, as our teacher St. Augustine puts it,

---

[137] 1 Cor. 15:41–42.
[138] Song of Songs 1:3.
[139] This seems illogical, since the unjust masters would presumably not be in heaven.
[140] Ps. 81:6.

"The mobility of these bodies will be great as their happiness. Wherever the spirit wants to be, there without fail will the body be."[141] Therefore you may believe, my much desired soul, that wherever you will want to go then, you will be able to do so the more freely for having been so tightly restricted now. And, if I may color with human sentiment even this pure intellection, these supreme gifts of Christ's love, which cannot enter into the heart of man:[142] with your holy lady St. Edith and the whole chorus of sisters, all those her convent has educated for Christ, you will see from Heaven your Wilton. You will also see this cell of yours, no longer a cell but a splendid palace – provided that, by despising yourself as unworthy, you merit this favor through Christ's grace. For then heaven and earth, and Christ himself and all his possessions, will belong to all his elect who for the love of him either voluntarily spurned earthly things, or were shut out from them by godless possessors. But the godless will be taken from the earth and will inherit the tortures of tartarus. In vain do they steal what is not theirs with their insatiable gullets, in vain do they glory in their wealth and abundance, when in the end all godlessness will be eradicated and the holy and just will inherit the earth, too; for the good Lord will not suffer for them to lose that which they had renounced for his name's sake. For how could they lack anything who receive Christ as their inheritance, or are found worthy to be joint heirs with Christ? "How," says the apostle, "has the Father not also, with the son, given you all things?"[143] When the predators have been ejected, "Blessed are the meek, for they shall inherit the earth."[144] But this new earth, along with the new heaven, will not be as it is now, filthy, thorny, and venomous. It will be such as befits those splendid bodies: a blessed, luminous, salvific, sun-filled, gracious land of the living, adorned with living flowers and everything beautiful, full of all sweet fragrances and all the delights of God's paradise. It will flow with milk and honey and sweet nectar. The rivers and even the seas will turn to milk; all storms will be scattered, and the waters will be becalmed in eternal tranquility. Then your Wilton will be a huge, spacious city, generously bounded by a glass wall, surmounted by a gleaming fortress of

---

[141] Sermon 242:5–10 (PL 38:1140–42; St. Augustine, *Sermons on the Liturgical Seasons*, trans. Sister Mary Sarah Muldowney, R.S.M. [New York: Fathers of the Church, 1959], 267).
[142] 1 Cor. 2:9.
[143] Romans 8:32.
[144] Mt. 5:4.

gemstone towers, erected not for fighting but as a lookout of glory, whence the daughters of Zion can look out over their whole England. Her gates will be pearls and all her doors of gold. The temple will shine with jasper, chrysolite, beryl, amethyst, and all precious stones, outshining in dignity the temple of the old Solomon, for it was constructed with new craftsmanship by our new Solomon. Whenever she wants, your mighty queen Edith will come down there, proud in the chamber of the great Christ. She will bring her beloved spouse there together will his most excellent friends the angels and archangels, apostles and martyrs, with Roman and English kings and prelates, with her father Edgar and her brother Edward, with Thekla, Agnes, Cecilia, and Argina, Catherine, and a great host of virgins, and her entire family of Wilton, all those the Lord has raised to dignity in his kingdom.

And the greatest mother-in-law, Mary, will not disdain to be present at her son's wedding. She will celebrate there with her daughter-in-law, as will all those who love the Lord with her, singing to the Lord in eternal joy and delight; you, too, will sing a new song with them in the church of the saints.[145]

Thus the saints will rejoice in glory, will delight in their chambers, and will build the cities of Juda, and anything will belong to anyone and everything to everyone. Choirs will be everywhere, everywhere songs, everywhere feastdays, applause, jubilation, rejoicing, heavenly feasts, the epithalamia of spotless nuptials; everywhere a glorious fellowship of angels and men, an intimate companionship of the higher powers with humans; nowhere solitude, nowhere an absence of joys, nowhere any lack of any good thing. Everyone will be everywhere, and even though one may be wiser than another, all will be wise, just as all will be holy, all will be just, all will be chaste, all will be children of God. All will know all languages, but most commonly they will speak in their one mother tongue, Hebrew, so that there will be one commonwealth uniting all. There will be great harmony between angels and virgins, inseparable friendship, inestimable love, untold sanctity in holy embraces and kisses. Between youths and virgins, men and women, married and unmarried, there

---

[145] The idea is that St. Edith is a "sponsa Christi," bride of Christ, and/or that the entire church is – both the *familia* of Wilton and the universal church. For substitutions of this sort, see my "Closed Doors: An Epithalamium for Queen Edith, Widow and Virgin," in *Constructions of Widowhood and Virginity in the Middle Ages*, ed. Angela J. Weisl and Cindy Carlson (New York: St. Martin's Press, 1999), 71–73.

will be a union as perfect and sinless as it is holy, chaste, and blessed, as it is exempt from any corrupt appetite and free from any contagion of sin. "The young man shall dwell with the virgin," says the Lord through the prophet,[146] and the youths and virgins, the old with the young, will praise the name of the Lord alone, for the Lord alone will be exalted on that day, and he alone will be king over all.

Everyone's thoughts and everyone's hearts will be clearly visible to all. Everyone will openly speak his innermost thoughts, and the Lord will unlock all breasts and open them to his light, and the sweet tokens of affection will speak directly to each other and respond to each other, with no cloud of sinful thoughts interposing itself; for all suspicions and all stumbling blocks have been drowned in Styx.[147] This is why we must now live with such sincerity as we would appear before the highest majesty of heaven and earth. "Blessed are the pure of heart, for they will see God."[148] Everywhere, therefore, in heaven and on earth, and in every heart, God will be seen. Wherever you turn, wherever you go, you will find the joy of the divine vision, and you will see the Lord with your eyes open or closed. "And they shall teach no more every man his neighbor, saying: know the Lord; for all shall see me, from the least of you to the greatest, says the Lord."[149] And do not let mysterious words frighten you, which sometimes appear off-putting to those who do not understand them. For the same one who says, "no man has seen God at any time" also says, "we shall see him as he is" – not as great as he is, which no creature could ever comprehend, but as will be sufficient for the capacity of every one of us.[150] "And no man has ascended to heaven, but he that descended from heaven": that is, no one except the head and the body, no one except Christ and Christians, his members.[151] And: "flesh and blood cannot possess the kingdom of God,"[152] that is: until it is liberated from servitude to sin and corruption, and until the corruptible puts on incorruptibility and the mortal immortality. If this our earthly sun can fill with its rays the entire world with all houses . . . as the whole sea [can fill] every vessel,[153]

---

[146] Is. 62:5.
[147] This echoes various themes of the book's opening pages: the wish for a chaste and licit union with Eva, and the banishment of suspicious minds.
[148] Mt. 5:8.
[149] Jer. 31:34.
[150] 1 John 4:12, 3:2.
[151] 1 John 3:13.
[152] 1 Cor. 15:50.
[153] Parts of this sentence seem illegible in the ms., and Talbot left a lacuna.

cannot the author of all light, the sun of eternal joy, illuminate every-thing everywhere with his whole and full being? "I fill heaven and earth," he says.[154]

To see this joy, o sweet offspring of my soul, sigh, pant, strive with great humility, with inextinguishable love, with untiring labor, with incessant prayer. Wash your bodily dress with the twin sources of your tears, so that as soon as you lay it down you may receive it back more blessedly, and can appear before the Lord without stains or creases. May you be allowed to see your Savior eternally, first only in spirit, then in the double robe of body and soul. The angels desire to gaze on him,[155] and the more they see him the more ardently they burn with desire to see him. This satiety never breeds boredom, but increases everlasting desire. To see him is life, salva-tion, satiety, joy, peace, and endless end of all desire.

It is love that has forced me to go on for so long; but at some point I must put an end to my prolix garrulity. If you know the bowels of mercy,[156] take pity on your bereaved Goscelin, whom you loved as your soul's abode in Christ, but whom you have shaken to the foun-dations with your departure, and evicted from all consolation of the present life. But let me not obscure with the fog of my lamenting the splendor of the joys I just described. Please pray for me that I may receive god's forgiving mercy forever, and pardon for my sins. Even though you are far removed from my worthlessness now, may I be so happy one day to see you in the blessed light, full of joy.

MAY YOU RECEIVE ALL THAT YOUR SOUL DESIRES.

---

[154] Jer. 23:24.
[155] 1 Peter 1:12.
[156] Phil 2:1, Col. 3:12.

Interpretive Essay: Inclusae Exclusus: Desire, Identification and Gender in the *Liber Confortatorius*

Goscelin's long, idiosyncratic letter called the *Liber Confortatorius* – the book of encouragement and consolation – begins with this striking salutation: "Inclusae exclusus, solitarie a mundo solitarius in mundo, quem Christus et caritas noverit, unice anime scribit": "The excluded to the enclosed; the solitary in the world to the solitary from the world; one who is known to Christ and to Love, writing to his only soul." This magnificent formula beautifully captures the contradictory moves of Goscelin's letter: the play on inside and outside, his painful and complete separation from his "only soul," and his desire to identify with her, even merge with her. While the *Liber Confortatorius* is primarily a document of spiritual guidance, or spiritual formation, as Barbara Newman puts it, it is in many ways more about the advisor than about the advisee.[1] Goscelin is trying to work on his own "formation," giving shape to his shattered self, and one way in which he achieves this formation is to identify closely with his "unica anima," the recluse Eva.

The *Liber Confortatorius* (like the later and better-known letters to anchoresses, Aelred of Rievaulx's De *Institutione Inclusarum* and the anonymous *Ancrene Wisse*) is self-consciously in the tradition of St. Jerome's letters of counsel to his female friends. In his capacity as priest and teacher, Goscelin instructs and counsels Eva, suggests readings, spiritual practices, meditations, strategies for managing and harnessing the rigors of a solitary life. But, as Goscelin himself points out, the book is more about him than about her; the "comfort" of the title is for him at least as much as for her.[2] It is as much his attempt to come to terms with his loss as it is a treatise of spiritual

---

[1]   Barbara Newman, "Flaws in the Golden Bowl: Gender and Spiritual Formation in the Twelfth Century," *Traditio* 45 (1989–90): 111– 46.

[2]   "Confortatorius," "confortare," etc., are not quite like the English word "comfort," but closer in meaning to the word "fortis" (strong) from which they are derived; they are perhaps more accurately translated as "encourage," "strengthen," "reinforce." "Consolare"/"Consolatio" are the more common words for "console"/ "consolation." But in context, the meaning here seems close enough to "consolation."

advice. Goscelin devotes the first of the four books to overcoming his grief and writing himself into the traditional role of spiritual advisor. But even then, the *Liber Confortatorius* remains concerned with his loss, his hopes of recovery (such as they are), his relationship with her. Especially in the early part of the book, the model and intertext of Augustine's *Confessions* is more prominent than Jerome. Goscelin recommends it for Eva's reading, but more importantly uses it as a role model for himself. The result is an interesting cross between the second-person address of Jerome's letters and the I, the insistent first-person-ness of Augustine – a confessional, autobiographical style which Guibert of Nogent and Abelard were to adapt some decades after Goscelin.[3] Goscelin is, as it were, addressing his *Confessions* not to God but to Eva, the very person he is counseling.

This confessional quality changes the dynamics of the advisor-advisee relationship quite considerably. Jerome's letters, Aelred's book for his sister, and the *Ancrene Wisse* are unidirectional. The relationship between Goscelin and Eva is perhaps not so much mutual (since Eva doesn't answer) as it is reflexive. The positions of advisor and advisee become interchangeable: the advisor offers guidance and consolation, even redemption, but wants it to rebound on himself; he offers them to himself in the guise of offering them to the advisee. It is therefore necessary for the *exclusus* to identify strongly with the *inclusa*, even to merge with her, a desire that is beautifully embodied in the ambiguous address, "anima mea," "my soul," which means both him and her.

Partly for these reasons, the *Liber Confortatorius* is not as rigidly gendered as the other anchoritic advice books. It has little or none of the rhetoric, suggested by Jerome and perfected by Aelred and the *Ancrene Wisse*, that genders the very institution of anchoritism female. There were male anchorites, but, as Ann K. Warren has shown, females always outnumbered them, in some periods quite considerably.[4] To my knowledge, there are no texts addressed to male recluses that are comparable to *De Institutione Inclusarum* or the *Ancrene Wisse*; and texts that mention male anchorites or narrate their lives do not dwell on the physical fact of their enclosure as the rules for the females do.[5] Aelred and the *Ancrene Wisse* author

---

[3]   *The Letters of Abelard and Heloise*, trans. Betty Radice (Harmondsworth: Penguin, 1974); *A Monk's Confession: The Memoirs of Guibert of Nogent*, trans. Paul Archambault (University Park: Pennsylvania State University Press, 1996).

[4]   Ann K. Warren, *Anchorites and Their Patrons in Medieval England* (Berkeley: University of California Press, 1985), 18–20.

[5]   A partial exception is the letter by Peter the Venerable to the male recluse Gislebertus (c. 1134?), which does dwell on the image of the cell, seeing it as a

portray enclosure as specific to and appropriate for women, both for their own protection and as a kind of penitential discipline for their problematically female bodies, speech, and imagination. The recluse is encouraged to think of the cell as a metonymy of her own body, as impenetrable as she should be virginal; the cell's windows are thought of as dangerous and endangered orifices which must be guarded with extreme care.[6] The male advisor imagines the female *inclusa*, thus contained and immobilized, as an Other, radically separate from himself, whom he can assist or control, and onto whom he can project all sorts of sexual anxieties of his own, but with whom he certainly does not identify – even if, as Susan Greer Fein has argued for Aelred of Rievaulx, he may wish to see her as his other half, his complement, and thus participate in her femaleness and spirituality.[7] Nonetheless the strategy for achieving that participation is a strict separation. The advisor, as Fein also shows, is everything the recluse is not. She is inside, he is outside. She is restricted to a small cell, he is free in his movements. She is dead to the world, he still lives in the world. She is a laywoman, he is a priest. She is female, he is male. She is constantly tempted by her flesh, her irrational desires, while he portrays himself as rational, intellectual, and detached. Even where he respects her and takes her seriously, even where he acknowledges her superior holiness and humbly requests her prayers, he is still the father, and she is the child.

Goscelin wrote about sixty years earlier than Aelred, and his relative lack of interest in Eva's virginity and chastity, as well as his greater emphasis on her intellectual life, is in part simply generational. Aelred's and the *Ancrene Wisse*'s interest in these matters is part of a general tendency from the twelfth century onwards to stress chastity as the female virtue par excellence, and even to restrict

refuge, a tomb, a microcosm, a way to keep out the world and filter what should or should not come to the recluse's attention, even a wall guarding his virtues – but not, as Aelred and the *Ancrene Wisse* do, as a metonym for the recluse's chastity and inviolate body. (Letter 20, "Ad servum Dei Gislebertum Silvanectis inclusum," in *The Letters of Peter the Venerable*, ed. Giles Constable [Cambridge: Harvard University Press, 1967], 1:27–42.)

6   Elizabeth Robertson, "The Rule of the Body: The Feminine Spirituality of the *Ancrene Wisse*," *Seeking the Woman in Late Medieval and Renaissance Writings: Essays in Feminist Contextual Criticism*, eds. Sheila Fisher and Janet E. Halley (Knoxville: University of Tennessee Press, 1989), 109–34.

7   Susanna Greer Fein, "Maternity in Aelred of Rievaulx's Letter to His Sister," in *Medieval Mothering*, eds. John Carmi Parsons and Bonnie Wheeler (New York: Garland, 1996), 139–56.

women's spirituality to the guarding of their virginal bodies.[8] But it is also because of the nature of his consolatory project that Goscelin has little use for the rhetoric of rigid separation. Since he needs to be both outside and inside the enclosure, giving and receiving his own consolation and advice, he needs to blur the strict separation of outside and inside. He says he envies her cell – though, tellingly, not her confinement in it: he wishes he had a "little refuge," but "with a little door," for he needs the larger space of a church as well. Images of entering her enclosure recur, with all their erotic suggestiveness; and his repeated fantasy, expressed both directly and obliquely, is to become one with Eva. For the same reasons, Goscelin needs to blur the gender distinction. "Anima mea," in both its senses, is female, and the many *exempla* of family relationships cited in the book – siblings, or parents and children – cross gender lines in all directions. Somewhat disconcertingly, Goscelin needs to fudge not only gender lines but also the directionality of certain family relations – especially that of birth. Since everything, in his scenario, needs to be reciprocal, he has to imagine – hard though that may be – a mutual birthing, in which both Eva and he can be "mother" and "child." (Fathers, interestingly, play a negligible role.) Scholars like Caroline Bynum have taught us that medieval spiritual writing does frequently and easily cross gender lines and plays freely with emotionally and erotically charged imagery;[9] and it is presumably that same ease which sanctions Goscelin's rhetoric here. Such crossings could be at least in part consoling and empowering to men and women.[10] But the gender crossings in the *Liber Confortatorius*, if one looks closely at their precise inflections, do not always seem easy, or even fully sanctioned. Whether they are consoling or empowering, and to whom, is also open to question.

The overt and conscious drift, the official storyline of the *Liber Confortatorius*, is one of sublimation. Goscelin puts his *dilectio*, his

[8] This tendency has been much discussed and well documented in recent scholarly literature. See, for example, Barbara Newman, "Flaws in the Golden Bowl: Gender and Spiritual Formation in the Twelfth Century," *Traditio* 45 (1989–90): 111–46 and Elizabeth Robertson, "The Rule of the Body: The Feminine Spirituality of the *Ancrene Wisse*."
[9] Caroline Walker Bynum, "Jesus as Mother, Abbot as Mother, in *Jesus as Mother: Studies in the Spirituality of the High Middle Ages* (Berkeley: University of California Press, 1982), 110–69.
[10] Bynum, "Jesus as Mother," 154–59; Pamela Sheingorn, "The Maternal Behavior of God: Divine Father as Fantasy Husband," in *Medieval Mothering*, eds. John Carmi Parsons and Bonnie Wheeler (New York: Garland, 1996), 77–99.

parental feelings, his desire for the *inclusa*, and his grief over her loss to a legitimate and constructive use: to propel himself (and Eva) past such earthly attachments to God. It is a good Augustinian move. Like Augustine's *Confessions*, the *Liber Confortatorius* is autobiographical in that it is an act of self-construction, of not only exploring one's life but writing a life for oneself. Goscelin – as Augustine does at times – portrays himself as broken, demolished down to the foundation, *enervus*, *insulsus*, weak-jointed and helpless, a nobody, a nothing washed up at the doorstep of Eva's cell. Through her prayers (at times he addresses her exactly as he might address the Virgin Mary, asking for her intercession), she can build him back up, give him shape, make him into something, or at any rate ask God to do so:

> But the Lord has rejected me and destroyed me, and my days are vanished like smoke. He has made me to waste away like a spider's web, and cut short my years like a spider's thread. . . . How can I console you in your loneliness with my exhortations, when I am more in need of consolation myself, or am even inconsolable? How can I, who am down, raise up the upright one? How can I, the sick one, help the healthy one, I, the troubled one, assist the secure one? But I have the building materials of comfort in you, which I do not find in myself.   (pp. 33–34)

Metaphors of building recur throughout the book. Goscelin not only wants to help Eva build her spiritual edifice but wants to build himself back up from the utter ruin of his abandonment.

Appropriately, as the prefatory hexameter quatrain tells us, the *Liber Confortatorius* moves in four progressively ordered books, which build on each other, from total desolation (Book I) to a fight with the demons (Book II), to a casting-out of depression ("fastidiae" or "tedia") (Book III), to an extended eschatological vision (Book IV). This grand finale is a rhapsodic description of the new heaven and the new earth, where all are made whole no matter how fragmented they were; where all distinctions are erased, and all become one. Goscelin's imagination falters a little at this final step. He struggles with the paradoxes of an egalitarian heaven that must nonetheless be depicted in hierarchical terms. The heaven he paints for himself and for Eva is a familiar one, a transfigured version of their past happiness at the convent of Wilton, where she was a young oblate and he her tutor. With touching unintentional humor, he pictures a Heavenly Wilton on the model of the Heavenly Jerusalem, as a kind of English division of heaven, with its "familia" of saints living together in a sweet and casual harmony. St. Edith, the patron saint, will come and go as she pleases, sometimes bringing along Christ, her bridegroom, Mary, her mother-in-law, and a long list of English national saints (p. 148). But these inconsistencies and homey touches serve only to highlight, not to destroy, this vision of plenitude and oneness.

The official story, then, moves forward towards a definite, indeed eschatological conclusion. The final beatitude, to be sure, is projected far into the future, and for now Goscelin remains "destroyed down to the foundations and exiled from all the comforts of the present life," as he says even at the very end of the *Liber Confortatorius*, where one might expect him to have achieved his consolation. But even though the resolution is distant, it gives the narrative direction, teleology, and closure.

Nonetheless, there is another side to the story which does not seem to progress towards resolution, in which Goscelin's desire for Eva, his wish to enter her cell and unite with her, is never transcended. Goscelin tries to write himself free from Eva, carefully distinguishing between him and her, her fulfillment and his sorrow. He uses the familiar consolatory topos that it is the bereaved, not the dead, who need consolation – a topos that allows for grief but also helps to distance the living from the dead: "Tu in portu es, ego fluctuo . . ." "You are safely in the harbor, I founder; you are at home, I am shipwrecked; you have built your nest in a rock, I slide about in the sand" (p. 34). Other passages move from closeness to distance, describe the process of a painful letting-go. The odd birth imagery that crops up throughout the book has precisely this function. Goscelin recalls how he used to imagine that one day, in heaven, he would be holding her in his lap; now he would be content to see her in Abraham's lap.[11] If the initial fantasy conveys maternal intimacy, the second one implies distance: he is now Dives seeing Lazarus across the great abyss, though unlike Dives he says he is content.[12] Goscelin, the mother, has let Eva go to her father – though a very maternal father. Yet despite these attempts to emphasize their separation, he cannot, or will not, pull himself away from her.

The unresolved side of this complex love story is accompanied by guilt, oblique apologies, a constant pleading for absolution. It proceeds indirectly, by *exempla* and images, usually introduced apropos of something quite different, as if just slipping out of Goscelin's

[11] Sheingorn, "The Maternal Behavior of God," 79–81.
[12] Cf. Luke 16:19–31.

busy subconscious. For example, the theme of unification, of two-in-one, frames the entire book at the beginning and end and reappears in the guise of numerous stories and references: Sabinus and Sabina, the unnamed virgin martyr and her gallant rescuer, Alexander the hermit and his foster child. Throughout the book, Goscelin tries out family or quasi-family relations that could permit him to get closer to Eva – siblings in particular, both male and female. He confesses that he has always envied Eadgyth, Eva's closest friend at Wilton, both for her physical proximity to Eva and for her intimacy with her. He likes stories of twins. A very poignant instance of twinning occurs in Goscelin's discussion of the Last Judgment, where all will rise in their perfect bodily shape, no matter what their imperfections or mutilations in life – even Siamese twins. There is, says Goscelin, the example of a "double man" with a single soul: he was fused at the torso, back-to-back, but had four arms and four legs. Conversely, there once was a single woman with a double soul, that is, with two upper bodies fused from the waist down (p. 139). It is this example he dwells on: "They" (or she?) lived in beautiful harmony, conversing with herself, and when one of her died, the other faithfully carried her dead other half around with her. Goscelin just leaves this *exemplum* hanging in the air. He briefly comments, in one sentence, on whether this double (or single?) woman will rise as one or as two. But we are left to complete the thought. The story begins to resonate with Goscelin's expressions of desire for Eva and his wish for a heavenly, guilt-free union with her, and we cannot help but note the sexual suggestiveness of imagining that heavenly union as two twin-sister souls "fused from the waist down."

The *Liber Confortatorius* can be read, aside from its "official" content, as a web of subtexts, interconnected allusions and cross-references, strands of half-articulated themes and oblique metaphors. To demonstrate some possible paths through this network, I will concentrate primarily on Book I, in which Goscelin attempts to work through his grief, to settle into the more staid and accepted role of St. Jerome, advisor to holy women. In the same book, he also establishes the imagery that permits his identification and fusion with Eva, thereby subverting the Jerome project even as he works on it. I would like to follow two central maneuvers in this first book, each playing off a famous and conspicuous intertext.

The first maneuver is Ovidian. Or, rather, there are two different Ovidian intertexts at work here, though they are not unconnected. The first, fainter one, seems at first quite unlikely: the *Amores*, with its constant preoccupation with women behind closed doors. In a way, the *Liber Confortatorius* is a non-comical, spiritualized version of the paraclausithyron, a comical classical genre: the lament of the shut-out lover.[13] The classical *exclusus amator* camps out at his beloved's locked door, often quite drunk, vowing not to go away so she may find him in the morning, miserable and unshaven, and take pity on him. He rails against her, her guardians, the door, the lock, the bolts. He physically attacks the door. Ovid, of course, likes the bawdy potential of this image, where getting through the door, penetrating the lady's space, is a fairly obvious metonymy for a sexual conquest, albeit in this case a frustrated one. Clearly, Goscelin would not want to stress this sexual aspect. But we may hear it faintly in the background, since other aspects of the paraclausithyron are clearly present: the guilt-inducing lament, the persistent vigil, the abject self-abasement.

The other Ovidian reminiscence in the *Liber Confortatorius* hinges on Eva's and Goscelin's mutual and multiple exiles. Ovid's poems about his exile in Tomus[14], and perhaps even more the image of the banished poet, remained well-known and influential throughout the Middle Ages. Why Ovid was banished is unclear to this day. He hints that one official, stated reason – though surely not the real one, or not the main one – was his "immoral" *Ars Amatoria*. Hence the speculation developed in late Antiquity, and it never went away, that the real reason may also have been amatory: that, for instance, Ovid may have been involved in an illicit or unwise affair with a member of the imperial family. Whether or not these speculations are valid, the idea of being exiled for a forbidden love is subtly and covertly articulated in the *Liber Confortatorius*. Goscelin's language of forbidden love and exile is clearly prompted by guilt, though it must be remembered that his fantasies and metaphors bear a very uncertain relationship to "what really happened" – something we cannot know.

Exile in general, however, is an overt and important theme, and it resonates for both Eva and Goscelin. Goscelin places their specific exile stories into a general framework of Augustine's metaphysical exile on the one hand (we are never at home until we rest in God)

---

[13] See Ovid, *Amores* 1.6; Frank Olin Copley, *Exclusus Amator: A Study in Latin Love Poetry* (Madison: American Philological Association, 1956).

[14] Ralph Hexter, *Ovid and Medieval Schooling* (Munich: Arbeo-Gesellschaft, 1986), 83–109; Giorgio Brugnoli, "Ovidio e gli esiliati carolingi," in *Atti del Convegno Internazionale Ovidiano, Sulmona maggio 1958*, vol. 2 (Roma: Istituto di Studi Romani, 1959), 209–16.

and, on the other hand, a broad canvas of historical exiles from the Bible to the present day. Goscelin observes that because of the Norman presence in both England and Southern Italy, and the common practice of international political marriages, many people in his time find themselves settling far from their homelands (pp. 41–42).[15] Goscelin's and Eva's own situation is rich in ironies: he has remained in exile (England) for her sake, even after the end of his original mission to accompany Bishop Herman (see Introduction, p. 5). Yet Eva has now left England, leaving him a double exile: "The mother soul [i.e., Goscelin!] who gave birth to you with heaving womb, who shunned her desired homeland for your sake as if it were an exile, and loved her exile as a homeland, who did so much and bore so much in the hope of our mutual presence, now complains that you have left her behind, in a cruel and insulting manner of which she thought your love quite incapable" (p. 26). Eva's voluntary exile is also a multiple one: her exile from England, her homeland (which is so only in a limited sense, as Goscelin remarks, since both her parents are foreign-born); her exile from her spiritual second home, Wilton, and her surrogate family there; her doubled exile from the world as not only a recluse, but a recluse in a foreign land.

This web of exiles gives Goscelin the opportunity for the Ovidian move – gendered and directional – of trying to be present (though absent) to her in his writing:

O my soul, dearer to me than the light, your Goscelin is with you, in the inseparable presence of the soul. He is with you, undivided, in his better part, that part with which he was allowed to love you, that part which cannot be hindered by any physical distance. He salutes you in Christ with an everlasting greeting. . . . Since your soulmate [unanimis tuus] cannot and does not deserve to visit you in the flesh, he now seeks you out with anxious letters and long laments. God's provident mercy has given us this consolation, that, though distant in space, we can be present to each other in faith and in writing. And these torments of separation, which I deserved through my crimes – a letter shuttling back and forth can reconnect us and keep us warm. Also, the tenacious page speaks more edifyingly than the fluid tongue. You have relinquished me and banished me from your sight, but your love will be able to see me in your reading and to

15 For a recent overview of medieval Norman culture and expansionism, see Marjorie Chibnall, *The Normans* (Oxford: Blackwell, 2000).

take in my voice and my sighing words, using your eyes for
ears. (p. 21)

This passage rewrites Ovid's *Tristia*, particularly the poems to his
wife, in Christian terms: it links the hope for a higher, purer reunion
to Ovid's topos of the letter, the poem, making him vicariously present to his beloved. That Goscelin's letter does have erotic valence is
suggested at the very beginning, in his insistence that there is nothing improper about it, and that it is meant for Eva alone. Even as he
insists on privacy, he is of course quite conscious of us, the other
readers. But the disclaimer makes us feel as if we should not really
be there, or that we are only tolerated; and it immediately banishes
any unsympathetic or suspicious readers:

> If by any chance this pilgrim letter, entrusted to uncertain
> winds but commended to God, should stray into alien hands,
> I pray that it may be returned to her for whom alone it is
> manifestly intended, lest someone appropriate what is not
> meant for him. This secret between two people is sealed
> with Christ as mediator, offering in sacrifice nothing but vir-
> ginal simplicity and pure love. Far be from this pure
> encounter the whisperer of scandal, the lecherous eye, the
> pointing finger, the spewer of hot air and the dirty snickerer.
> The story is long, the words are awkward and feeble; he who
> does not like it should not read it, and should leave alone
> what was not written for him. (pp. 19–20)

Of course, not only Ovid the exiled husband, but also Ovid the
exclusus amator can play the game of presence-through-writing; and
when the *exclusus amator* writes, the poet/lover's presence can be
insistent, even unwelcome and intrusive. The *exclusus amator* is
therefore played down, and Ovid the exile is, not surprisingly, the
more visible and more "official" presence here. Goscelin even imitates a famous passage from the *Tristia*, where Ovid addresses his
Rome-bound poem: "If someone asks about me, you will say, / I live,
but you will add that I don't flourish . . ." Goscelin, addressing Eva,
says, "And whenever you should chance to think of me and wonder,
perhaps, 'he was once dear to me – what may he be doing now?' this
page will always answer, 'he is sighing.' "[16]

Yet both Goscelin and Eva are exiles, and this complicates the
Ovid-in-Tomus scenario of the exile writing home to his wife, his

---

[16] *Tristia* 1:17 (Ovid, *Sorrows of an Exile*, trans. A. D. Melville [Oxford: Clarendon,
1992] 1).

friends, his city. The Ovidian reminiscences replicate Ovid's situation in that Goscelin has crossed the sea to get where he is now.
But they also and especially reverse Ovid's situation in that *Eva* has
now left and crossed the sea. She has as much claim to being Ovid
as Goscelin does. This mixing of roles disrupts the gendering of
the image. It is no longer clear who left whom, who is the active
(though unwilling) exile and who the passive stay-at-home.
Moreover, the gendered and phallic overtones of the presence-
through-writing, the image of the male writer intruding into the
woman's space, using his stylus or pen, are now blurred. They are
still there, but they are muted, even muddled. Goscelin does stress
directionality: it is he who is coming to her ("adest Goscelinus
tuus"). But he also pictures a two-way exchange, a "letter shuttling
back and forth" – even though in reality there seems to have been
no reply.

The second and more visible intertext is an Augustinian and generally familial one, which, interestingly, hinges on the concept of
motherhood, that is, on the figure of Monica. Most of Goscelin's
symbolic moves in this regard have ample precedent in the
Confessions. Monica is doubly the mother of Augustine: physically
and, through her prayers and tears, spiritually. She is doubled and
supplemented in the *Confessions*, as Robert O'Connell has shown,
by Isaiah's "mothering God," a nurturing, nourishing figure.[17]
(Goscelin, too, quotes some of Isaiah's "mothering" verses, p. 35.)
The presence in the *Liber Confortatorius* of maternal images is
therefore not surprising in itself. But, as in the Ovid model, Goscelin
literally needs to have it both ways: he needs to be both Augustine
and Monica. When he first introduces Augustine, he calls him "the
great creator of many volumes" – which makes him like Goscelin,
the prolific writer. Evoking the efficacy of Monica's prayers for her
son, Goscelin quotes the famous line from the *Confessions*, "Absit ut
harum lacrimarum filius pereat" – "It cannot be that the son of these
tears should be lost" (p. 31). Goscelin, as we have seen, foundering
and sliding, in need of consolation and reshaping, is the wayward
son, and he asks Eva for her prayers and tears: that is the primary
point of the passage, which is entitled "The fruit of prayer" ("fructus
orationis"). Yet Eva is also Augustine. *She* is the wayward one, having left furtively to board a ship and go overseas; it is his tears that

---

[17] Robert J. O'Connell, "Isaiah's Mothering God in St. Augustine's Confessions,"
    Thought 58 (1983): 188–206.

follow her. That would make him Monica. Indeed, up to that point,
that has been the direction of the imagery: Eva has been the child,
Goscelin the "mother."

The most overt use of mothering imagery is Goscelin's repeated
claim to have "given birth" to Eva spiritually, as Monica did to
Augustine. I have already cited a particularly striking instance of
Goscelin's spiritual motherhood (where he calls himself the "mother
soul who gave birth to you with heaving womb"), and there are many
others. He recalls the "partus dilectionis," that is, the birth of his love
for her but perhaps also his giving birth to her in love, as he watched
her make her profession as a nun. It is a poignant and daring scene,
in which he conceives her and gives birth to her, falls in love and
gives her away in marriage all at once:

> But when you walked up to the Lord's wedding, with trepi-
> dation, the penultimate of fourteen virgins, with glittering
> candles like the stars and constellations above; when, before
> a large crowd waiting in solemn silence, you put on the
> sacred vestment, it was as if from the fiery throne of God sit-
> ting above his cherubim, I was struck to the quick with this
> wondrously beautiful epithalamium: "I am given in mar-
> riage to him whom the angels serve, and he has wedded me
> with his ring." I was touched by the heavenly dew and wept
> in tearful fervor. And as I continued to witness your silence,
> your careful continence, your singing of the psalms and the
> praises of your teacher, my desire was inflamed even more.
> I arranged for you to be present at the upcoming dedication
> of the church, since I wanted you to benefit from such a
> great sacrament. Do continue to practice diligently what I
> then, as if giving birth, instilled in your ear: "Weep before
> the lord."   (p. 23)

This passage of course leaves the birth image rather oblique.
Goscelin may be "giving birth" to the quotation, or to the idea that
he installs in young Eva's mind. In fact, while he does frequently
speak of birth, he rarely calls himself her "mother" outright; if he
does he often leaves or belatedly supplies a way out of that identification. Sometimes he operates within triangles of shifting personae,
which do and do not place him in the position of the mother. For
instance, he recalls frequent visits to Wilton with the "father," bishop
Herman. The bishop, apparently fond of Eva also, would greet her
by hugging her and reciting, in jest, "Eva, mater viventium," "Eva,
mother of all the living." To which Goscelin would reply, "No, the
other Eva was the mother of all the living; this one will be the

daughter of the living" (p. 26). I confess that I do not get the joke. But Eva's mother/daughterhood is at issue here, and if Herman is the father and Eva is *not* the mother, then who is?

A more audacious set of images and correspondences involves Jesus on the Cross. The reproachful argument is that no one – no saint, no martyr, not even Jesus – left his or her loved ones so utterly without consolation as Eva has done. "Stabat iuxta crucem illa mater singularis . . ." "Next to the cross stood that singular mother, regarding him with tearful gaze as he was transfixed with the sins of the world – him to whom alone she alone, peerless virgin, had given birth, the immaculate to the holy, the one to the one, the unique to the unique" (p. 28). Christ, deeply moved to pity, would like to embrace her, and could if he so chose. But his hands must remain nailed to the cross if the Redemption is to go forward; therefore, he instead commends her to John. Goscelin reflects on the familiar tableau of threefold virginity: "The savior, Jesus, who himself is the virgin's virginity, in the middle, embracing, as it were, with each arm a virgin of each sex." How are we to translate the tableau? Eva, Goscelin immediately informs us, is and is not Christ in this picture. Christ, he begs her to remember, is radically different from anyone else in the scene: she is not to think of him as "one of the three" but rather "a third one in addition to the two" under the cross. He is thus not really available for identification. Nonetheless, he has "deigned to offer himself as an exemplar to be followed," in this case clearly an exemplar for Eva, an example of how she should have treated her "family" even as she did her own work of redemption. So if Eva is and is not Christ, then the mother of Christ/not Christ would have to be Goscelin, for lack of a better candidate. John of course would be the more obvious, and safer, part for him. But he does not volunteer that identification, and so far he has been portraying himself – and only himself – not only as the birth-giver but also the bereaved one, i.e., in this picture, Mary. He then briefly interrupts himself to try out the role of David mourning for Absalom; or perhaps it is the role of Absalom being mourned for by David, since what is at issue is the father daring to ask God's pardon for his sinful son. (And Eva, indeed, would then be the father, David.) After that, Goscelin makes, without much conviction, a late nomination for the part of Mary under the Cross: "Mater Wiltonie," the mother abbess: "You have left behind much lamentation for the Mother of Wilton, for your sisters, your parents, and all of us" (p. 30). Thus, anyone who balks at Goscelin in the role of Mary can now settle on "Mater Wiltonie" – as indeed modern readers of the *Liber Confortatorius* have generally done.[18] But it is an awkward reading, since that precise connection is never made, and the abbess is introduced very late; she had not been mentioned and was not available when the "stabat mater" tableau was first drawn for us. Goscelin's styling of himself as Mary, then, is tentative, and it has, as it were, "deniability." There is another, safer candidate available for the part of Mary, if we should want one; Goscelin can then take refuge in the part of John, which is left entirely open. Yet the idea of him as mother – and not just any mother – is firmly implanted in our minds.

The opposite idea – Eva as Goscelin's mother – often addresses his sense of abandonment. He would *like* her to be Mary interceding for Goscelin the sinner, or Monica to his Augustine; he asks her to adopt those roles. But perhaps she is really more like the early Christian saints Felicitas and Perpetua, both of whom give up mother-hood in order to, as he says, "give birth to the martyr's crown": Felicitas, who is pregnant, prays for and obtains an early delivery so that she can be executed together with her friends. Perpetua, on the other hand, is nursing an infant; on his last visit to her in prison, her pagan father makes a last, tearful appeal to her to give up her faith for her child's sake. When she refuses he forcibly takes the baby away from her. Perpetua is rewarded for her heroic stance by a vision of her little brother, who died in infancy; now she is shown that through her intercession he has been cured of his disfiguring illness and is happily playing in heaven (pp. 54–55). This *exemplum* serves among other things as the standard encouragement to a religious woman to trade real motherhood for spiritual motherhood, as when Goscelin encourages Eva towards the end of the book to "conceive, give birth to and nourish" Christ (p. 135).[19] But it also offers a vari-ation on the mother-child theme for Eva and Goscelin: if she has rejected him as her child, he can be her baby brother. Thus, the story plays on both his abandonment and his consolation: his sense that she has sacrificed him to her vocation and his hope that her con-tinued attention, however distant, will redeem him.

---

[18] There is also a suggestion of the common image of the convent as mother or the church as mother. See Joseph C. Plumpe, *Mater Ecclesia: An Inquiry Into the Concept of the Church as Mother in Early Christianity* (Washington, D. C: The Catholic University of America Press, 1943); Sebastian Tromp, S.J., "Ecclesia sponsa virgo mater," *Gregorianum* 18 (1937): 3–29 and my "Closed Doors: An Epithalamium for Queen Edith, Widow and Virgin," in *Constructions of Widowhood and Virginity in the Middle Ages*, ed. Angela J. Weisl and Cindy Carlson (New York: St. Martin's Press, 1999), 73.

[19] See Otter, "Closed Doors," 71–74.

The connected paradoxes of double exile and mutual motherhood are the main rhetorical trick of Goscelin's self-consolation. He is both the *exclusus* and the *inclusa*; she, as his "unica anima," is both inside and outside of him. Whether the rhetoric "works" as a consolation is not certain; while the book's official text takes off and soars, and ends on a jubilant note, the subtext I have been describing remains sad, and does not appear to be moving forward. It is "tenacious," as Goscelin says of his "pagina," his text. But the rhetoric does accomplish, or tries to accomplish, a number of things. In one way it is a sort of narcissistic fantasy, of the kind Nancy Partner has diagnosed in Guibert of Nogent's autobiographical work.[20] Guibert shares with Goscelin the abandonment "in the world" by a maternal figure, for his mother entered a convent when he was twelve years old. Following Partner's lead, Goscelin's work could be seen as attempting a kind of self-engendering without any father, in which he is the child and the mother as well.

But in Goscelin's case the elimination of father figures not only enhances Goscelin's self-sufficiency; it also protects Eva. By rights, Eva should be Goscelin's daughter and he her father. But fathers do not especially interest Goscelin, and many of the fathers mentioned in passing are in some way a threat to their children. Perpetua's father is a poignant and deeply sympathetic figure, but he attempts to divert his daughter from her path to sanctity. Jephtha sacrifices his child; Abraham comes close. David does not exactly sacrifice Absalom, but Absalom dies in a war against his father. Goscelin, when he is Eva's father and teacher, sees himself as an irritant or even a vague threat to her. He reminds her of their first encounters, "how I first vexed you [as] a child" – literally, "when I first irritated your childishness" ("tuam irritaverim infantiam") – "certain that I could easily correct such a pious soul" (p. 23). Presumably he recalls disciplining her when she was a small child, for the context here is teaching her how to read. The tone here is light-hearted, and the reference is to a commonplace school scene and a childish tantrum. Yet the choice of verb, "irritaverim," is interesting, especially as it stands alone, not as part of a list of possible roles he took towards her. Perhaps, to Goscelin, being Eva's father is not only distant – mother, sibling, especially twin seem more intimate choices – but simply too dangerous.

---

[20] Nancy Partner, "The Family Romance of Guibert of Nogent: His Story/Her Story," in *Medieval Mothering*, eds. John Carmi Parsons and Bonnie Wheeler (New York: Garland, 1996), 359–79.

Near the end of the book, Goscelin tells the only extended father-anecdote in the whole work, and its implications for Goscelin and Eva are indeed disturbing: it is the story of Alexander the hermit, in the style of the popular literature of the Desert Fathers, but not attested there. Goscelin himself says he has learnt it "from singing and reciting, not from reading." (It seems close, in many respects, to the well-known story of Mary the Harlot and the hermit Abraham;[21] if this is the story Goscelin is half-remembering and mis-remembering here, then his transformation of the story is very interesting indeed.) Alexander's temptation consists in the devil bringing him an abandoned baby girl, whom Alexander nurtures and raises. When she is grown, Alexander has sex with her and makes her pregnant. Again at the devil's prompting, Alexander decides that the only way out of the scandal is to murder the girl. The next thing that happens, only thinly motivated in the narration, is that Alexander gets his hands stuck in a cleft tree, and in this position remains miraculously alive for many years, until the girl's real father happens by. From Alexander's narrative, the father figures out that the girl must have been his. Taking pity on the hermit, he exhumes the body and finds it incorrupt. When he touches the hermit with the girl's undecayed finger, he is freed from his tree; rejoicing he looks forward to the day they can be reunited in heaven, "inseparabili nexu dilectionis," "with an inseparable bond of love" (pp. 130–33).

The only part of this astonishing story that Goscelin really wishes to contemplate is the ending, the promise of forgiveness and a loving reunion in heaven – in language that echoes his initial wish for a loving reunion with Eva. The official reason he gives for telling it is a moral one: we – or specifically Eva – should not presume on our own goodness but rejoice that God's mercy can wipe out even the gravest sin. He wants it to be a story generally about "sanctity fallen to temptation but built up again from ruin." Even though the temptation, sin, and ruin are the male hermit's (in the Mary-the-harlot story, it is the girl who falls), even though Alexander specifically identifies his sin as "the crime of corrupter and penetrator [percussoris]," Goscelin prefers to address this story to Eva, not – officially – to himself. For it is of course easily recognized as a figurative rendition of perhaps not what happened to Eva and Goscelin but what could have happened; and that, despite the happy ending, is perhaps simply too uncomfortable to dwell on. Better to bracket the father-daughter

[21] Helen Waddell, *The Desert Fathers*, Vintage Spiritual Classics (New York: Random House, 1998), 197–209.

story, and the story of an illicit sexual relationship, and return to the safer terrain of two soulmates united in heaven.

The hope for oneness in the afterlife is the ultimate but distant goal of Goscelin's self-refashioning. By freely mixing roles, genders, generations, Goscelin has gendered himself both male and female, and throughout the book of the Exclusus writing to the Inclusa, he is in some way addressing himself. He is addressing not only his grief over losing Eva but also his sense of exile, his personal restlessness, indeed the human condition of never feeling completely at one with oneself. In that respect, Eva, "my only soul," is the name Goscelin gives to a part of himself, and to the everlasting desire Augustine describes at the beginning of the *Confessions*. As a person, Eva thus becomes even more inaccessible: she is, in a sense, a part of Goscelin, and an elusive one at that. Despite her undoubted historicity and despite what must have been an extraordinary strong, independent personality, she threatens to be completely subsumed in the psyche of her lover and advisor – and that makes her silence in this dialogue even more poignant.

Suggestions for Further Reading

This listing is intended primarily for beginning students in the field of medieval devotional literature. It concentrates on English-language materials or English translation of foreign texts wherever possible, although a few indispensable or particularly interesting texts in other languages have been included. Additional references can be found in the notes.

Primary Texts

C. H. Talbot, ed. "The Liber Confortatorius of Goscelin of Saint Bertin." *Studia Anselmiana* 37; Analecta Monastica, 3rd ser. (1955): 2–117.
  The only published edition to date.

Aelred of Rievaulx. "A Rule of Life for a Recluse." Trans. Mary Paul Macpherson. *Aelred: Treatises and the Pastoral Prayer*. Cistercian Fathers Series 2. Kalamazoo: Cistercian Publications, 1971.
  Translation of one of the earliest, most important and most studied texts on anchoritism.
Anchoritic Spirituality: Ancrene Wisse *and Associated Works*. Eds. Anne Savage and Nicholas Watson. New York: Paulist Press, 1991.
  A modern translation of the full text of the thirteenth-century Middle English *Ancrene Wisse* ("Guide for Anchoresses"), with associated texts.
[Goscelin of St. Bertin.] "La légende de Ste Édith en prose et vers par le moine Goscelin." Ed. A. Wilmart. *Analecta Bollandiana* 56 (1938): 5–101, 265–307.
  Of Goscelin's hagiographic works, the closest in subject matter and literary ambition to the *Liber Confortatorius*. In Latin. No translation available.
Guibert of Nogent. *A Monk's Confession: The Memoirs of Guibert of Nogent*. Trans. Paul Archambault. University Park: Pennsylvania State University Press, 1996.
  A first-person account by a monk contemporary with Goscelin and Eva. Another enlightening comparison. (See the essay by Partner, below.)
Hilarii versus et ludi. Ed. John Bernard Fuller. New York: Holt, 1929.
  Includes Hilarius's poem commemorating Eva.

The Letters of Abelard and Heloise. Trans. Betty Radice. Harmondsworth: Penguin, 1974.

A famous pair of clerical lovers. See Introduction.

The Life of Christina of Markyate. Ed. and trans. C. H. Talbot. Oxford Medieval Texts. Oxford: Clarendon, 1959.

The Life of a twelfth-century English anchoress, by a monk who knew her. An extremely engaging book and a good companion reading to the *Liber Confortatorius*, focusing on the woman's experience.

Medieval English Prose for Women: Selections from the Katherine Group and Ancrene Wisse. Eds. Bella Millett and Jocelyn Wogan-Browne. Oxford: Clarendon, 1992.

An anthology similar to Savage's and Watson's, with the advantage of providing facing-page original text and translation; but includes only a selection from *Ancrene Wisse*.

Medieval Saints: A Reader. Ed. Mary-Ann Stouck. Peterborough, Ont.: Broadview Press, 1999.

Includes translations of several texts of interest to students of the *Liber Confortatorius*: The Passion of Saints Perpetua and Felicitas, the Life of the twelfth-century Northern English hermit Godric of Finchale, and a good selection of lives of the Desert Fathers and Mothers.

Rollason, D. W. *The Mildrith Legend: A Study in Early Medieval Hagiography in England.* Leicester: Leicester University Press, 1982.

A discussion of one of Goscelin's hagiographic work, set in its literary, historical and institutional context. Includes edition of the Latin text, but no translation.

Other important sources and background texts of the Liber Confortatorius*:*

Augustine. *Confessions.* The most widely available translation is that by R. S. Pine-Coffin (Baltimore: Penguin Books 1961, and newer printings.)

Auteurs spirituels et textes dévots du moyen âge. Ed. André Wilmart. Paris, 1932.

The Church History of Rufinus of Aquileia: Books 10 and 11. Trans. Philip R. Amidon S. J. New York: Oxford University Press, 1997.

The Desert Fathers. Trans. Helen Waddell. London: Constable, 1936. Rpt. Vintage Spiritual Classics. New York: Random House, 1998.

Eusebius. *The History of the Church from Christ to Constantine.* Trans. G. A. Williamson. Baltimore: Penguin, 1965.

Handmaids of the Lord: contemporary descriptions of feminine asceticism in the first six Christian centuries. Trans. Joan M. Petersen. Kalamazoo: Cistercian Publications, 1996.

Includes several of Jerome's letters to women, among others the famous one to Eustochium.

Un maître de la vie spirituelle au XIe siècle: Jean de Fécamp. Eds. Jean Leclercq and Jean-Paul Bonnes. Paris: Vrin, 1946.

The Rule of St. Benedict (any edition/translation).

The Sayings of the Desert Fathers: The Alphabetical Collection. Trans. Benedicta Ward, SLG. London: Mowbray, 1975.

Discussions of Goscelin, Eva, the *Liber Confortatorius*

Barlow, Frank, ed. *The Life of King Edward Who Rests at Westminster.* 2nd ed. Oxford: Clarendon, 1992.

Includes full discussion of Goscelin's life and works (with bibliographical details), by way of presenting arguments for and against attributing this text to Goscelin. The text itself (Latin, with facing-page translation), is of great interest among other things for its discussion of Wilton.

Elkins, Sharon. *Holy Women of Twelfth Century England.* Chapel Hill: University of North Carolina Press, 1988.

Includes a short section on Eva (pp. 21–27).

Gransden, Antonia. *Historical Writing in England c. 550 to c. 1307.* Ithaca: Cornell University Press, 1974.

Includes short discussion of Goscelin's hagiographical work in its historical and cultural context (pp. 64–65, 107–11).

Latzke, Therese. "Robert von Arbrissel, Ermengard und Eva." *Mittellateinisches Jahrbuch* 19 (1984): 116–54.

Indispensable, especially on Eva's later life, usefully contextualized with a discussion of another contemporary advisor to religious women. The discussion of Goscelin's relationship with Eva is to be taken with a grain of salt (see Introduction). In German.

Olson, Linda. "Did Medieval English Women Read Augustine's *Confessiones*? Constructing Feminine Interiority and Literacy in the Eleventh and Twelfth Centuries." *Learning and Literacy in Medieval England and Abroad.* Ed. Sarah Rees Jones. Turnhout: Brépols, 2003. 69–95.

Roy, Gopa. "Sharpen Your Mind with the Whetstone of Books: The Female Recluse as Reader in Goscelin's *Liber Confortatorius*, Aelred of Rievaulx's *De Institutione Inclusarum* and the *Ancrene Wisse*." *Women, the Book and the Godly: Selected Proceedings of the St. Hilda's Conference, 1993.* Ed. Lesley Smith and Jane H. M. Taylor. Vol. 1. Cambridge: Brewer, 1995. 113–22.

Townsend, David. "Omissions, Emissions, Missionaries, and Master Signifiers in Norman Canterbury." *Exemplaria* 7 (1995): 291–315.

Interesting, instructive, provocative discussion of Goscelin's hagiographical works on Augustine of Canterbury, using queer theory.

Whalen, George. "Patronage Engendered: How Goscelin Allayed the Concerns of Nuns' Discriminatory Publics," in *Women, the Book and the Godly*, eds. Lesley Smith and Jane H. M. Taylor (Cambridge: D. S. Brewer, 1995), 123–35.

On Goscelin's writings about female saints and for female patrons and audiences.

Wilmart, André. "Eve et Goscelin." *Révue Bénédictine* 46 (1934): 414–38; 50 (1938): 42–83.

An indispensable account of Eva's and Goscelin's lives and discussion of the *Liber Confortatorius*. In French.

Anchoritism and Anchoritic Literature

Constable, Giles. "Eremitical Forms of Monastic Life." *Istituzioni monastiche e istituzioni canonicali in occidente (1123–1215)*. Milano: Vita e pensiero, 1980. 239–64.

Excellent overview.

Georgianna, Linda. *The Solitary Self: Individuality in the Ancrene Wisse*. Cambridge: Harvard University Press, 1981.

A seminal study on the spirituality, mentality and literary style of the *Ancrene Wisse*, raising many questions of direct or comparative interest for the *Liber Confortatorius*.

Gilchrist, Roberta. *Gender and Material Culture: The Archaeology of Religious Women*. London: Routledge, 1994.

Includes a chapter on anchorholds.

Warren, Ann K. *Anchorites and Their Patrons in Medieval England*. Berkeley: University of California Press, 1985.

The literature on anchoritism, enclosure and gender has grown enormously over the past several years. A few important titles, which will provide futher bibliographical hints:

Bartlett, Anne Clark. *Male Authors, Female Readers: Representation and Subjectivity in Middle English Devotional Literature*. Ithaca: Cornell University Press, 1995.

In particular, an important chapter on "Gendering and Regendering" in Aelred's *De Institutione Reclusarum* (pp. 34–55).

Horner, Shari. *The Discourse of Enclosure: Representing Women in Old English Literature*. Albany: State University of New York Press, 2001.

Includes a discussion of Christina of Markyate.

Hostetler, Margaret. "Designing Religious Women: Privacy and Exposure in the *Life of Christina of Markyate* and *Ancrene Wisse*." *Mediaevalia* 22 (1999): 201–31.

Kalve, Kari. " 'The Muthes Wit': Reading, Speaking, and Eating in the *Ancrene Wisse*." *Essays in Medieval Studies* 14 (1998): 39–49.

Newman, Barbara. "Flaws in the Golden Bowl: Gender and Spiritual Formation in the Twelfth Century." *Traditio* 45 (1989–90): 111–46.

A study of spiritual practices and spiritual advice given to men and women in the twelfth century.

Price, Jocelyn G. " 'Inner' and 'Outer': Conceptualizing the body in *Ancrene Wisse* and Aelred's *De Institutione Inclusarum*." *Medieval English Religious and Ethical Literature*. Ed. Gregory Kratzmann and James Simpson (Cambridge: D. S. Brewer, 1986), 192–208.

Robertson, Elizabeth. "The Rule of the Body: The Feminine Spirituality of the *Ancrene Wisse*." *Seeking the Woman in Late Medieval and Renaissance Writings: Essays in Feminist Contextual Criticism*. Eds. Sheila Fisher and Janet E. Halley. Knoxville: University of Tennessee Press, 1989. 109–34.

Discusses the focus on body and virginity in later anchoritic literature.

On the education, reading, and intellectual life of anchoresses:

Kauth, Jean-Marie. "Book Metaphors in the Textual Community of the *Ancrene Wisse*." *The Book and the Magic of Reading in the Middle Ages*. Ed. Albrecht Classen. New York: Garland, 1998. 99–122.

Millett, Bella. "Women in No Man's Land: English Recluses and the Development of Vernacular Literature in the Twelfth and Thirteenth Centuries." *Women and Literature in Britain, 1150–1500*. Ed. Carol M. Meale. Cambridge: Cambridge University Press, 1993.

Mentions the *Liber Confortatorius* in passing; provides some context for the reading program and reading habits recommended by Goscelin.

Further Bibliography:

Bella Millett. *The* Ancrene Wisse, *the Katherine Group, and the Wooing Group*. Annotated Bibliography of Middle English Literature II. Cambridge: D. S. Brewer, 1996.

An excellent bibliography on Middle English anchoritic literature, with many titles of interest to students of the *Liber Confortatorius*.

The Wider Intellectual Context

Bestul, Thomas. "St. Anselm, the Monastic Community at Canterbury, and Devotional Writing in Late Anglo-Saxon England." *Anselm-Studies* 1 (1983): 185–97.

Carruthers, Mary. *The Craft of Thought: Meditation, Rhetoric, and the Making of Images, 400–1200*. Cambridge: Cambridge University Press, 1998.
  Particularly the chapters "Remember Heaven: The Aesthetics of Mneme" and "Cognitive Images, Meditation, and Ornament."

Evans, G. R. *Anselm and a New Generation*. Oxford: Clarendon, 1980.
  Discusses the circle of St. Anselm of Canterbury and its philosophical and devotional interests.

Leclercq, Jean. *The Love of Learning and the Desire for God*. Trans. Catharine Misrahi. New York: Fordham University Press, 1961.
  A classic study of monastic reading and meditation.

McGuire, Brian Patrick. *Friendship and Community: The Monastic Experience 350–1250* (Kalamazoo: Cistercian Publications, 1988).
  Brief discussion of Goscelin and Eva (pp. 201–203). More importantly, a broad historical overview, centered on Aelred of Rievaulx, of the concept and practice of spiritual friendship and its erotic overtones.

Partner, Nancy. "The Family Romance of Guibert of Nogent: His Story/ Her Story." *Medieval Mothering*. Eds. John Carmi Parsons and Bonnie Wheeler. New York: Garland, 1996. 359–79.
  An excellent and programmatic psychoanalytical reading of an autobiographical text roughly contemporary with the *Liber Confortatorius*, with many interesting points of comparison.

Wenzel, Siegfried. *The Sin of Sloth: Acedia in Medieval Thought and Literature*. Chapel Hill: University of North Carolina Press, 1967.

Index

Library of Medieval Women

Already published

Christine de Pizan's Letter of Othea to Hector, *Jane Chance*, 1990

Writings of Margaret of Oingt, Medieval Prioress and Mystic,
Renate Blumenfeld-Kosinski, 1990

Saint Bride and her Book: Birgitta of Sweden's *Revelations*,
Julia Bolton Holloway, 1992; new edition 2000

The Memoirs of Helene Kottanner (1439–1440),
Maya Bijvoet Williamson, 1998

The Writings of Teresa de Cartagena,
Dayle Seidenspinner-Núñez, 1998

Julian of Norwich, Revelations of Divine Love and
The Motherhood of God, *Frances Beer*, 1998

Hrotsvit of Gandersheim: A Florilegium of her Works,
Katharina M. Wilson, 1998

Hildegard of Bingen: On Natural Philosophy and Medicine: Selections from
Cause et Cure, Margret Berger, 1999

Women Saints' Lives in Old English Prose, *Leslie A. Donovan*, 1999

Angela of Foligno's Memorial, *Cristina Mazzoni*, 2000

The Letters of the Rožmberk Sisters, *John M. Klassen*, 2001

The Life of Saint Douceline, a Beguine of Provence,
Kathleen Garay and Madeleine Jeay, 2001

Agnes Blannbekin, Viennese Beguine: Life and Revelations,
Ulrike Wiethaus, 2002

Women of the *Gilte Legende*: A Selection of Middle English Saints Lives,
Larissa Tracy, 2003

Mechthild of Magdeburg: Selections from *The Flowing Light
of the Godhead, Elizabeth A. Andersen*, 2003

The Book of Margery Kempe: An Abridged Translation,
Liz Herbert McAvoy, 2003

Guidance for Women in Twelfth-Century Convents, *Vera Morton with
Jocelyn Wogan-Browne*, 2003